T0328843

APPLICATIONS OF PRINCIPAL-AGENT THEORY TO AGRICULTURAL LAND USE POLICY

Lessons from the European Union

APPLICATIONS OF PRINCIPAL-AGENT THEORY TO AGRICULTURAL LAND USE POLICY

Lessons from the European Union

Rob Fraser

University of Kent, UK

Imperial College Press

Published by

Imperial College Press
57 Shelton Street
Covent Garden
London WC2H 9HE

Distributed by

World Scientific Publishing Co. Pte. Ltd.
5 Toh Tuck Link, Singapore 596224
USA office: 27 Warren Street, Suite 401-402, Hackensack, NJ 07601
UK office: 57 Shelton Street, Covent Garden, London WC2H 9HE

Library of Congress Cataloging-in-Publication Data
Fraser, Robert W., author.
   Applications of principal-agent theory to agricultural land use policy : lessons from the European Union /
Rob Fraser.
      pages cm
   Includes bibliographical references and index.
   ISBN 978-1-78326-675-3 (hardcover : alk. paper)
   1. Land use--Government policy--European Union countries. 2. Agency (Law)--European Union countries.
I. Title.
   HD590.5.F73 2015
   333.76--dc23

                                    2014050223

British Library Cataloguing-in-Publication Data
A catalogue record for this book is available from the British Library.

Chapter 2 was reprinted by permission of the publisher (Taylor & Francis Ltd, http://www.tandf.co.uk/journals).
Chapter 5 was reprinted by permission of Oxford University Press.

Typeset by Stallion Press
Email: enquiries@stallionpress.com

Printed in Singapore

To my family

Contents

Foreword

Over the past 50 years, agriculture has been strongly supported by governments in a number of major developed economies, particularly those of Europe, the United States and Japan. Farmers in these countries have benefited greatly from these policies, and the benefits have, broadly speaking, been maintained despite major changes in the rationales for providing support and in the mechanisms for providing it.

The changes in European agricultural policy in particular have been profound. As Rob Fraser explains, one of the principal objectives for creating the European Economic Community in 1957 was to deliver food security in the wake of terrible food shortages during World War 2. Agricultural productivity remained the main emphasis of European policy through the 1960s, 1970s and 1980s. However, this period saw the first emergence of a number of unintended consequences from the policy. Because the assistance to farmers was delivered via higher prices for agricultural products, there was massive over-production, resulting in cost blow-outs in Europe, degradation of Europe's agricultural landscape and damage to the livelihoods of poor farmers in developing countries. Further, the policy delivered its largest benefits to the largest farmers, who needed them least. It also created expectations and a strong vested interest amongst farmers for a continuation of the policy, placing a constraint on reforms ever since.

Nevertheless, reforms have occurred, including the introduction of "set-aside" policies (paying farmers to leave areas of their farms out of production), "uncoupling" of assistance from agricultural prices (which ultimately rendered set-aside redundant) and a growing emphasis on the delivery of social and environmental benefits as the rationale for assistance to farmers.

For each of these reforms, there have been additional unintended consequences. The initial set-aside policy, motivated solely by over-production, was observed to result in environmental benefits on those lands no longer used for agriculture.

The delivery of financial assistance through direct payments to farmers rather than through boosting prices has made the resulting wealth transfer from the broader community more transparent and perhaps less acceptable to the European public. Fraser reasons that this is likely to place increasing pressure on this aspect of the policy.

A third unintended consequence was that the introduction of payments for environmental and social benefits has helped to shield European farmers from increasing risk, which would otherwise have been a result of the de-coupling reform. Fraser examines in detail the complex interplay between agricultural policies and farming risks, and shows that it can be a major factor driving the outcomes of policy.

In this, and in other ways, the book highlights the need for clear thinking, analysis and evidence when policies such as these are being designed and implemented. Apart from the need to anticipate unintended consequences, effort is needed to achieve the goals of policy efficiently. It shouldn't be assumed that the best outcomes can be achieved easily through spending large sums of money. Generating farmer participation is relatively easy, with sufficient funding, but delivering public benefits can be much more challenging. Fraser highlights that complexities such as the risk of "moral hazard" (cheating), adverse selection (paying the wrong farmers) and information asymmetry (farmers knowing more about their own situation than governments do) all need to be accounted for if the public is to get the best value for money from its investment in agricultural payments. All too often, this doesn't occur, but Fraser gives policy makers the insights and conceptual tools needed to do so.

European agricultural policies will continue to evolve. As of 2014, the most likely direction of change appears to be towards further increased emphasis on delivery of public goods from agriculture as the justification for payments, rather than payments to farmers because they are farmers. In the context of the UK, in particular, Fraser argues that this change is appropriate, since food and energy can always be obtained through trade, but local environmental, aesthetic and recreational benefits cannot. If that occurs, one could imagine questions emerging as to why agriculture is privileged as a supplier of public goods, perhaps leading to competition for funding between agriculture and other potential providers of these types of goods. Another possibility, given the financial pressures still facing some European countries, is less funding for agricultural policy in general. Whatever happens, the ideas and analyses presented in this book will provide much-needed assistance, warnings and reality checks to European policy makers, and a powerful foundation for understanding these issues for students and future researchers.

David Pannell
Winthrop Professor
School of Agricultural and Resource Economics
University of Western Australia
November 2014

Chapter 1

Introduction

1.0 Background to this Book

As a policy economist I have been researching the design of agricultural land use policy within the European Union (EU) since the introduction of voluntary set-aside as part of the Common Agricultural Policy (CAP) in the late 1980s. This book contains primarily a collection of my published research, which analyses and evaluates the EU's agricultural land use policy as it has evolved over the last two decades from voluntary set-aside to "compliance" set-aside to environmental stewardship, and using the principal-agent methodology as a consistent framework of economic analysis. In addition the book contains an introduction both to the principal-agent methodology, and to the historical development of agricultural land use policy in the CAP, as well as literature-based introductions to each major part of the book (i.e. Parts A and B), and finally some reflections on policy and policy design lessons for the future from this research.

More specifically, following the introduction of voluntary set-aside in the late 1980s, attempts to use the CAP to directly manage land use began with the May 1992 CAP Reform, which introduced for the first time "compliance" set-aside, with the aim of requiring farmers to take land out of production so as to help reduce the over-production problems characterising EU agriculture at that time. However, set-aside was also subsequently seen to produce environmental benefits (such as reduced nitrate leaching from set-aside land) and this observation, combined with other social concerns about environmental degradation from agricultural production, saw over the next 10–15 years the CAP's financial support shifting increasingly towards agricultural land use management for environmental benefit (this is also known as the shift from "Pillar 1" to "Pillar 2"), whereby farmers were paid to take land out of production (i.e. "set-aside") to improve habitats for flora and fauna. This is now called "environmental stewardship" and is an increasingly important source of income for farmers both in the UK and elsewhere in the EU.

My research on set-aside in the 1990s was among the first to identify (and quantify) such environmental benefits from taking land out of production, and it subsequently has evolved into identifying and evaluating the benefits of existing environmental stewardship policies, both as aspects of agricultural land use policy in the CAP.

Within this context, the unifying methodological theme of my research has been the problem of "asymmetric information" which relates to the policy feature that the government (known as the "principal") is aiming to influence the farmer (known as the "agent") to deliver behaviour which achieves the government's policy objectives. Principal-agent theory is a mainstream economics methodology, which I have been a pioneer in applying in the context of EU agricultural land use policy. In this methodology the two sub-components of the asymmetric information problem are the "adverse selection" problem, and the "moral hazard" problem — both of which are aspects of designing a policy so that even though agents are acting in their best interests, this behaviour also coincides with what the principal wants them to do (called "goal alignment"). Technically, to remove the adverse selection problem a land use policy must be "incentive compatible" (so that the right choices of land use are made by the farmer), while to remove the moral hazard problem the land use policy must also be "compliance compatible" (so that the farmer doesn't just say they are doing the right thing with their land, but then cheat, and take the money and not do what they are being paid to do). My published research on set-aside during the 1990s and subsequently on environmental stewardship has consistently used principal-agent methodology to analyse and evaluate existing agricultural land use policy design (relating to both adverse selection and moral hazard), culminating with my Agricultural Economics Society Presidential Address on the moral hazard problem published in the *Journal of Agricultural Economics* in September 2013.

1.1 An Introduction to Principal-Agent Theory in Relation to Policy Design

According to Laffont and Martimont (2002), the first joint use of the terms "principal" and "agent" in the economics literature was by Arrow (1963): "the principal can never hope to completely check the agent's performance" (see Laffont and Martimont (2002)p. 2).[1] But the first formal exposition of the economic theory of the principal-agent problem was by Ross (1973). This seminal exposition was subsequently further developed by Grossman and Hart (1983) and by Rees (1985a, 1985b), and then more completely by Laffont and Tirole (1993). The most recent and comprehensive presentation of the economics of the principal-agent model is by Laffont and Martimont (2002).

The core concept of principal-agent theory is a "contract" between the principal and the agent whereby the principal pays the agent to deliver a prescribed action,

---

[1] Laffont and Martimont (2002) also acknowledge that these terms have their origins in the law literature relating to contracts, and particularly in the area of insurance markets.

and in return the agent delivers this action. Moreover, this theory identifies two main components to the specification of the principal-agent model:

(i) both the principal and the agent have goals (objectives), and these goals are not necessarily aligned with each other in the context of the consequences of the agent's actions, and

(ii) the principal has imperfect information about one or both of the agent's characteristics and their behaviour (in relation to their actions on behalf of the principal). Given the agent has perfect information about both their characteristics and their behaviour, this specification feature is called "asymmetric information".

Given this specification, principal-agent theory has been mainly applied in the economics literature to analyse policy design situations, whereby the "principal" is usually the government, and the agents are usually producers operating in a situation where there is some market failure which justifies a government policy intervention.[2]

1.1.1 *Policy design problems*

Within this policy design context principal-agent theory then identifies two main problems:

(i) adverse selection, and
(ii) moral hazard.

Each of these problems reflects both goal non-alignment and the lack of information on the part of the principal regarding the characteristics and/or behaviour of the agent, and each leads to a reduction in the efficiency of the principal's policy in managing its agents to achieve its objective(s) — a reduction in efficiency which could be due to one or both of: (a) increased costs of delivering prescribed actions and (b) reduced effectiveness of delivered actions.

Adverse selection

The problem of adverse selection has at its core some element of heterogeneity within the population of agents that impacts the efficiency of the principal's policy. Most commonly this is represented as heterogeneity *between* agents in their characteristics, although it can also relate to heterogeneity *within* an agent's own economic circumstances. In either case, by agents *choosing* to act (legally) in their own best interests, the principal will find that *adverse selection* is taking place, and

---

[2]See Laffont and Martimont (2002) for a discussion of the range of these applications. Note also that insurance markets are an important context in the literature where government policy considerations are not central.

as a consequence the efficiency of the policy is reduced. Note that if the heterogeneity that reduces policy efficiency is *between* agents, then adverse selection can take the form of differences between the agents who chose to participate in the principal's policy process, and those who choose not to participate, while if this heterogeneity is *within* an agent's own economic circumstances, then the adverse selection instead results from each participating agent's choice of actions within the context of the policy.

An additional aspect of the policy which needs to be considered in this context is whether participation by agents is compulsory or voluntary. In particular, if participation is voluntary then heterogeneity between agents can be an important cause of reduced policy efficiency if this efficiency is affected by selection bias among participating agents. Whereas if participation is compulsory, then only heterogeneity within the economic circumstances of agents can cause the efficiency of this policy to be reduced by adverse selection.

Moral Hazard

The problem of moral hazard has at its core a willingness on the part of one or more agents to act illegally with respect to the principal. More specifically, in the context of an agent participating in the principal's policy, this illegality takes the form of the agent accepting a benefit (e.g. a payment) from the principal in return for agreeing to undertake a policy-related action which has a cost to the agent, and then either not undertaking this action, or undertaking a modified form of the action (which is typically of lower cost to the agent). In either case, the agent accepts the risk that the illegal action will not be detected by the principal and therefore the agent will overall be better off. For the principal, it finds that each illegal action by an agent reduces the effectiveness of its policy.

Note in this case that the issue of whether participation by agents is compulsory or voluntary does not directly affect the extent of the moral hazard problem. However, an indirect effect can arise if, for example, compulsory participation has an effect on the willingness of agents to take the risk of behaving illegally.

1.1.2   *Set-aside: An illustration of the policy design problem*

The problems of adverse selection and moral hazard can be clearly illustrated within the context of a set-aside (or land diversion) policy which is used as an output control policy.[3]

---

[3]See Ervin (1988) for a discussion of the land diversion policy introduced as an output control policy in the US in 1985 (the "Acreage Reduction Program"), and its implications for a set-aside policy in the UK (subsequently introduced in the EU in 1988).

Reduced policy-efficiency in this context is referred to as "slippage", which was first defined by Gardner (1987) as:

$$\text{Slippage} = 1 - \frac{\%\ change\ in\ output}{\%\ change\ in\ acreage} \tag{1}$$

However, this definition fails to make the distinction between slippage attributable to adverse selection, and slippage attributable to moral hazard. In making this distinction, slippage attributable to the adverse selection by farmers of their lowest yielding land would be defined as:

$$\text{Slippage (Adverse Selection)} = 1 - \frac{\%\ change\ in\ output}{\%\ change\ in\ actual\ acreage} \tag{2}$$

while if we are also to take into account the possibility of farmers who state they are setting aside land, but in fact do not, then a comprehensive measure of slippage (i.e. accounting for both adverse section and moral hazard) would be:

$$\text{Slippage (Adverse Selection and Moral Hazard)}$$
$$= 1 - \frac{\%\ change\ in\ output}{\%\ change\ in\ stated\ acreage} \tag{3}$$

where:

$$\text{Slippage (Moral Hazard)} = \frac{\%\ change\ in\ output}{\%\ change\ in\ actual\ acreage}$$
$$- \frac{\%\ change\ in\ output}{\%\ change\ in\ stated\ acreage} \tag{4}$$

Using these definitions, if the percentage decrease in output is 10%, in stated acreage is 20%, and in actual acreage is 15%, then:

$$\text{Slippage (Adverse Selection and Moral Hazard)} = 50\%$$

with:

$$\text{Slippage (Adverse Selection)} = 33.3\%$$

and:

$$\text{Slippage (Moral Hazard)} = 16.7\%.$$

1.1.3   *Policy design solutions*

Each of the problems caused by the non-alignment of the principal's objectives and those of their agents and by the asymmetric information between the principal and their agents has a theoretical solution within the general framework of policy design which increases policy efficiency. The policy design solution to the adverse selection problem relates to the *incentive compatibility* features of the policy, while the policy design solution to the moral hazard problem relates to the *compliance compatibility* features of the policy.

Incentive compatibility features

The aim of designing a policy to be incentive-compatible is to align an agent's objective with that of the principal. Specifically, if a policy is designed to be incentive-compatible, then in choosing to act in their own best interests, agents will also be acting in the best interests of the principal. As a consequence, the choices of the agents will be consistent with achieving the objective of the principal, and policy efficiency will be increased.

Compliance compatibility features

Since in choosing to behave illegally an agent will be taking the risk of being detected by the principal, the aim of the design of a monitoring and penalties system is to discourage as many agents as possible from taking this risk, and as a consequence these agents would instead choose to behave legally with respect to the principal, thus increasing policy efficiency.

Finally, note that the specific details of the policy design solution to the slippage problem outlined in section 1.1.2 are presented in Chapter 8. But in general terms this solution involves both differentiating set-aside payments based on land quality so as to discourage the adverse selection of lower yielding land for set-aside, and discouraging moral hazard by expanding the monitoring and penalties system to include both the quality and quantity of set-aside land.

1.2   A Brief History of Agricultural Land Use Policy Within the Common Agricultural Policy

The purpose of this section is to provide a brief history (up until 2013) of agricultural land use policy as a component of the EU's Common Agricultural Policy (CAP).[4] And while the CAP is within a few years of its 50th birthday of operation, the CAP's agricultural land use policy has a comparatively shorter history, having been introduced in the form of voluntary set-aside as a production control mechanism in the CAP's "crisis years" of the late 1980s, when the cost of funding on-going production surpluses of the EU's major farm commodities threatened to derail the CAP's budget.

But the frequent "reforms" to the CAP since the late 1980s make even a partial historical account of its evolution a challenging task. In this context Ackrill (2000) presents an excellent account of the development of the CAP, but only up until the end of the 1990s, while Knudsen's (2009) perhaps more polemical account describes the CAP as "the agricultural subsidy and protection regime of the EU" (p. 2) — in effect a continuously evolving welfare regime for farmers!

---

[4]See Chapter 17 for a detailed discussion of the European Commission's recently released "CAP Reform 2014–2020".

Given this problem of on-going policy change, I think the most comprehensive and up-to-date account of the history of the CAP is that provided by the European Commission (EC) itself on its website:[5]

ec.europa/agriculture/cap-history/index_en.htm

In this account changes in the CAP are characterised as comprising three main stages:

(i) from 1957–"productivity",
(ii) from the May 1992 CAP reform — "competitiveness", and
(iii) from the Agenda 2000 CAP reform — "sustainability".

And in this account the CAP's agricultural land use policy is formally introduced as "compliance" set-aside within the package of the May 1992 CAP reforms to improve "competitiveness" in EU agriculture. This characterisation overlooks the earlier introduction of voluntary set-aside (in 1988), but in so doing emphasises the new (in 1992) *requirement* of set-aside in order to receive "compensatory payments" for reductions in price support, which themselves were central to the May 1992 CAP reform package. Moreover, the "sustainability" characterisation represents the formal creation of "Pillar 2" as part of the CAP, and the explicit recognition of farmers as "environmental stewards", who became (in 2003) not just *required* to keep their land in "good agricultural and environmental condition" in order to receive ("decoupled") direct payments, but also offered further financial incentives to protect and enhance their provision of environmental goods and services on their land.

And looking ahead to the CAP beyond 2013 we can already see proposals to shift more of the CAP's budget from Pillar 1 to Pillar 2, thereby further strengthening the role of the CAP's agricultural land use policy as one of supporting environmental "sustainability", with farmers as central providers of environmental benefits from this support.[6]

But if we go back to the 1980s to what the EC calls the CAP's "crisis years", then with the benefit of hindsight we can clearly see the beginnings of the agricultural land use policy process by which farmers have now come to be seen as "environmental stewards", rather than as "destroyers" of the environment as they were then.

Recalling that the first stage of the CAP is characterised by the EC as "productivity", we are reminded that one of the principle objectives of creating the European Economic Community in 1957 was to deliver "food security". As a consequence, farmers were encouraged to increase their production with a range of market intervention measures which were designed to provide price support (e.g.

---

[5]Note also that this account is regularly updated. In addition, it contains links to a large number of relevant policy documents.

[6]See, for example, on Defra's website: "Reforming the Common Agricultural Policy to ensure a fair deal for farmers, consumers and taxpayers" (https://www.gov.uk/government/policies/reforming-the-common-agricultural-policy-to-ensure-a-fair-deal-for-farmers-consumers-and-taxpayers). See also Chapter 17.

tariffs and intervention purchasing). And given this price support, it follows that farmers did take steps to increase their production, both by the intensification and the extensification of their land use. This "productivity" stage continued successfully through the 1960s and 1970s, at which point on-going production surpluses began to become apparent, initially in the dairy sector, but by the early 1980s extending across the range of the EU's major farm commodities.

Moreover, these production surpluses can now be seen as the cause of two separate concerns which developed during the 1980s. The first was the policy concern relating to the CAP's budget, which was required to fund the (supported) prices of surplus farm commodities. The second was a social concern, relating to the perceived negative effect of the intensification and extensification of agricultural land use on the environment.

More specifically, the first concern led to the realisation that steps needed to be taken to control farm production within the EU. In addition, in the 1985 Farm Bill, a "land diversion" policy was introduced in the US as a production control mechanism (see Ervin, 1988). As a consequence, the EU took its first step into the domain of an agricultural land use policy by introducing voluntary set-aside in 1988. This embryonic policy offered a "carrot" to farmers in the form of set-aside payments to take a proportion of their land out of production. However, given the level of these payments compared with the foregone production income (with supported prices) from set-aside land, the incentive for farmers to engage with the policy was very weak, and the uptake was therefore very low (see Chapter 2).

Meanwhile, developing alongside this policy concern was the social concern about environmental degradation caused by the intensification and extensification of agricultural land use. In relation to intensification, supported prices gave farmers the incentive to increase yields with the addition of fertiliser, leading specifically to the problem of nitrate leaching. In addition, this price support encouraged farmers to maximise the area of their land under production, thereby leading to the destruction of habitats (e.g. hedgerows and native woodland).

This social concern gave rise to calls in the academic literature for "conservation set-aside" to be introduced — i.e. to deliver a policy "win-win" by encouraging farmers to take land out of production which would also deliver environmental benefits (see, for example, Gasson and Potter, 1988). And while there is no doubt that the formal introduction of voluntary set-aside as an agricultural land use policy in 1988, and its modification in the May 1992 CAP reform to "compliance" set-aside, was driven primarily by the EU's on-going production surpluses and the associated crisis in the CAP's budget, this social concern in the 1980s was undoubtedly a precursor to the subsequent policy process in the late 1990s which led to the introduction of the environmental "sustainability" stage of the CAP with the Agenda 2000 reforms.[7]

---

[7]This social concern also led to the introduction of some early forms of environment-orientated policies such as "Environmentally Sensitive Areas" and "Countryside Stewardship" in the UK.

But while this social concern about the negative impact of farming on the environment was developing further into the 1990s, so was the policy awareness that the CAP's voluntary set-aside scheme was not delivering production control. In this context, the EC's website detailing the history of the CAP (see above) contains an excellent package of information about the development of the May 1992 CAP reform (known also as the "MacSharry reform"). More specifically, it was acknowledged that price support was at the centre of the production surplus problem, and so this needed to be reduced — in so doing particularly encouraging the de-intensification of agricultural land use. In addition, the evolution of the CAP's agricultural land use policy from voluntary to "compliance" set-aside was intended particularly to encourage the de-extensification of agricultural land use. And although the only risk to "compliance" set-aside was that farmers would choose to forego their "compensatory payment" for reduced price support in order to keep all their land in production, this risk proved to be extremely low (see Chapters 3 and 4).

As a consequence, the implementation of the May 1992 CAP reform during the 1990s saw the amelioration of the EU's production surplus problem. And while "compliance" set-aside played its role in this process, academic analysis of the land use response of farmers to their set-aside requirement also revealed the policy "win-win" anticipated by the movement for "conservation set-aside" in the 1980s (see Chapter 7).

This combination of a reduced CAP budget concern, and the growing social awareness of the environmental impacts of agricultural land use, led to increased support for further CAP reform to raise the profile of environmental considerations in its operation — hence the "sustainability" stage of the CAP introduced with the Agenda 2000 reform.

The creation of "Pillar 2" was central to the Agenda 2000 CAP reform, and provided explicit financial support for the "integration of environmental concerns into agricultural policy" (see the Agenda 2000 reform page of the EC's "History of the CAP" website detailed above). And although within this reform set-aside was retained as an agricultural land use policy, increasingly farmers were encouraged to see their set-aside land in terms of the policy "win-win" — i.e. production control plus environmental benefit. Moreover, as noted previously, this policy impetus towards "environmental stewardship" by farmers was maintained with the 2003 CAP reform, which both "de-coupled" direct payments from production and introduced "cross-compliance" whereby farmers were required to keep their land in "good agricultural and environmental condition" in order to receive their direct payments. In addition, there was a further shift of CAP financial support from Pillar 1 to Pillar 2 — known as "modulation", resulting in the development of voluntary environmental stewardship schemes such as England's "Higher Level Stewardship Scheme" (HLS).

So successful was the re-focussing of the CAP's agricultural land use policy towards environmental "sustainability", that the decision was taken in 2008 to abolish set-aside. By this time production surpluses were a thing of the past, and social support for farmers to be incentivised to protect and enhance environmental goods and services had become commonplace. Moreover, given the increased exposure of farmers to production income risk from market price volatility (following reduced price support), farmers themselves were becoming increasingly attracted to the certain income stream associated with participating in environmental stewardship schemes — with schemes such as the English HLS becoming increasingly important to farmers in determining their agricultural land use. So much so that it is now a common sight to see "field margins" and "buffer strips" side-by-side with crops as joint features of agricultural land use.

References

Ackrill, R. (2000) *The Common Agricultural Policy*. Sheffield: Sheffield Academic Press.

Arrow, K. (1963) Research in management controls: A critical synthesis. In: Bonini, C., Jaediche, R. and Wagner, H. (eds.) *Management Controls: New Directions in Basic Research*. New York: McGraw-Hill, 317–327.

Ervin, D. E. (1988) Cropland diversion (set-aside) in the US and UK, *Journal of Agricultural Economics* 39(2): 183–196.

Gardner, B. L. (1987) *The Economics of Agricultural Policies*. New York: Macmillan Publishing Company.

Gasson, R. and Potter, C. (1988) Conservation through land diversion: a survey of farmers' attitudes, *Journal of Agricultural Economics* 39(2): 340–351.

Grossman, S. and Hart, O. (1983) An analysis of the principal-agent problem, *Econometrica* 51(1): 7–45.

Knudsen, A-C. (2009) *Farmers on Welfare: The Making of Europe's Common Agricultural Policy*. Ithaca and London: Cornell University Press.

Laffont, J-J. and Martimont, D. (2002) *The Theory of Incentives: The Principal-Agent Model*. Princeton and Oxford: Princeton University Press.

Laffont, J-J. and Tirole, J. (1993) *A Theory of Incentives in Procurement and Regulation*. Cambridge: MIT Press.

Rees, R. (1985a) The theory of principal and agent: Part 1, *Bulletin of Economic Research* 37(1): 3–26.

Rees, R. (1985b) The theory of principal and agent: Part 2, *Bulletin of Economic Research* 37(2): 75–97.

Ross, S. (1973) The economic theory of agency: The principal's problem, *American Economic Review* 63: 134–139.

PART A

SET-ASIDE AS AN AGRICULTURAL LAND USE POLICY IN THE EUROPEAN UNION

Introduction to Part A

As discussed in Chapter 1, set-aside was introduced as a new land use policy component of the EU's CAP in 1988. It survived in various forms through the 1990s and, despite an initial proposal to reduce its rate to zero as part of the Agenda 2000 CAP reforms, it limped on until being completely abolished in 2008. Moreover, by this time the role of a land use policy as a component of the CAP had broadened and matured into what is now known as environmental stewardship (whereby farmers are offered payments to provide environmental goods and services), primarily under the banner of "Pillar 2" support first introduced as part of the Agenda 2000 CAP reforms (see Part B).

However, academic interest within the EU in set-aside developed several years before its formal introduction, perhaps stimulated by the introduction of a "land diversion" policy in the US as part of the 1995 Farm Bill, but certainly as part of a growing awareness within the EU that the CAP had by the 1980s become too successful in stimulating food production, and that something needed to be done to reduce the growing production surpluses. An early important contribution to the academic debate about set-aside was provided by Ervin (1988) which largely represents a reflection on the (recent) US experience of land diversion as a production control policy, and its implications for the UK. Note this article also cites a range of mainly unpublished papers on the topic of set-aside, primarily by authors based at Wye College (Allan Buckwell and Clive Potter, among others — see Ervin, 1988).

A central preoccupation of the academic debate at the time was whether farmers would choose to participate in a voluntary set-aside policy, given this would mean forgoing (uncertain) production income in return for (certain) set-aside payments. For example, Gasson and Potter (1988) represents the findings of a survey of English (cereal) farmers' willingness to accept set-aside payments as compensation for forgone production income (an early application of the Contingent Valuation Methodology in the UK). In particular, this survey found that farmers would need to be offered a set-aside payment "midway between the average gross margins for winter and spring wheat" in order to be willing to set aside their land (p. 344).

This issue of the level of compensation required to be incentive-compatible with participation in a voluntary set-aside scheme is central to the analysis in Chapter 2 — which finds that because EU cereal farmers were at that time highly protected from world price fluctuations by price support mechanisms, the level of cropping income risk was very low. As a consequence, the substitution of certain set-aside payments for uncertain cropping income held little attraction for cereal farmers — unless set-aside payments were roughly in line with average gross margins. Moreover, given that these payments (set by the European Commission) were estimated at the time to be only 82% of UK average gross margins, it was no surprise that UK uptake of set-aside in 1989 was less than 1% of arable land (Agra Europe, 1989).

Note in this context that the research reported in Chapter 2 was subsequently developed by Hope and Lingard (1992) to allow for a more complex specification of production conditions, and including an analysis of regional differences across England — although the expectations of poor uptake were largely confirmed by this development.

Moreover, this poor uptake of voluntary set-aside was not confined to the UK — in its first year of operation less than 1% of arable land was taken out of production across the EU (Agra Europe, 1989). As a consequence, the production surplus problem continued throughout the period of negotiations leading up to the resolution of the May 1992 CAP reforms (also known as the "MacSharry reforms"), and so this on-going problem was no doubt influential in the decision to modify the existing voluntary set-aside scheme by linking it to the introduction of compensation payments for reductions in price support, which themselves were the centrepiece of the May 1992 CAP reforms (see Fraser, 1991). In effect this linking, whereby participation in set-aside became a requirement for receiving the compensation payments, was the first instance within the CAP of what is now commonly known as "cross-compliance", whereby specific payments made to farmers are made conditional on agricultural land use requirements specified for those farmers. As such this change in the land use policy component of the CAP meant that participation in set-aside became a "stick" rather than a "carrot" to farmers aimed at production control, and heralded the introduction of a still-continuing "compliance" feature to the CAP's land use policy.

All of which raised two questions in academics' minds at the time:

(i) was the threatened withholding of compensation payments a big enough "stick" to encourage participation in set-aside by EU farmers?
(ii) largely as a consequence, how successful would the May 1992 CAP reform of set-aside be as a production control policy?

The first question was considered by Froud and Roberts (1993) in their theoretical examination of the cereal industry supply curve in the presence of "compliance set-aside". They concluded that, above some market price for cereals, farmers would choose to forgo the compensation payments in order to receive production income from all their land, thereby creating a "kink" in the industry supply curve.

This issue of participation is considered further in Chapter 3, where it is shown that for current (at the time) market conditions and proposed levels of compensation payments associated with reductions in price support, the payments made to farmers for their participation in set-aside (i.e. in addition to the compensation payments) could be reduced to 30% of their existing levels and farmers would still be willing to participate in set-aside. As a consequence, this analysis concludes that a high level of participation across the EU could be expected for the new "compliance" set-aside policy.

Further support to this prediction is provided by the empirical analysis in Chapter 4 where Froud and Robert's (1993) "opting-in" price in the market for cereals, below which farmers would choose to participate in set-aside, is estimated to be more than double the existing market price for cereal at the time. Moreover, in the final chapter relating to the participation question (Chapter 5), the role of market price uncertainty in determining participation is examined and found to be only a minor consideration for farmers largely because, even with the proposed reductions, price support provided to EU cereal farmers by the CAP would remain at relatively high levels, thus insulating them to a large extent from market price instability.

Turning next to the second question outlined above, Ervin (1988) had already flagged the problem with the US land diversion scheme of "slippage" (see also Hoag *et al.*, 1993), which is associated with reduced cost-effectiveness in production control, and this problem also attracted the attention of academics analysing the CAP's set-aside policy.

As outlined in Chapter 1, slippage in the context of a policy of output reduction using land input reduction as an instrument is where the percentage reduction in output achieved is less than the percentage reduction in land input (see Gardner, 1987). And using principal-agent theory, this problem has its origin in the concept of the "incentive compatibility" for heterogeneous agents to behave in the way the principal wants them to. This framework was adopted by Bourgeon *et al.* (1995) in their theoretical analysis of the efficiency of the CAP's set-aside policy with heterogeneous farmers, and used to argue that a fully voluntary scheme would be more cost-effective than the (existing) "mandatory" scheme because it would encourage participation of the least efficient farmers.

Moreover, this ground-breaking use of the principal-agent framework to analyse a set-aside policy in a situation of land heterogeneity provided the stimulus for the research reported in the remaining three chapters of Part A. First, Chapter 6 develops further the role of land heterogeneity in reducing the effectiveness of the CAP's set-aside policy. More specifically, while Bourgeon *et al.* (1995) considers the role of land heterogeneity *between* farms, Chapter 6 expands this role to include land heterogeneity *within* farms. On this basis it is shown that, when faced with "compliance" set-aside which compensates farmers on the basis of "reference yields", it is in farmers' best interests to set aside their least productive land. In principal-agent theory this behaviour is called "adverse selection", and Chapter 6 is the first evaluation of this problem and its contribution to slippage within the CAP's set-aside policy.

But Chapter 7 then shows that the slippage "cloud" has a "silver lining" in the form of reduced nitrate leaching. In particular, a farmer's least productive land is often composed of light soils, which are also those that contribute most to nitrate leaching from the use of fertiliser to improve cereal yields. Therefore, by taking this land out of production to satisfy their set-aside requirement and have least impact on their production income, farmers are actually making the best choice of land to set aside in order to reduce nitrate leaching. This chapter represents the first demonstration of such "auspicious selection" of land by farmers from the perspective of environmental benefit, a behaviour which was to become increasingly central to the CAP's agricultural land use policy after the Agenda 200 reforms and the introduction of environmental stewardship support under "Pillar 2".

Finally in Part A, Chapter 8 represents an early, but fully developed, application of principal-agent theory to the analysis of the CAP's agricultural land-use policy. Focussed in this case on the "compliance" set-aside policy, the analysis in this chapter extends its focus beyond just the problem of "adverse selection" considered by Bourgeon *et al.* (1995) and Chapter 6, to also consider the problem of "moral hazard", which is also important to the efficiency of "compliance" set-aside. As outlined in Chapter 1, within principal-agent theory "moral hazard" refers to cheating behaviour, whereby the agent informs the principal that they are going to undertake a required action (e.g. set aside land), and takes the payment associated with this action, but then does not undertake the required action (e.g. keeps the land in production), in the hope of their non-compliance going undetected. Chapter 8 outlines these problems within the context of "compliance" set-aside, and then demonstrates how this policy can be re-designed to introduce both "incentive compatibility" and "compliance compatibility" for participating farmers. These twin solutions to the twin problems of "asymmetric information" identified in principal-agent theory will be seen to be prominent in the analysis in Part B of the CAP's agricultural land use policy as it evolved from simply a set-aside policy to the more complex land use policy known now as environmental stewardship.[1]

---

[1] Although not considered here, a further issue associated with modifying the flows of income to farmers brought about by the introduction of "compliance" set-aside is that of the distribution of income across farmers. This issue was considered within the EU by Allanson (1993), and see also Gissen (1993) for the US.

References

Agra Europe, 17 November 1989, No. 1364.

Allanson, P. A. (1993) The impact of the modulation proposal on the MacSharry plan for the reform of the cereal regime, *European Review of Agricultural Economics* 20(1): 99–109.

Bourgeon, J-M., Jayet, P-A. and Picard, P. (1995) An incentive approach to land set-aside programs, *European Economic Review* 39: 1487–1509.

Ervin, D. E. (1988) Cropland diversion (set-aside) in the US and UK, *Journal of Agricultural Economics* 39(2): 183–196.

Fraser, R. W. (1991) Price-support effects on EC producers, *Journal of Agricultural Economics* 42(1): 1–10.

Froud, J. and Roberts, D. (1993) The welfare effects of the new EC set-aside scheme, *Journal of Agricultural Economics* 44(3): 496–501.

Gardner, B. L. (1987) *The Economics of Agricultural Policies.* New York: Macmillan Publishing Company.

Gasson, R. and Potter, C. (1988) Conservation through land diversion: a survey of farmers' attitudes, *Journal of Agricultural Economics* 39(2): 340–351.

Gisser, M. (1993) Price support, acreage controls and efficient redistribution, *Journal of Political Economy* 101(4): 584–611.

Hoag, D. L., Babcock, B. A. and Foster, W. E. (1993) Filed-level measurement of land productivity and programme slippage, *American Journal of Agricultural Economics* 75(1): 181–189.

Hope, J. and Lingard, J. (1992) The influence of risk aversion on the uptake of set-aside, *Journal of Agricultural Economics* 43(3): 401–411.

Oxford Agrarian Studies, Vol. 19, No. 1, 1991

Chapter 2

'Nice Work if You Can Get It': an Analysis of Optimal Set-aside

ROB FRASER

ABSTRACT *This paper presents a model of the optimal set-aside decision of a risk averse producer which takes account of the trade-off between the certain return to set-aside land and the higher (in expectation) but more uncertain return to cropping. The model is applied to the case of European wheat production. The ratio of set-aside premium to expected net revenue per hectare required for producers to find it optimal to set-aside the qualifying proportion of land is shown to be both very close to unity and relatively insensitive to changes in key parameter values. By contrast, once attractive set-aside premiums have been established, it is shown that the optimal set-aside proportion of land is relatively sensitive to these values.*

1. Introduction

In an attempt to reduce cereal production the European Commission introduced a set-aside programme for cropping areas in 1988–89. This programme differs from that applying in the USA in that for the US programme continued price support is conditional on setting-aside croppable land, whereas the EC programme is voluntary.[1] The principal requirement seems to be that "to qualify, farmers must fallow at least 20% of cropping areas".[2] In return, they receive a fixed premium (in ECU/ha) designed to compensate them for the associated loss of income. Initial take-up of the scheme appears to have been disappointing since the Commission has subsequently adopted a proposal to increase the level of funding. In its first year only 434 000 ha (0.9% of arable land) was taken out of production across the Community, well short of the Commission's target of 1 000 000 ha by 1990.[3]

The aim of this paper is to present a model of optimal set-aside for an individual producer. The model is based on that contained in Fraser (1990) and characterizes the optimal set-aside decision as one which takes account both of the relationship between the certain return to set-aside land and the uncertain return to cropping, and of producer attitudes to risk.[4]

The model is presented in section 2 and is then applied to the case of European wheat production in section 3. It is argued that producers require a very high ratio (close to unity) of set-aside premium to expected net revenue from cropping in order to be induced to set-aside the required minimum of 20% of cropping area. Moreover,

Rob Fraser, University of Warwick and Department of Economics, University of Western Australia, Nedlands, Western Australia 6009, Australia. This paper was written when the author was a Visiting Fellow in the Department of Economics at the University of Warwick. The author is grateful to the editor and an anonymous referee for helpful comments.

62   Rob Fraser

this result is shown to be relatively insensitive to changes in the key parameter values of the model. By contrast, once attractive premiums have been established, the optimal set-aside area is shown to be relatively sensitive to parameter changes so that, for example, a small change in cropping revenue uncertainty can bring about a large change in optimal set-aside area. The paper concludes with a brief summary.

2. The Model

It is assumed that the producer has two alternatives for generating income, either uncertain cropping income or certain set-aside premiums. The former depends both on the uncertain net revenue per unit of output and the uncertain level of yield per hectare. It is further assumed that the producer's total land area is of homogeneous quality, and that there is no scope for productivity improvement by factor intensification on cropped land.[5] On this basis the producer's income (π) can be represented by:

$$\pi = c\alpha\Theta L + s(1-\alpha)L \tag{1}$$

where:

c = uncertain new revenue per unit of output;
Θ = uncertain yield per hectare;
$E(\Theta) = 1$ (expected yield per hectare is assumed to equal unity);
L = area of land;
α = share of land cropped (i.e. not set-aside);
s = premium for set-aside land per hectare.

Taking account of a possible covariance between uncertain net revenue and uncertain yield ($\text{cov}(c,\Theta)$) means expected income ($E(\pi)$) is given by:

$$E(\pi) = \bar{c}\alpha L + \text{cov}(c,\Theta)\alpha L + s(1-\alpha)L \tag{2}$$

where:

$\bar{c}$ = expected net revenue per unit of output.

In addition, the variance of income ($\text{Var}(\pi)$) may be approximated by:[6]

$$\text{Var}(\pi) = \alpha^2 L^2 \sigma_c^2 + \bar{c}^2 \alpha^2 L^2 \sigma_\theta^2 + 2\bar{c}\alpha L \, \text{cov}(c,\Theta) \tag{3}$$

where:

σ_c^2 = variance of net revenue per unit of output;
σ_θ^2 = variance of yield per hectare.

It is further assumed that the producer's expected utility of income ($E(U(\pi))$) is given by a second-order Taylor series approximation about expected income:

$$E(U(\pi)) = U(E(\pi)) + \tfrac{1}{2}U''(E(\pi)).\text{Var}(\pi). \tag{4}$$

The optimal set-aside decision is given by differentiating (4) with respect to α and equating to zero:

$$U'(E(\pi)) \cdot \frac{\partial E(\pi)}{\partial \alpha} + \tfrac{1}{2}U'''(E(\pi)) \cdot \text{Var}(\pi) \cdot \frac{\partial E(\pi)}{\partial \alpha}$$

$$+ \tfrac{1}{2}U''(E(\pi)) \cdot \frac{\partial \text{Var}(\pi)}{\partial \alpha} = 0. \tag{5}$$

On the basis of (2) and (3) the derivatives in (5) are given by:

$$\frac{\partial E(\pi)}{\partial \alpha} = (\bar{c} - s)L + \text{cov}(c, \Theta).L \tag{6}$$

$$\frac{\partial \text{Var}(\pi)}{\partial \alpha} = 2\alpha L^2(\sigma_c^2 + \bar{c}^2\sigma_\theta^2) + 2\bar{c}L\,\text{cov}(c,\Theta). \tag{7}$$

Because the behaviour of a risk neutral producer is characterized by constant marginal utility of income:

$$U''(E(\pi)) = 0$$
$$U'''(E(\pi)) = 0$$

so that (5) reduces to (6). Consequently, as (6) is independent of α, the risk neutral producer's decision is simply to either crop all land or set-aside all land depending on whether expected net revenue per hectare is greater than or less than the set-aside premium:

$$\bar{c} + \text{cov}(c,\Theta) \gtrless s. \tag{8}$$

By contrast, if it is assumed that (6) is positive, then for the risk averse producer ($U''(E(\pi)) < 0$) the optimal set-aside decision involves a trade-off at the margin between the higher expected income from cropping and the associated increased variance of income.[7] Clearly then, the producer's attitude to risk plays an important role in how this trade-off is evaluated. Also important are the levels of revenue and yield variability, particularly as it can be seen from (6) and (7) that higher levels not only increase the variability of income but also, in the case of a negative covariance, reduce the expected income from extra cropping.

In the next section this trade-off is evaluated in the specific context of European wheat production.

3. Application to European Wheat Production

In order to apply the model to the example of European wheat production, equation (5) must be evaluated using the appropriate industry data and a precise form of the producer's utility function. In what follows it is assumed that this utility function is of the constant relative risk aversion form:

$$U(\pi) = \frac{\pi^{1-R}}{1-R}. \tag{9}$$

The principal feature of the behaviour of individuals with this form of utility function is that their willingness to pay for insurance is a constant proportion of their expected income.[8] However, the sensitivity of the results to alternative assumptions about the utility function will be examined.

The required industry-related data are the coefficient of variation of yield per hectare, the coefficient of variation of net revenue per unit of output, and the correlation coefficient between yield and net revenue. The coefficient of variation of European wheat yield was calculated in Fraser (1991) to be 6.5% over the period 1981–84. This value is consistent with the 6.4% calculated by Singh & Byerlee (1990) for wheat grown in irrigated/well watered temperate zones between 1976 and 1986.

64   *Rob Fraser*

However, specifying the coefficient of variation of net revenue per unit of output from wheat is more difficult. With the CAP price support programme in operation, the coefficient of variation of (de-trended) producer prices for wheat in Europe was calculated in Fraser (1991) to be only 5.0% over the period 1981–84. By contrast, the coefficient of variation of world wheat prices was calculated in Hazell *et al.* (1990) to be 23.1% over the period 1949–87. In addition, it can be argued not only that changes to the CAP price support programme in recent years have meant that European wheat producers are now subjected to a higher proportion of the instability in world wheat prices, but also that (somewhat more speculatively) the world wheat price has itself become more unstable since 1984. Moreover, the distinction between net revenue and price per unit of output needs to be borne in mind, particularly as a given level of coefficient of variation of price typically implies a higher associated level of coefficient of variation of net revenue.[9] Because of this lack of clarity regarding the appropriate level of the coefficient of variation of net revenue from European wheat production, in what follows a broad range of possible values is considered. The Hazell *et al.* (1990) estimate of 23.1% is taken as a central case, with the Fraser (1991) estimate of 5.0% as a lower bound, and the Hazell *et al.* (1990) estimate for the world sugar price of 41.6% as an upper bound, this latter value being the highest estimate for all agricultural products. Finally, the correlation coefficient between yield and net revenue is assumed to equal −0.12. This value is estimated in Fraser (1991) for wheat producer prices and yield and is consistent with Europe's relatively small share of world wheat exports (averaging about 15% during the 1980s).

Given that producers are required to set-aside a minimum of 20% of cropping area to qualify for the programme, the approach taken here has been to calculate the ratio of set-aside premium to expected net revenue per hectare which induces a producer to decide that it is optimal to set-aside the required 20% of land. This clearly represents the minimum premium needed to induce the producer's participation in the programme. In particular, on the basis of the specifications outlined above, and setting:

$$L = 100$$

equation (5) is solved for that value of:

$$s/(\bar{c} + \mathrm{cov}(p, \Theta)) \tag{10}$$

which gives:

$$(1 - \alpha)L = 20.$$

In Table 1 the value in (10) is calculated for two different values of attitude to risk (R) and the specified range of coefficients of variation of net revenue (CV_c).[10]

Table 1. Ratio of premium to expected net revenue per hectare set-aside (%)

	R	
CV_c (%)	0.3	0.9
5.0	99.84	99.52
23.1	98.62	95.93
41.6	95.77	88.06

An Analysis of Optimal Set-aside 65

It can be seen from Table 1 that for the central case of CV_c equal to 23.1%, the premium required to induce 20% set-aside is a very high proportion of expected net revenue per hectare for both less and more risk averse producers although, as expected, the required ratio is lower for the more risk averse producer.[11] However, this representation of the results tends to exaggerate the similarity of the behaviour of the two types of producers. An alternative representation is that, for the central case, a producer with $R=0.3$ would be willing to pay up to 1.38% of expected income from 20% of his land for a guarantee that this expectation would be fulfilled on that land, whereas a producer with $R=0$ would be willing to pay 4.07% for the same guarantee. Hence, the more risk averse producer is willing to pay almost three times as much as the less risk averse producer for the same 'insurance' policy.

In addition, Table 1 shows that this result is robust not just with respect to the producer's attitude to risk, but also with respect to the coefficient of variation of net revenue per unit of output. In particular, the required ratio differs by less than 12% between the extremes of risk aversion and variability. A stylized graphical representation based on these results which shows the general relationship between the required ratio, risk aversion and variability is contained in Figure 1.

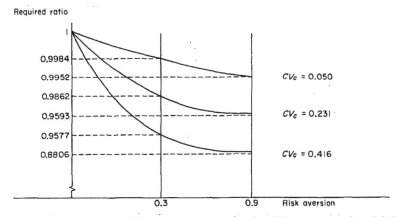

Figure 1. General relationship between required ratio, risk aversion and variability.

To test the sensitivity of the results to alternative specifications of the utility function, consider two other commonly used forms:

(i) $U(\pi) = -e^{-A\pi}$

(ii) $U(\pi) = -(m - k\pi)^2$.

Specification (i) is known as the constant absolute risk aversion form, and (ii) is known as the quadratic form.[12] Table 2 contains the required ratios for the central case of CV_c equal to 23.1% for each of the forms of utility function, where the required ratios have been calculated at the reference values for risk aversion of R equal to 0.3 and 0.9.[13] It is clear from Table 2 that the required ratios are also insensitive to the assumed form of the utility function.

A final indication of the relative insensitivity of the required ratio to significant changes in key parameter values is contained in Table 3 where the required ratios

66   *Rob Fraser*

Table 2. Required ratio of premium to expected net revenue per hectare for each form of utility function (%)

	R	
$U(\pi)$	0.3	0.9
$\pi^{1-R}/1-R$	98.62	95.93
$-e^{-A\pi}$	98.61	95.86
$-(m-k\pi)^2$	98.61	95.80

Table 3. Required ratio of premium to expected net revenue per hectare for a range of qualifying proportions of set-aside land (%)

	R	
Qualifying proportion (%)	0.3	0.9
10	98.45	95.47
20	98.62	95.93
30	98.79	96.40

applying to the central case of CV_c equal to 23.1% but for a range of qualifying proportions of set-aside land are reported.

For example, Table 3 shows that halving the qualifying proportion of set-aside land to 10% only reduces the required ratio by between 0.17 and 0.46% depending on the producer's attitude to risk. Similar to Figure 1, a stylized graphical representation based on these results which shows the general relationship between the required ratio, risk aversion and the qualifying proportion of set-aside land is contained in Figure 2.

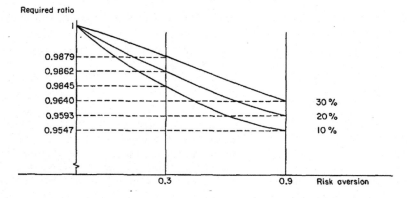

Figure 2. General relationship between required ratio, risk aversion and qualifying proportion of set-aside land.

However, Table 3 also suggests that, unlike the required ratio, the optimal proportion of set-aside land may be relatively sensitive to changes in parameter values once attractive levels of premium have been established. In particular, for the more risk averse producer ($R=0.9$) an increase in premium of less than 1% of expected net revenue per hectare (i.e. from 95.47 to 96.40) is sufficient to triple the optimal level of set-aside land, while for the less risk averse producer this occurs for an increase in required ratio of less than 0.4% (i.e. from 98.45 to 98.79). This suggestion is further supported by the following results. First, for CV_c equal to 23.1%, at the level of premium which induces the less risk averse producer to set-aside 20% of land (i.e. 98.62% of expected net revenue per hectare), the more risk averse producer finds it optimal to set aside 73% of land. Second, an increase in CV_c of only about 10% to 25.5% (with unchanged ratio of premium to expected net revenue per hectare) increases the optimal set-aside proportion by over half from 20% to 34% for both producers.[14] The optimal set-aside proportion therefore appears to be relatively sensitive not just to the ratio of premium to expected net revenue, but also to the variability of net revenue and to the attitude to risk of the producer. But this sensitivity is conditional on the established premiums being at a level sufficient for producers to find it optimal to set-aside some land.

4. Conclusion

This paper has presented a model of the optimal set-aside decision of a risk averse producer which takes account of the trade-off between the certain return to set-aside land and the higher (in expectation) but more uncertain return to cropping. The model was applied to the case of European wheat production.

It was argued that the ratio of set aside premium to expected net revenue per hectare required for producers to find it optimal to set-aside the qualifying proportion of land (20% in the European case) is very close to unity. Moreover this ratio was shown to be relatively insensitive to the level of variability of net revenue, the specification of the utility function and the level of risk aversion of producers and the qualifying proportion of set-aside land. By contrast, it was also shown that, once attractive set-aside premiums have been established, the optimal proportion of set-aside land is relatively sensitive to changes in key parameter values.

Further research is required, however, before the results in this paper can be used to explain or predict the actual level of interest of producers in setting-aside cropping land. In particular, apart from the producer's required ratio as has been calculated here, the other factors determining the decision to set-aside a given area of land are the expected net revenues (per hectare) on that land and the premium on offer for land set-aside. Moreover, although the required ratio has been shown to be a relatively stable value, and although the premium on offer for land set-aside will be known, determining the proportion of total cropping land which could be set-aside requires an evaluation of the distribution of expected net revenue per hectare across this land. Once this distribution is known, the proportion of land set-aside is indicated by the proportion of the distribution which lies below a value equal to the product of the premium and the inverse of the required ratio. While such an evaluation is beyond the scope of this paper, it would seem a worthwhile topic for future study.

Notes

1. See Ervin (1988) for details.

68   Rob Fraser

2. *The Agricultural Situation in the Community 1988 Report*, p. 20.
3. *Agra Europe*, 17 November 1989, p. E1. In the UK 55 000 were set-aside in 1988–89, also representing 0.9% of arable land.
4. The analysis of optimal set-aside contained in Hope & Lingard (1990) explicitly excludes the role of uncertainty and risk aversion in determining the set-aside decision.
5. To the extent that these assumptions do not apply in reality, scope exists for the programme to fail to achieve output reductions proportional to the area of land set-aside.
6. The variance of the product of two random variables, say X and Y, is approximately equal to:

$$\bar{Y}^2\sigma_X^2 + \bar{X}^2\sigma_Y^2 + 2\bar{X}\bar{Y}\,\text{cov}(X,Y)$$

where:

$\bar{X}$=mean of X
$\bar{Y}$=mean of Y.

See Mood *et al.* (1974, p. 181) for more details. Equation (3) is based on:

$X=\alpha Lc$ $(\bar{X}=\alpha L\bar{c})$
$Y=\Theta$ $(\bar{Y}=1)$.

In addition, since α and L are non-random:

$$\sigma_X^2 = \alpha^2 L^2 \sigma_c^2.$$

7. Although the typical covariance in agriculture is negative, it is unlikely to be a dominant factor so that (7) can be expected to be positive.
8. It is straightforward to check that: $R = -U''(\pi)\cdot\pi/U'(\pi)$. See Newbery & Stiglitz (1981, p. 74) for more details of this form of utility function.
9. With costs usually known, they reduce the expected level of revenue, but not its variability.
10. Newbery & Stiglitz (1981) survey empirical evidence relating to the value of R and conclude that for Indian farmers it typically varies between 0.5 and 1.2. Bond & Wonder's (1980) evidence suggests values between 0 and 0.45 for Australian farmers.
11. This result is consistent with the survey evidence reported in Gasson & Potter (1988) which suggests English farmers would need to be offered a set-aside premium "midway between the average gross margins for winter and spring wheats" (p. 344) in order to be willing to set-aside land. Moreover, the ratios are well above the 82% estimated by the European Commission for the UK. See *Agra Europe*, 17 November 1989, p. E2.
12. Newbery & Stiglitz (1981, p. 74) discuss these forms in detail and argue that they are less appealing than the constant relative risk aversion form. In particular, specification (i) features a willingness to pay for insurance which is constant regardless of expected income, while specification (ii) requires the additional restriction that $m>k\pi$ in order for the marginal utility of income to remain positive.
13. This requires adjusting the values of A, m and k so that $R=0.3$ and 0.9 at the optimum in equation (5) as R is not constant for the constant absolute risk aversion and quadratic forms.
14. More precisely, 34.0% for $R=0.9$ and 33.7% for $R=0.3$, reflecting the more risk averse producer's stronger preference for stable income.

References

Agra Europe (1989) 17 November, No. 1364.

Bond, G. & Wonder, B. (1980) Risk attitudes amongst Australian farmers, *Australian Journal of Agricultural Economics*, 24, pp. 1–15.

Ervin, D.E. (1988) Cropland diversion (set-aside) in the US and UK, *Journal of Agricultural Economics*, 39, pp. 183–196.

European Commission (1989) *The Agricultural Situation in the Cmmunity 1988 Report* (Luxembourg, EC).

Fraser, R.W. (1990) Producer risk, product complementarity and product diversification, *Journal of Agricultural Economics*, 41, pp. 103–107.

Fraser, R.W. (1991) Price support effects on EC producers, *Journal of Agricultural Economics*, 42, pp. 1–10.

Gasson, R. & Potter, C. (1988) Conservation through land diversion: a survey of farmers' attitudes, *Journal of Agricultural Economics*, 39, pp. 340–351.

Hazell, P.B.R., Jaramillo, M. & Williamson, A. (1990) The relationship between world price instability and the prices farmers receive in developing countries, *Journal of Agricultural Economics*, 41, pp. 227–241.

Hope, J. & Lingard, J. (1990) The economics of set-aside: linear programming analysis, *Farm Management*, 7, pp. 315–325.

Mood, A.M., Graybill, F.A. & Boes, D.C. (1974) *Introduction to the Theory of Statistics*, 3rd edn (Kogakusha, McGraw-Hill).

Newbery, D.M.G. & Stiglitz, J.E. (1981) *The Theory of Commodity Price Stabilisation* (Oxford, Clarendon Press).

Singh, A.J. & Byerlee, D. (1990) Relative variability in wheat yields across countries and over time, *Journal of Agricultural Economics*, 41, pp. 21–32.

Chapter 3

SET-ASIDE PREMIUMS AND
THE MAY 1992 CAP REFORMS

R. Fraser*

This paper considers the linking of participation in the set-aside programme to the receipt of a compensatory payment for proposed reductions in European Community price support announced in May 1992. It is shown that in this situation set-aside premiums should lie between a lower bound sufficient to deter opting-out in favour of full cropping, and an upper bound approximately equal to a level sufficient to induce voluntary participation in the programme. The initial level of Community price support and the extent of reductions from this level are shown to be the main factors determining the gap between the upper- and lower-bound premiums. The impact of removing the compensatory payment system is also examined.

1. Introduction

In an earlier paper (Fraser, 1991a) the author examined the issue of the set-aside premiums required for the voluntary participation of European Community (EC) wheat growers in the Common Agricultural Policy (CAP) set-aside programme. A model of land allocation between cropping and set-aside was combined with data on the level and variability of Community wheat prices and production. For wheat growers with a range of attitudes to risk, it determined the minimum set-aside premiums (as a percentage of expected net revenue per hectare) required for these growers to be willing to trade off uncertain cropping income for certain set-aside premiums on a given percentage of their land.

However, a central feature of the May 1992 CAP reforms was a modification to the existing set-aside programme, linking participation to the receipt of a 'compensatory payment' for proposed reductions in price support.[†] In effect, this reform converts the Community set-aside programme from a voluntary one to one of compulsory participation (in order to receive the compensatory payment), in parallel with the features of the US Acreage Reduction Program.

Moreover, this reform alters the relationship between set-aside premiums and the cropping income alternative. In the case of voluntary participation, the set-aside premiums were required to be at least equal to a *minimum* percentage of expected net revenue per hectare in order to induce participation. With

* Dr Rob Fraser is a Senior Lecturer at The University of Western Australia. I am grateful to Allan Buckwell, an anonymous referee and the Editor for helpful comments. Thanks also go to seminar participants at Wye College and the Universities of Cambridge and Manchester.

† See *Agra Europe* May 22, 1992 pp.P1-15 '...over the period to 1997... (t)he individual producer will be fully compensated for this loss of potential income through direct compensatory payments' (p.P1). However '(w)hat is still not clear is the life of the compensatory subsidy system' (p.P15).

participation made compulsory in order to receive the compensatory payment, the set-aside premiums should not exceed a *maximum* level if they are to avoid being unnecessarily remunerative. That is to say, if participation in set-aside is a requirement for receiving the compensatory payment, it is wasteful of EC budget funds to set premiums at a level which would in other circumstances induce voluntary participation. In addition, the attractiveness of set-aside premiums becomes dependent on the relative sizes of the (uncertain) cropping income forgone on set-aside land and the associated compensatory payment. Participation is only a requirement for receiving the compensatory payment; thus, if set-aside premiums are not sufficiently remunerative, a wheat grower may opt out altogether, in favour of cropping all land and forgoing the compensatory payment rather than setting aside 15% of land and receiving this payment.

Consequently, the May 1992 reforms mean that established set-aside premiums (as a percentage of expected net revenue per hectare) should now lie between a lower bound necessary to deter farmers from opting-out of the set-aside programme, and an upper bound above which the requirement of 15% set-aside would have been achieved without making the receipt of the compensatory payment conditional upon participation in the set-aside programme. Moreover, the size of the lower bound is of particular significance as it represents the extent to which set-aside premiums could be reduced to effect budgetary savings without putting at risk the control of production associated with the set-aside programme.

The aim of this paper is to analyse the roles of the determinants of the size of these upper- and lower-bound premiums. The model set out in Section 2 identifies the following four determinants of these bounds:

(i)   the attitude of Community wheat growers to uncertain prices and yield (i.e. their 'risk-aversion')

(ii)   the level of wheat price uncertainty

(iii)   the level of EC price support (relative to expected world wheat prices)

(iv)   the presence or not of the compensatory payment for reduced price support based on the area of land not set aside.

However, the numerical analysis of Section 3 shows that the upper bound is relatively insensitive to all these determinants, and that the lower bound is only sensitive to the level of EC price support and the presence or not of the compensatory payment. The paper ends with a brief summary.

2.   Model and Data

In Fraser (1991a), a producer is assumed to have two alternatives for generating income, either uncertain cropping income or certain set-aside premiums. Cropping income depends on an uncertain price per unit of output, an uncertain yield per hectare, and certain production costs per hectare. In the context of the May 1992 reforms, the producer may have a third source of income: the compensatory payment for reduced price support. With this specification, the producer's income (π) can be represented by:

$$\pi = p\alpha\Theta L - r\alpha L + s(1 - \alpha)L + c\alpha L \qquad (1)$$

R. FRASER

where: p = uncertain price per unit of output

Θ = uncertain yield per hectare ($E(\Theta)=1$)

L = area of land

α = share of land cropped (i.e. $1-\alpha$ = share of set-aside land)

r = certain production costs per hectare

s = premium for set-aside land per hectare

c = the compensatory payment per hectare of land not set aside for producers participating in the set-aside programme.

It is shown in Fraser (1991b) that, if the underlying (world) price distribution is assumed to be normal, then in the presence of price support at level $\hat{p}$ the expected level ($E(p_u)$) and variability ($Var(p_u)$) of producer prices are given by:

$$E(p_u) = F(\hat{p})\hat{p} + (1 - F(\hat{p}))[\bar{p} + \sigma_p Z(\hat{p})/(1 - F(\hat{p}))] \tag{2}$$

$$Var(p_u) = (1 - F(\hat{p}))\, \sigma_p^2 \{1 - [Z(\hat{p})/(1 - F(\hat{p}))]^2 + ((\hat{p} - \bar{p})/\sigma_p).$$
$$Z(\hat{p})/(1 - F(\hat{p}))\} + (1 - F(\hat{p}))F(\hat{p})\{\hat{p} - [\bar{p} + \sigma_p Z(\hat{p})/(1 - F(\hat{p}))]\}^2 \tag{3}$$

where: $\hat{p}$ = the support price

$F(\hat{p})$ = cumulative probability of price being less than or equal to $\hat{p}$

$\bar{p}$ = mean of the underlying (world) price distribution

σ_p = standard deviation of the underlying price distribution (σ_p^2 = variance)

$Z(\hat{p})$ = ordinate of the standard normal distribution at $\hat{p}$.

Producer's expected utility of income $[E(U(\pi))]$ is represented by a second-order Taylor series approximation about expected income ($E(\pi)$):

$$E(U(\pi)) = U(E(\pi)) + \tfrac{1}{2} U''(E(\pi)).Var(\pi) \tag{4}$$

where $Var(\pi)$ = variance of income. On this basis, the optimal set-aside decision (in the absence of any policy constraints such as a conditional compensatory payment) is given by differentiating (4) with respect to α and equating to zero:[*]

$$U'(E(\pi)).\frac{\partial E(\pi)}{\partial \alpha} + \tfrac{1}{2}U'''(E(\pi)).Var(\pi).\frac{\partial E(\pi)}{\partial \alpha} + \tfrac{1}{2}U''(E(\pi)).\frac{\partial Var(\pi)}{\partial \alpha} = 0 \tag{5}$$

In (4) expected income and the variance of income can be represented using (2) and (3) by (see Mood, Graybill and Boes, 1974, p. 181):

$$E(\pi) = E(p_u).\alpha L + Cov(p_u,\Theta).\alpha L - r\alpha L + s(1 - \alpha)L + c\alpha L \tag{6}$$

---

[*] Concavity of the utility function, which applies if the producer is assumed to be risk-averse ($U''(\pi)<0$), ensures that the second-order condition for a maximum is satisfied.

$$\text{Var}(\pi) = \alpha^2 L^2 \text{Var}(p_u) + (E(p_u))^2 \alpha^2 L^2 \sigma_\Theta^2 + 2 E(p_u)\alpha L \, \text{Cov}(p_u,\Theta) \qquad (7)$$

where: σ_Θ^2 $\quad$ = variance of yield

$\quad\quad$ $\text{Cov}(p_u,\Theta)$ = covariance between producer price and yield.

The derivatives in (5) are given by:*

$$\frac{\partial E(\pi)}{\partial \alpha} = (E(p_u) - r - s + \text{Cov}(p_u,\Theta))L \qquad (8)$$

$$\frac{\partial \text{Var}(\pi)}{\partial \alpha} = 2\alpha L^2(\text{Var}(p_u) + (E(p_u))^2 \sigma_\Theta^2) + 2 E(p_u)L \, \text{Cov}\,(p_u,\Theta) \qquad (9)$$

In the situation of a voluntary set-aside programme, it can be seen from (5), (8) and (9) that, for a risk-neutral producer $(U''(\pi) = 0, U'''(\pi) = 0)$, the decision is to crop all land or set-aside all land depending on whether the set-aside premium is less than or greater than expected net revenue per hectare:

$$s/[E(p_u) - r + \text{Cov}(p_u,\Theta)] \lessgtr 1 \qquad (10)$$

For a risk-averse producer $(U''(\pi) < 0)$, the optimal set-aside decision involves a trade-off at the margin between the higher expected income from cropping (i.e. (10) is less than unity) and the associated increased variance of income. In addition, for a given level of set-aside (i.e. $1 - \alpha$) and a given level of risk-aversion, the ratio in (10) can be chosen such that (5) is satisfied. The value of the ratio derived in this way (with $(1 - \alpha)$ equal to the set-aside requirement and including unconditionally the amount of the compensatory payment as part of $E(\pi)$) represents the upper bound for the set-aside premium in the situation of a compulsory (i.e. in order to receive the compensatory payment) set-aside programme.

By contrast, the lower bound can be found by reducing the value of the ratio in (10) until the value of expected utility in (4) given on the basis of the set-aside requirement, and with the amount of the compensatory payment added to $E(\pi)$, is equal to the value of expected utility with all land cropped (i.e. $\alpha = 1$), and no compensatory payment.

In the case of both bounds, the amount of compensatory payment can be calculated by using (2) to determine the impact on expected producer prices of the reduction in price support ($\hat{p}$) and multiplying this change by the expected output from land not set aside.† For the purpose of numerical analysis of these upper and lower bounds, the utility function is specified as (Pope and Just, 1991; Fraser, 1991a):

$$U(\pi) = \frac{\pi^{1-R}}{1-R} \qquad (11)$$

---

* Note that, although c is included in (6) for producers participating in the set-aside programme, the optimal set-aside decision in (5) is made in the absence of any policy constraints. Consequently, marginal expected profit is independent of c.

† According to *Agra Europe*, the amount of output on which compensation is payable is referred to as the 'subsidy entitlement quota' and this quota is based on average regional yields rather than individual yields (May 22, 1992 p. P1).

Table 1 Values Relating to Price and Output Uncertainty for European Community Wheat Production

CV_p	23.1%*
CV_Θ	6.5%†
$\hat{p}$	1.1$\hat{p}$‡
ρ	−0.12§

Notes:
* Coefficient of variation of world wheat prices calculated by Hazell, Jaramillo and Williamson (1990) for the period 1949-87.
† Coefficient of variation of Community wheat yield calculated by Fraser (1991b) over the period 1981-84. Singh and Byerlee (1990) estimate 6.4% for wheat grown in irrigated/well watered temperature zones between 1976 and 1986.
‡ $\hat{p}/\bar{p}$ estimated in Fraser (1991b) for Community wheat over the period 1981-84. Brown (1990) provides a similar estimate.
§ Estimated in Fraser (1991b) for Community wheat.

where: R = the producer's (constant) coefficient of relative risk-aversion

$$= -U''(\pi)\pi/U'(\pi).$$

Application to Community wheat can be achieved by using the industry data contained in Table 1 and by setting the value of L equal to 100 and the value of r equal to zero.* Finally, on the basis of the May 1992 CAP reforms, the set-aside requirement (i.e. $1 - \alpha$) is set equal to 15% of croppable land, and the 'phased-in' reductions in price support are set in total to equal about 30% of the initial level.

In this context, the roles of the determinants of the size of the upper and lower bounds for set-aside premiums can be evaluated by varying the specified values of CV_p, R and $\hat{p}/\bar{p}$, and by including or removing the compensatory payment.

3. Numerical Results

Table 2 contains estimates of upper- and lower-bound set-aside premiums (as percentages of expected net revenue per hectare) using the 'base case' parameter values detailed in Section 2. The Table features two levels of risk-aversion, $R=0.3$ and $R=0.9$ (see Fraser, 1991a), three 'phased-in' reductions in the level of Community price support from a given initial relative to expected world price (initial $\hat{p}/\bar{p} = 1.1$), and possible removal of the compensatory payment at the end of the phasing-in period ($\hat{p}/\bar{p}$ reduced by about 30% to 0.8). While the upper-bound set-aside premium is lower in a situation of higher risk-aversion, overall it is relatively insensitive to the level of risk-aversion, the level of price support and the presence or not of the compensatory payment. The lower-bound premium is also relatively insensitive to the level of risk-aversion, but both the extent of reductions in the level of Community price support and the presence or not of the compensatory payment are important determinants of the size of the lower-bound premium.

* For the numerical analysis, the following definition is used:

$$Cov(p_u, \Theta) = \rho\sigma_{pu}\sigma_\Theta \qquad (12)$$

where: ρ = correlation coefficient between producer prices and yield
   σ_{pu} = standard deviation of producer prices
   σ_Θ = standard deviation of yield.

Table 2   Base Case Estimates of the Impact of Reduced Price Support on Upper- and Lower-Bound Set-Aside Premiums for Community Wheat*

Ratio of Level of Price Support to Expected World Price ($\hat{p}/\bar{p}$)		Risk Aversion Coefficient (R)		Total Decrease in Expected Producer Price (% $E(p_w)$)
		0.3	0.9	
1.1	Upper Bound	99.70	99.09	
	Lower Bound	99.67	99.01	
1.0	Upper Bound	99.53	98.59	
	Lower Bound	69.11	68.05	−5.09
0.9	Upper Bound	99.30	97.93	
	Lower Bound	45.22	43.62	−8.69
0.8	Upper Bound (CP)†	99.08	97.27	
	Lower Bound (CP)	29.17	27.02	−10.94
	Upper Bound (NCP)‡	98.98	97.00	
	Lower Bound (NCP)	98.90	96.75	

Notes: * Premium as a percentage of expected net revenue per hectare.
        † CP = compensatory payment included.
        ‡ NCP = compensatory payment removed.

Table 3   Sensitivity of Estimates of Upper- and Lower-Bound Set-Aside Premiums to Increased World Price Uncertainty* (CVp increased from 23.1% to 35%)

Ratio of Level of Price Support to Expected World Price ($\hat{p}/\bar{p}$)		Risk Aversion Coefficient (R)		Total Decrease in Expected Producer Price (% $E(p_w)$)
		0.3	0.9	
1.1	Upper Bound	99.38	98.15	
	Lower Bound	99.32	98.00	
1.0	Upper Bound	99.11	97.37	
	Lower Bound	71.28	69.32	−4.66
0.9	Upper Bound	98.79	96.43	
	Lower Bound	46.76	44.04	−8.37
0.8	Upper Bound (CP)†	98.44	95.44	
	Lower Bound (CP)	26.77	23.33	−11.17
	Upper Bound (NCP)‡	98.28	94.98	
	Lower Bound (NCP)	98.13	94.59	

Notes: * Premium as a percentage of expected net revenue per hectare.
        † CP = compensatory payment included.
        ‡ NCP = compensatory payment removed.

Because successive reductions in the level of price support are associated with increases in the size of the compensatory payment (to reflect the size of the fall in expected producer price associated with each fall in price support: see the last column of Table 2), opting-out of the set-aside programme becomes less attractive. Specifically, whereas with the initial level of price support (and therefore a zero compensatory payment) the only consequence of opting-out is a slight increase in the variability of income due to 100% rather than 85% cropping, with the final level of price support a compensatory payment equal to 10.94% of the initial expected producer price multiplied by expected output is forgone by opting-out. As a result, the ratio of set-aside premium to expected net revenue per hectare can be reduced from about 99% to about 28% and still give producers sufficient financial incentive to remain in the set-aside programme. However, if the compensatory payment is removed at the end of the phasing-in period, then the lower-bound premium reverts approximately to its initial level.

Next consider the sensitivity of this pattern of results to the level of uncertainty of world prices. The results in Table 3 have been calculated on the basis of a coefficient of variation of world price of 35% (instead of 23.1%). A comparison of Tables 2 and 3 shows that the estimates are relatively insensitive to the level of uncertainty of world prices with all estimates altered by less than 9% in the case of $R=0.3$ and by less than 14% in the case of $R=0.9$, despite the 50% increase in the coefficient of variation of world price. However, this insensitivity is consistent with the insensitivity of the results to the level of risk-aversion: increases in uncertainty or in risk-aversion have a similar effect on producer welfare.

Finally, consider the sensitivity of this pattern of results to the initial level of Community price support relative to expected world price. The results in Table 4 have been calculated on the basis of the initial situation featuring a ratio of the Community support price to expected world price of 1.3 (instead of 1.1). They show once again the relative insensitivity of the upper-bound premium to all parameter values. However, the lower-bound premiums following reductions in price support are significantly smaller than those in Table 2. This reflects the larger size of compensatory payment required in this situation to compensate producers fully for the associated reductions in their expected price (compare the last column in Tables 2 and 4).

Table 4   Sensitivity of Estimates of Upper- and Lower-Bound Set-Aside Premiums to the Initial Level of Community Price Support Relative to Expected World Price* (Initial $\hat{p}/\bar{p}$ increased from 1.1 to 1.3)

Ratio of Level of Price Support to Expected World Price ($\hat{p}/\bar{p}$)		Risk Aversion Coefficient (R)		Total Decrease in Expected Producer Price (% $E(p_w)$)
		0.3	0.9	
1.3	Upper Bound	99.86	99.60	
	Lower Bound	99.85	99.56	
1.2	Upper Bound	99.82	99.46	
	Lower Bound	60.05	59.64	−6.55
1.1	Upper Bound	99.71	99.15	
	Lower Bound	20.82	20.17	−12.21
1.0	Upper Bound (CP)†	99.58	98.74	
	Lower Bound (CP)	0§	0	−16.66
	Upper Bound (NCP)‡	99.50	98.52	
	Lower Bound (NCP)	99.46	98.40	

Notes: *   Premium as a percentage of expected net revenue per hectare.

   †   CP = compensatory payment included.

   ‡   NCP = compensatory payment removed.

   §   In this situation the set-aside premium could instead be a tax of almost 15% and still deter opting-out.

4.   Conclusion

As a consequence of the May 1992 CAP reforms, set-aside premiums should lie between a lower bound sufficient to deter opting-out in favour of full cropping (and forgoing the compensatory payment), and an upper bound approximately equal to the previous (voluntary participation) lower bound. The model of the set-aside decision presented in Section 1 formed the basis of a numerical analysis in Section 2 of the role of four factors in determining the size of the upper- and lower-bound premiums: the level of world price uncertainty; the level of producer risk-aversion; the level of Community price support relative to expected world price; and the presence or not of the compensatory payment. It was shown that the size of the upper-bound premium is relatively insensitive to all four determinants. By contrast, the size of the lower-bound premium was shown to be relatively sensitive both to the initial level of Community price support relative to expected world price, and to the extent of reductions in price support from this level. In particular, a higher initial level of price support and/or larger reductions from this initial level mean that larger compensatory payments are required for producers to be fully compensated for the loss of expected income associated with such reductions. As a consequence, larger budgetary savings from reductions in set-aside premiums are possible without inducing producers to opt-out of the set-aside programme. However, removing the compensatory payment also removes the main disincentive to opting-out and therefore eliminates any scope for the EC to effect budgetary savings via reduced set-aside premiums without putting at risk the objective of production control.

References

Agra Europe (1992). 22 May, No. 1492.

Brown, C. G. (1990). Distributional Aspects of CAP Price Support. *European Review of Agricultural Economics,* 17(3), 289-302.

Fraser, R. W. (1991a). 'Nice Work If You Can Get It': An Analysis of Optimal Set-Aside. *Oxford Agrarian Studies,* 19(1), 61-69.

Fraser, R. W. (1991b). Price-Support Effects on EC Producers. *Journal of Agricultural Economics,* 42(1), 1-10.

Hazell, P. B. R., Jaramillo, M. and Williamson, A. (1990). The Relationship Between World Price Instability and the Prices Farmers Receive in Developing Countries. *Journal of Agricultural Economics,* 41(2), 227-41.

Mood, A. M., Graybill, F. A. and Boes, D. C. (1974). *Introduction to the Theory of Statistics.* 3rd Edition, McGraw-Hill, Kogakusha.

Pope, R. D. and Just, R. E. (1991). On Testing the Structure of Risk Preferences in Agricultural Supply Analysis. *American Journal of Agricultural Economics,* 73(3), 743-48.

Singh, A. J. and Byerlee, D. (1990). Relative Variability in Wheat Yields Across Countries and Over Time. *Journal of Agricultural Economics,* 41(1), 21-32.

Chapter 4

PARTICIPATION IN SET-ASIDE:
WHAT DETERMINES THE OPTING IN PRICE?

D. Roberts, J. Froud and R. W. Fraser*

This paper analyses the decision facing Community farmers of whether or not to participate in the voluntary rotational set aside scheme. For each individual producer, an "indifference price" for cereals can be identified at which the expected profit from either opting in or out of the scheme is identical. An expected utility model is used to investigate the influence of various factors on the level of indifference price and hence the uptake of set aside. Empirical analysis, based on FBS farm level data, suggests that this price is relatively insensitive to the uncertainty faced by the farmer and the farmer's attitude to risk. It is, however, sensitive both to the key policy variables and to the farm's cost structure and yield. The results presented help explain the initial high take up of set aside in England.

1. Introduction

Recent policy decisions and statements from the European Commission suggest that the set aside scheme, introduced to the arable regime of the CAP as part of the 1992 MacSharry reforms, is set to continue well beyond its initial three years of implementation. The introduction of set aside has been met with mixed reactions. On the one hand, it has been argued that set aside was "neither a necessary nor desirable" component of the CAP reform package, rather an admission that the price level that continues to be supported by border protection is still too high (Josling, 1993). On the other hand, one could argue that the flexibility provided by set aside proved critical in the successful completion of the Uruguay Round of GATT negotiations. Classified as production neutral, and thus exempt from the domestic farm support reductions agreed as part of the final GATT deal, the arable compensation payments linked to set aside have provided the Community with the option of reducing internal support prices whilst increasing compensation payments should the level of export subsidies near their agreed limit. Either way, it is highly likely that the rules by which the set aside scheme is implemented will be manipulated in the future which will, in turn, influence the level of participation in the scheme.

* Dr D. Roberts is a Research Fellow, Centre for Rural Development, University of Aberdeen, Ms J. Froud is a lecturer in the Department of Accounting and Finance, the University of Manchester, and Dr R. Fraser is an Associate Professor in the Faculty of Agriculture, University of Western Australia and a Hallsworth Fellow in the School of Economic Studies, the University of Manchester.

Journal of Agricultural Economics
47 (1) (1996) 89-98

Participation during the 1993 crop year, the first year of the scheme, seems to have varied significantly between member states. Whilst 4.7 million hectares of arable land in the EU (9.6% of the total arable base area) was withdrawn from cereal production as a result of set-aside, UK farmers set aside 12.6% of their national base area, and Spanish farmers, who have the third largest arable base area in the community, only withdrew 9.9% from production (Home Grown Cereals Authority, 1994). However, since small farms are excluded from the set aside requirement under the so-called "simplified scheme",* these differences will reflect not only national participation rates but also the distribution of cereals area by farm size together with regional yield differences (Allanson, 1993).

Focusing on producers whose base arable area exceeds the simplified scheme's maximum entitlement, this paper analyses the decision of whether or not to participate in the post-May 1992 rotational set aside scheme. Assuming that a farmer makes this choice on the basis of the expected utility of profits, in section 2 an "indifference price" is identified at which participating in or opting out of the scheme are equally desirable. An expected utility model is then used to investigate the influence of various factors on the level of the indifference price and hence the uptake of set aside. The empirical analysis, in section 3, investigates the situation during the first year of the scheme's implementation, 1993/94, and is based on farm level FBS data relating to English cereal producers. Finally some concluding remarks are given in section 4.

2.   The Model of the Set Aside Decision

A key characteristic of the post-1992 CAP cereals regime is that participation in the set aside scheme is voluntary with compensation payments made to induce farmers to withdraw land from production. It follows that every individual arable producer in the community now faces a choice – either to join the scheme, set aside a fixed proportion of their base arable area but receive compensation for doing so or, alternatively, forfeit the compensation payments but maintain flexibility on their arable production. In order to investigate this participation decision, a model, based on Fraser (1993) is developed which characterises the decision as a choice between more and less uncertain profit alternatives.

Specifically, on the assumption that the farmer produces only one output which is subject to uncertain yield and price, a non-participating farmer has profit (π_0) given by

$$\pi_0 = p_u \theta L - r_0 L \tag{1}$$

where p_u = uncertain producer price,

       θ = uncertain yield,

       r_0 = total cost per hectare,

       L = area of land in hectares.

---

* The simplified scheme allows producers to claim area compensation payments up to a given number of hectares (calculated from regional yields) without setting aside land provided they meet eligibility criteria. In England, for example, those growing less than 15.51 hectares of supported crops are eligible for this so-called simplified scheme. Alternatively, producers growing more than this area may claim on part of their cropping under the simplified scheme, thus excluding themselves from the general set-aside scheme.

whereas a farmer who chooses to participate in the set aside scheme will have profit (π_i) given by

$$\pi_i = p_u \theta \alpha L - r_i \alpha L + (1 - \alpha)sL + \alpha cL \qquad (2)$$

where r_i = total cost per hectare of a participator,

$(1 - \alpha)$ = the set aside requirement,

c   = price compensatory payment per hectare,

s   = set aside premium per hectare.

In what follows it is assumed that, in the short run, the total cost per hectare of a participating farmer, r_i, is greater than that of a non-participator, r_0, since the former is allocated to a smaller area of land (αL as opposed to L). The short run focus of the model is, in part, justified by the uncertainty of the current policy environment.

Thus with FC representing total fixed costs and assuming that the variable costs per hectare of a participator and non-participator are identical, then

$$r_0 - \frac{FC}{L} = r_i - \frac{FC}{\alpha L}$$

rearranging and letting β represent the share of fixed costs in total costs for full cropping, that is,

$$\beta = \frac{FC}{r_0 L}$$

it can be shown that

$$r_i = r_0 \left[\frac{1 - (1 - \alpha)(1 - \beta)}{\alpha} \right] \qquad (3)$$

Taking expectations of equations (1) and (2), and subtracting the expected profits of a participator from that of a non-participator, it can be shown that

$$E(\pi_0) - E(\pi_i) = (1 - \alpha)E(p_u)E(\theta)L + (1 - \alpha)cov(p_u,\theta)L$$
$$- (1 - \alpha)(1 - \beta)r_0 L - (1 - \alpha)sL - \alpha cL \qquad (4)$$

where $E(p_u)$ = expected producer price,

$cov(p_u,\theta)$ = covariance between producer price and yield.

This equation captures the essential decision facing arable farmers. That is, if the farmer is risk neutral, then the decision of whether or not to participate in the set aside scheme depends on whether the right-hand-side of equation (4) exceeds or is less than zero. Moreover, increasing the world market price and hence the expected producer price, $E(p_u)$, from an initial level at which participation in the set aside programme is more profitable will, at some leveL, equate (4) to zero. The expected price corresponding to this equality is the so-called indifference price of the farmer, the price at which he or she would receive the same level of profit as either a participator or non-participator.* For expected prices above (below) this level, opting out of (into) the scheme is the preferred decision.

Equation (4) suggests a number of factors that will influence the level of the indifference price and hence participation in the set aside scheme. Three of these factors are policy parameters. Specifically, a decrease in the set aside requirement, $(1 - \alpha)$, or an increase in either the level of set aside premiums, s, or the level of price compensation, c, can be expected to increase the indifferenc price, and *ceteris paribus,* make participation in the scheme more attractive. More interestingly, the equation indicates some of the farm specific characteristics that will influence the decision of whether to opt in or out of the scheme. The higher total costs per hectare, r_0, the higher will be the indifference price of an individual. However, equation (8) indicates that it is not just total costs per hectare that influence the level of indifference price but also the share of fixed costs in total costs, β. Since opting to set aside land means that fixed costs have to be spread over a smaller area, the higher the level of β, *ceteris paribus,* the lower the indifference price. Consequently, a farmer with a higher total cost per hectare may have a lower indifference price than a farmer with lower total costs per hectare if the latter also has a lower share of fixed costs in total costs.† The level of expected yield, particularly in relation to the regional reference yield used by the Commission in the calculation of compensation payments, is also shown to influence the level of indifference price. Finally, the price will be reduced by either a larger positive or smaller negative covariance between price and yield.

Since the level of set aside and price compensation payments are pre-determined whilst the level of producer price and yield are uncertain, the level of risk aversion could, *a priori,* be expected to influence whether or not a producer chose to participate in the scheme. Relaxing the assumption of risk neutrality, the variance of equations (1) and (2) are given by

$$\text{var}(\pi_0) = E(\theta)^2 L^2 \text{var}(p_u) + E(p_u)^2 L^2 \text{var}(\theta) + 2L\text{cov}(p_u,\theta)E(p_u)E(\theta) \quad (5)$$

and

$$\text{var}(\pi_i) = \alpha^2 E(\theta)^2 L^2 \text{var}(p_u) + \alpha^2 E(p_u)^2 L^2 \text{var}(\theta) + 2\alpha L\text{cov}(p_u,\theta)E(p_u)E(\theta) \quad (6)$$

where $\text{var}(p_u) = $ the variance of the producer price, and

$\text{var}(\theta) = $ the variance of yield‡.

Barring the case where the covariance between price and yield is not only negative but of a magnitude such that it dominates the sum of the first two terms, equations (5) and (6) indicate that profits are more variable for a non-participating farmer than a farmer who opts to set aside land. Consequently,

---

* The concept of an indifference price is developed in Lee and Helmberger (1985) whilst Froud and Roberts (1993) use it to illustrate the nature of the supply curve for cereals under the new set aside regime.

† For example, if $r_0 = 100$, $\beta = 0.75$, $(1 - \alpha) = 0.15$ and $L = 100$, then the cost term in equation (4) equals -375. Whereas, if $r_0 = 80$, $\beta = 0.5$, $(1 - \alpha) = 0.15$ and $L = 100$ then this term equals -600.

‡ Equations (5) and (6) are derived using the formula for approximating the variance of a function of two random variables, given in Mood *et al.* (1974).

ceteris paribus, a risk averse farmer can be expected to have a higher indifference price than a risk neutral farmer. In addition, they reveal that the indifference price of a risk averse farmer is increased by either an increase in the variance of producer price, $var(p_u)$, or the variance of yield, $var(\theta)$.

Finally, if the underlying world price distribution is assumed to be normal, then the continued presence of a price support scheme under the reformed cereals regime – guaranteeing farmers a minimum price for their output – affects the expected level and variability of producer prices. This, in turn, influences the level of the indifference price for an individual producer. Specifically, it can be shown (Fraser, 1993) that

$$E(p_u) = F(\hat{p})\hat{p} + (1 - F(\hat{p}))[\bar{p} + \sigma_p Z(\hat{p})/(1 - F(\hat{p}))] \tag{7}$$

and

$$var(p_u) = (1 - F(\hat{p}))\sigma_p^2\{1 - [Z(\hat{p})/(1 - F((\hat{p}))]^2 + ((\hat{p} - \bar{p})/\sigma_p)Z(\hat{p})/(1 - F\hat{p}))\}$$
$$+ (1 - F(\hat{p}))F(\hat{p})\{\hat{p} - [\bar{p} + \sigma_p Z(\hat{p})/(1 - F(\hat{p}))]\}^2 \tag{8}$$

where $\hat{p}$ =   the minimum guaranteed price (the intervention price),

     $F(\hat{p})$ = the cumulative probability of price being less than or equal to $\hat{p}$,

     $\bar{p}$ =   the mean of the world market price distribution,

     σ_p =   the standard deviation of the world market price distribution, and

     $Z(\hat{p})$ = the ordinate of the normal distribution at $\hat{p}$.

The presence of a minimum guaranteed price, $\hat{p}$, means that the expected producer price is higher than the world market price because of the removal of low world market price outcomes from the producer price distribution. As $\bar{p}$ increases, $E(p_u)$ will also increase, with the difference between the two prices decreasing, since $\hat{p}$ will become less and less significant in determining the level of the expected producer price. From equation (8), a reduction in the level of minimum guaranteed price, $\hat{p}$, will increase the variance of the producer price and thus, as argued above, increase the indifference price of risk averse farmers thus making set aside a more attractive option.

3. Empirical Analysis

In order to investigate the importance of the various factors described above on the level of indifference price, it was assumed, following Fraser (1993), that the farmer's expected utility of profit $(E(U(\pi)))$ is represented by the mean variance framework:

$$E(U(\pi)) = U(E(\pi)) + \frac{1}{2}U''(E(\pi))var(\pi) \tag{9}$$

whereas the utility function was specified by the constant relative risk aversion form:

$$U(\pi) = \frac{\pi^{(1-R)}}{1-R} \qquad (10)$$

where $R = -U''(\pi).\pi/U'(\pi)$ and R is set equal to 0.3.

Table 1 details the base parameter values used in the analysis. Whilst the parameters, c, s, $(1-\alpha)$, and $\hat{p}$ correspond to the actual levels of these policy parameters during 1993/94, the values relating to price and output uncertainty in world wheat markets were taken from Fraser (1993). The values of the remaining parameters relating to the farm characteristics β, L, $E(\theta)$, $cv\theta$ and r_o were based on analysis of the Farm Business Survey (FBS) national data set for England and Wales and held within the ESRC Data Archive.* Specifically, average values of the farm characteristics for both English specialist cereals and general cropping producers were calculated on the basis of four years of data 1986/87 to 1990/91. This is reasonably consistent with the period used by MAFF (1987/88 to 1991/92) to calculate the reference yield for England of 5.93 tonnes per hectare. Together, these two types of farms account for approximately seventy five per cent of cereal production in England. The farm-specific parameter values in Table 1 relate to the average of specialist cereals producers.

Table 1   Initial Parameter Values

Policy Parameters, 1993	Market uncertainty parameters*	Farm Characteristic parameters (England; specialist cereals)
c = 148.25 ECU per hectare	$CV\bar{p}$ = 23.1%	β = 0.617
s = 266.85 ECU per hectare	ρ = −0.12†	L = 123 ha
$(1-\alpha)$ = 0.15	$CV\theta$ = 0.074	r_o = 777.78 ECU/ha
$\hat{p}$ = 117 ECU per tonne		$E(\theta)$ = 5.977 t/ha

* Taken from Fraser, 1993, apart from $CV\theta$, the coefficient of variation in cereal yields, which was calculated from FBS data.

† Correlation coefficient between price and yield.

Feeding base level values of the parameters into the model, an indifference price of 243.59 ECU per tonne was identified for English specialist cereals producers, that is, only at this price level were the expected levels of utility from participating or not participating in set aside the same. Since this was much higher than the market price for cereals it implies that participation in set aside for 1992/93 would be very high, as indeed was the case during the first year of the scheme's implementation.

Sensitivity analysis on the basis of actual differences between farm characteristics, policy and uncertainty factors was carried out to determine which parameters have the greatest impact upon the indifference price. Table 2 reports the results of this sensitivity analysis.

The indifference price is shown to be relatively insensitive to all the elements of uncertainty in the model as well as to the level of the farmer's risk aversion.† For instance, a 50 per cent increase in the coefficient of variation of yield leads to only a 0.49 per cent increase in indifference price, whilst a 50 per cent increase in the coefficient of variation of world price increases the indifference price by only 2.95 per cent. An increase in the degree of a farmer's risk aversion, R, of 50 per cent again increases the indifference price only slightly, by 1.54 per cent. Thus the addition of the elements of uncertainty to the model

* Ministry of Agriculture, Fisheries and Food, (1993).

† Such insensitivity is consistent with the findings in Fraser (1993) who was focusing on the bounds within which compensation payments could be set by EC policy makers so as to avoid either wasteful budgetary expenditure or deterring participation.

Table 2   **Sensitivity of the Indifference Price to Changes in the Farm, Policy and Uncertainty Parameters**
(Based on average values for specialist cereals producers; $E(p_u)$ = 243.59 ECU/t

Parameter (Base values in parenthesis)	Value of $E(p_u)$ resulting from change in parameter (ecu/t) (% change in parenthesis)		
	+ 10%	+50%	+100%
R (0.3)	244.37 (+0.32)	247.34 (+1.54)	
ρ (−0.12)			244.12 (−1.68)
CVp̄ (0.231)	244.98 (+0.57)	250.78 (+2.95)	
CVθ (0.074)		244.79 (+0.49)	
r° (777.87)	249.51 (+2.43)	274.48 (+12.68)	
ß (0.617)	235.54 (−3.30)	203.50 (−16.46)	
E(θ) (5.977)	221.34 (−9.13)	161.39 (−33.75)	
s (260.85)	248.08 (+1.84)	266.05 (+9.22)	
c (148.25)	257.73 (+5.80)	314.49 (+29.11)	
(1−α) (0.15)	228.48 (−6.2)	188.44 (−22.64)	161.40 (−33.74)
p̂ (117)	243.47 (−0.05)	238.66 (−2.02)	

do not have a significant effect upon the indifference prices estimated and equation (4) by itself can be taken as a reasonable basis on which to evaluate a farmer's indifference price.*

The indifference price is more sensitive to the value of the individual producer's expected yield with a 10 per cent increase in yield reducing the indifference price by slightly less than 10 per cent. More surprisingly perhaps, the fixed costs proportion is also a significant determinant of the indifference price: an increase in ß of 10 per cent (from 0.617 to 0.679) reduces indifference price by 3.30 per cent. An increase in the total level of costs r_o has a slightly less marked but positive impact on indifference price.

With regard to the policy parameters, the indifference price is more sensitive to changes in c, the price compensation, than to s, the set aside payment, since c will be received on a much greater proportion of the land. The set aside requirement $(1-\alpha)$ also has a significant effect upon indifference price with a 10 per cent increase leading to a reduction of almost 6.2 per cent in the price. Finally, Table 2 shows that the level of minimum guarantee price, p̂, has a negligible impact on the level of indifference price given the other factors involved in the participation decision.

Further analysis revealed some regional differences in the level of indifference price of specialist cereal producers depending on, primarily, expected yields and costs.† Table 3 focuses on farms within the Eastern England EU region which is the most important region for specialist cereal

---

* On its own. equation (4) produces an estimate of indifference price of 234.9 ECUs per tonne for specialist cereal producers illustrating that allowing for risk in the model increases the indifference price by only 3.7 per cent.
† Indifference prices ranged from an average of 234 ECUs per tonne in the Cambridge FBS region to 26° ECUs per tonne in the Newcastle region.

Table 3   Indifference Prices for Specialist Cereal Farms in the Eastern England EC Region

Size Group (BSU)	Cereal Area (ha)	Expected Yield* (t/ha)	Fixed Cost Prop'n	Total Cost ecu/ha	$E(p_w)$
≤16	25.93	5.722	0.647	673.77	242.6
16-24	46.09	5.325	0.597	804.75	278.6
24-40	72.10	5.731	0.610	871.37	262.4
40-100	136.77	5.917	0.630	782.61	244.5
≤100	293.59	6.271	0.644	785.13	229.1
All Farms	130.42	5.899	0.626	823.45	248.9

* A value of 0.066 for the coefficient of variation of the yield is assumed throughout.

producers in terms of both area and output. It illustrates, in particular, that as market prices fall it will be the largest, highest yielding farms with the greatest values of β, which will be the last to join the set aside scheme. Alternatively, should market conditions improve, it will be this category of farms that are first to opt out and return to full arable production.

The average farm parameter values for general lowland cropping farms generated a similar pattern of estimates for the indifference price as the specialist cereal producers but at an overall higher level due to different farm characteristics. In particular, the national average opting out price for such producers is 252 ECU per tonne, with values of 245 ECUs per tonne for farms in the Cambridge FBS region.

Following the first year of the set aside scheme in 1993/94 there has been a gradual reduction in the intervention price offset by increases in c, the price compensation and s, the set aside payment. As shown in Table 4, as these parameters are adjusted, the level of the indifference price for specialist cereal farms is increased and set aside becomes more attractive. However, an increase in the set aside requirement from 15 to 20 per cent of the base acreage leads to a significant lowering of the indifference price in each of the three years considered, implying that for any given level of market price, farms would be less likely to participate in the set aside scheme. Hence increasing the set aside

Table 4   Impact of Indifference Price of the Transitional Arrangements
Specialist Cereals Producers
(ecu/t)

Year	Compensation Payment	Set Aside Payment	Intervention Price	$E(p_w)$ with: Set Aside at 15%	Set Aside at 20%
1993/94	25	45	117	243.59	201.15
1994/95	35	57	108	312.38	253.75
1995/96	45	57	100	369.31	293.74

proportion, even with increases in compensation payments, set aside becomes less attractive. However, the lowest indifference price is still in excess of current market prices suggesting that English cereal growers will still participate in set aside.*

* Given that the estimated indifference prices are so high compared with EU market prices, it is interesting to identify the combination of values to farm parameters which may give rise to a decision not to opt into the set aside scheme. For instance, with the same values of the risk and policy parameters as previously, and with total costs per hectare of 600 ECU/t a fixed cost proportion of 0.65 and expected yield of 10t/ha, an indifference price of 134 ECU/t is obtained. Similarly, with total costs of 550 ECU/t, fixed cost proportion of 0.7 and expected yield of 10.5 t/ha, an indifference price of 123 ECU/t is obtained from the model.

4. Conclusions

Analysis has focused on the decision facing arable producers of whether or not to participate in the arable rotational set aside scheme of the CAP. In section 2, an indifference price was identified at which an individual producer could expect the same level of profit either by opting in or out of the scheme and several factors were noted which could, potentially, influence the level of indifference price and hence the uptake of set aside.

Empirical analysis based on the FBS national dataset, indicated the sensitivity of the indifference prices to the levels of the various factors and, importantly, suggested that the level of indifference prices for English specialist cereal and general cropping farmers are high in relation to actual market prices. The findings are thus consistent with the high uptake of set aside in England in the first year of the scheme's operation. Virtually all cereal producers chose to participate in 1993/94 with 94.8 per cent of the estimated base area which would be eligible for set aside at 15 per cent entered into the programme, allowing for the effects of the small producer exceptions under the simplified scheme, the old five year set aside and the cereals, oilseeds and protein crops forage area claims to satisfy stocking rate criteria in the livestock sector (Home Grown Cereals Authority, 1993). Consistent with the finding of Fraser (1993), in the case of English producers there is clear indication that there is considerable potential for reducing levels of price and set aside compensation payments and increasing the set aside requirement, without leading to any significant loss of take up. Alternatively, the results have implications when considering the required level of increases in set aside proportions and/or reductions in EC support prices should the Community fail to meet the necessary reductions in subsidised exports required by the 1993 GATT agreement.

Although analysis focused on the most important categories of arable producers in the UK (producing approximately seventy five per cent of total arable production in England) the most obvious limitation of the model presented and the estimates produced is the assumption of a single output producer. This is highlighted by actual behaviour in the first year of the scheme. The reduction in cereals area was proportionately less than the area set aside due to the substitution of cereals for other crops in the rotation. Further, whilst it was assumed in the analysis that the level of policy parameters was predetermined, the set aside requirements and compensation payments are themselves not certain but subject to exchange rate risk and, in the longer term, political risk. Nevertheless, the analysis identifies the factors influencing participation in set aside, in particular the most important farm characteristics which, in turn, could be useful in explaining both participation rates as new, alternative types of set aside are introduced (for example, non-rotational and guaranteed set aside) and the varying levels of uptake in set aside in different regions or member states of the Community.

References

Allanson, P. A. (1993). The Impact of the Modulation Proposal on the MacSharry Plan for the Reform of the Cereal Regime, *European Review of Agricultural Economics*, **20**, 99-109.

Fraser, R. W. (1993). Set Aside Premiums and the May 1992 CAP Reforms, *Journal of Agricultural Economics*, **44(3)**, 410-417.

Froud, J. and Roberts, D. (1993). The Welfare Effects of the New EC Set Aside Scheme: A Note, *Journal of Agricultural Economics*, **44(3)**, 496-501.

Home Grown Cereals Authority (1993). *Market Information*, 13th December, 1993.

Home Grown Cereals Authority (1994). *Market Information*, 14th March 1994.

Josling, T. (1993). The Reform of the CAP and the Industrial World, Plenary Paper Presented at
    the 7th European Association of Agricultural Economics Congress, Stresa, September 1993.
Lee, D. R. and Helmberger, P. G. (1985). Estimating Supply Response in the Presence of Farm
    Programs, *American Journal of Agricultural Economics*, 67(2), 193-203.
Ministry of Agriculture, Fisheries and Food Economic (Farm Business) Division (1993). *Farm
    Business Survey 1982- (Computer File)*, ESRC Data Archive, Colchester.
Mood, A. M., Grayhill, F. A. and Boes, D. C. (1974). *Introduction to the Theory of Statistics*, 3rd
    Edition, McGraw-Hill, Kogakusha, Japan, p.181.

Chapter 5

The impact of price support on set-aside responses to an increase in price uncertainty*

ROB FRASER

The University of Western Australia

(received January 1992, final version received May 1993)

Summary

This paper examines the impact of increased price uncertainty on the decision to set aside croppable land. It is shown that the standard response of increased set-aside may not occur if the commodity in question is also subject to a price-support policy. In this situation, conflicting effects on the set-aside decision arise because an increase in underlying price uncertainty may increase not just the variability but also the expected level of producer prices.

Keywords: price support; set-aside; price uncertainty.

1. Introduction

The choice between setting aside and cropping land can be characterised as a choice between safe and risky alternatives (Fraser, 1991a). In this context, an increase in the level of uncertainty of the risky alternative can be expected to result in a shift in behaviour towards the safe alternative by risk averse agents (Hey, 1981: 40–43).

The aim of this paper is to demonstrate that such a conclusion does not necessarily follow if a price-support policy is in operation for the commodity in question because in this situation an increase in underlying price uncertainty increases not just the variability but also the expected level of producer prices, thereby resulting in conflicting effects on the desirability of setting aside land. The next section outlines the theoretical basis of these conflicting effects and the paper concludes with some comments on their significance for actual policy situations.

*   I am particularly grateful to two anonymous referees for helpful comments on earlier versions of this paper.

European Review of Agricultural Economies
21 (1994) 131–136

0165–1587/94/0021–0131
© Walter de Gruyter, Berlin

132   *Rob Fraser*

2. Analysis

The model of the set-aside decision presented below is based on Fraser (1991a). In this model a farmer has two alternatives for generating income, either uncertain cropping income or certain set-aside premiums. Cropping income depends on an uncertain price per unit of output, an uncertain level of yield per hectare and (assumed to be) certain production costs per hectare. With this specification the farmer's income (π) can be represented by:

$$\pi = p\alpha\theta L - r\alpha L + s(1 - \alpha)L \tag{1}$$

where:

  p = uncertain price per unit of output
  θ = uncertain yield per hectare
  L = area of land
  α = share of land cropped (i.e., $1 - \alpha$ = share of land set aside)
  r = certain production costs per hectare
  s = premium for set-aside land per hectare.

It is further assumed that the farmer seeks to maximise the expected utility of income $[E(U(\pi))]$ and that the farmer's expected utility of income can be approximated by a means-variance formulation:

$$E(U(\pi)) = U(E(\pi)) + \tfrac{1}{2}U''(E(\pi)) \cdot Var(\pi) \tag{2}$$

where:

  $E(\pi)$ = expected income
  $Var(\pi)$ = variance of income.

It should be recognised that although the first of these assumptions is common in the literature on producer behaviour under uncertainty (e.g., Hey, 1979, chs. 17–23), it represents an alternative to 'safety-first' concerns which may be present among farmers and which are arguably the main rationale for price-support policies (e.g., Arzac, 1976). However, it is felt that with the focus of such concerns being on 'downside risk', their inclusion would only highlight the potential for conflict between the policies of price-support and set-aside. Consequently, the approach taken here is to adopt the commonly-used expected utility framework as being both simpler and less prescriptive of the model's implications. In addition, regarding the mean-variance assumption, Meyer (1987) provides arguments supporting the use of this formulation while Hanson and Ladd (1991) extend this support to include situations (such as below) where truncated probability distributions are involved.

On this basis, the optimal set-aside decision is given by differentiating (2) with respect to α and equating to zero:[1]

$$U'(E(\pi)) \cdot \frac{\partial E(\pi)}{\partial \alpha} + \tfrac{1}{2}U'''(E(\pi)) \cdot Var(\pi) \cdot \frac{\partial E(\pi)}{\partial \alpha} + \tfrac{1}{2}U''(E(\pi)) \cdot \frac{\partial Var(\pi)}{\partial \alpha} = 0$$

(3)

The incorporation of a price support policy will modify the distribution of the price of output (p). It is shown in Fraser (1991b) that if the underlying price distribution is assumed to be normal, then in the presence of a price-support policy which guarantees to purchase any output which fails in the market to achieve a specified minimum price the expected level $(E(p_u))$ and variability $(Var(p_u))$ of producer prices are given by:

$$E(p_u) = F(p_f)p_f + (1 - F(p_f))[p_e + \sigma_p Z(p_f)/(1 - F(p_f))]$$

$$Var(p_u) = (1 - F(p_f))\sigma_p^2 \{1 - [Z(p_f)/(1 - F(p_f))]^2$$

$$+ ((p_f - p_e)/\sigma_p) \cdot Z(p_f)/(1 - F(p_f))\}$$

(5)

$$+ (1 - F(p_f))F(p_f)\{p_f - [p_e + \sigma_p Z(p_f)/(1 - F(p_f))]\}^2$$

where:

p_f = the support price
$F(p_f)$ = cumulative probability of price being less than or equal to p_f
p_e = mean of the underlying price distribution
σ_p = standard deviation of the underlying price distribution $(\sigma_p^2 = variance)$
$Z(p_f)$ = ordinate of the standard normal distribution at p_f.

Given this situation, consider the impact on the distribution of producer prices of an increase in the underlying level of uncertainty of prices (σ_p^2) as represented in Figure 1.[2] In this figure the initial underlying distribution (marked 1) is truncated at p_f by the price support policy so that the expected producer price is given by $E(p_u)^1$ (which exceeds p_e) and the variance of producer prices by equation (5) (which is less than σ_p^2). A mean-preserving increase in σ_p^2 is then represented by distribution 2 which, given the increased probability of price support at p_f as well as the increased probability of prices above $E(p_u)^1$, has the effect of increasing not only the variance of producer prices (given by (5)), but also the expected level of producer prices as indicated by $E(p_u)^2$. Clearly, such changes have a conflicting impact on the attractiveness of cropping for risk averse farmers.

It follows that this conflict may affect the optimal set-aside decision. On the basis of equation (1) and assuming expected yield per hectare is equal to unity $(E(\theta) = 1)$, expected income and the variance of income can be represented by (Mood, Graybill and Boes, 1974: 181):

$$E(\pi) = E(p_u) \cdot \alpha L + Cov(p_u, \theta) \cdot \alpha L - r\alpha L + s(1 - \alpha)L$$

(6)

$$Var(\pi) = \alpha^2 L^2 Var(p_u) + (E(p_u))^2 \alpha^2 L^2 \sigma_\theta^2 + 2E(p_u)\alpha L \, Cov(p_u, \theta)$$

(7)

134   *Rob Fraser*

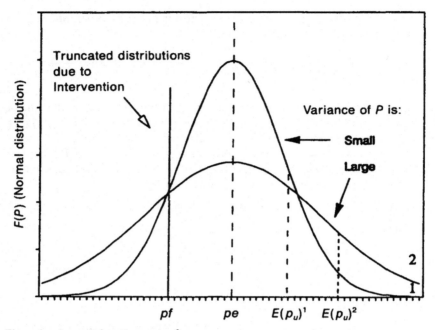

Figure 1.   *Impact of an increase in* σ_p^2

where:

$$\sigma_\theta^2 = \text{variance of yield}$$
$$Cov(p_u, \theta) = \text{covariance between producer price and yield,}$$

so that the derivatives in equation (3) are given by:

$$\frac{\partial E(\pi)}{\partial \alpha} = (E(p_u) - r - s + Cov(p_u, \theta))L \tag{8}$$

$$\frac{\partial Var(\pi)}{\partial \alpha} = 2\alpha L^2 (Var(p_u) + (E(p_u))^2 \sigma_\theta^2) + 2E(p_u)L \, Cov(p_u, \theta). \tag{9}$$

Because an increase in the underlying variance of prices increases both the variance and the expected level of producer prices in the presence of a price support policy, it also increases both the marginal expected income and the marginal variance of income from extra cropping and, therefore, less set-aside.[3] Consequently, the overall impact on the optimal set-aside decision will depend on the relative magnitude of these two marginal effects. In addition, equation (3) suggests that the overall impact will depend on the farmer's risk aversion as this determines the (utility) weight attached to each of the marginal effects. Finally, it should be emphasized that the key determinant of this conflict is the level of the support price. If this price was at such a low level that it did not significantly modify the farmer's price distribution, then an increase in underlying price uncertainty would simply increase producer price uncertainty and therefore increase the optimal level of set-aside among risk-averse farmers. Only if the support price is high enough relative to the underlying mean will there be a significant (positive) impact of increased uncertainty on expected producer prices and therefore the possibility of a risk-averse farmer being encouraged to increase cropping levels.

3. Conclusion

This paper has examined the issue of the impact of increased price uncertainty on the decision to set aside croppable land. While the standard response of risk-averse agents to an increase in the uncertainty of the risky alternative is to shift towards the safe alternative, the analysis showed that farmers may not respond in this way if the commodity in question is subject to a price-support policy. In particular, if the level of the support price is sufficiently high relative to the expected world price, then an increase in underlying price uncertainty will lead to an increase in expected producer prices, and therefore in expected income from cropping, which dominates the negative effect of increased variability of cropping income and results in an increase in the desirability of cropping.

However, this theoretical finding was achieved using hypothetical set-aside and price support policies. As a consequence, the relevance of the finding to, for example, the set-aside decisions of European Community producers, who benefit from a price support policy based on intervention purchasing but under more complex rules, is unclear. Nevertheless, set-aside and price support as represented in the theoretical analysis are arguably central features of these producers' actual policy situations and therefore the view taken here is that the theoretical finding may be a good starting point for analysing such situations. In particular, because it suggests a potentially perverse relationship between actual policies which are of considerable importance to Community agriculture, it would seem that further research is warranted in order to clarify the distinction between the hypothetical policy context of this paper and the actual policy situation facing European Community producers.

Notes

1. Concavity of the utility function, which applies if the farmer is assumed to be risk averse ($U''(\pi) < 0$), ensures the second-order condition for a maximum is satisfied.
2. I am indebted to the anonymous referee for suggesting this representation. Note that for ease of exposition the more uncertain distribution has been given a special shape relative to p_f and $E(p_u)$[1]. However equations (4) and (5) characterise the more general case.

136   *Rob Fraser*

3. If the covariance in (6) and (7) is negative, there will also be an indirect effect in the opposite direction.

References

Arzac, E. R. (1976). Profits and safety in the theory of the firm under price uncertainty. *International Economic Review* 17(1): 163–171.

Fraser, R. W. (1991a). "Nice work if you can get it": an analysis of optimal set-aside. *Oxford Agrarian Studies* 19(1): 61–69.

— (1991b). Price-support effects on EC producers. *Journal of Agricultural Economics* 42(1): 1–10.

Hanson, S. D. and Ladd, G. W. (1991). Robustness of the mean-variance model with truncated probability distributions. *American Journal of Agricultural Economics* 73(2): 436–445.

Hey, J. D. (1979). *Uncertainty in Microeconomics.* Oxford: Martin Robertson.

— (1981). *Economics in Disequilibrium.* Oxford: Martin Robertson.

Meyer, J. (1987). Two-moment decision models and expected utility maximisation. *American Economic Review* 77(3): 421–430.

Mood, A. M., Graybill, F. A. and Boes, D. C. (1974). *Introduction to the Theory of Statistics,* (3rd edition) Kogakusha: McGraw-Hill.

Chapter 6

LAND HETEROGENEITY AND THE EFFECTIVENESS OF CAP SET-ASIDE

Hild Rygnestad and Rob Fraser*

The May 1992 reform of the CAP included a choice for farmers between set-aside options. This paper examines the question of whether or not this choice feature has exacerbated the slippage problem associated with the set-aside policy in the context of heterogeneous land quality. A model is developed which provides a basis for determining both a farmer's preferred choice of set-aside option, and the implications of this choice for output reduction. A numerical application of the model suggests a strong tendency for farmers to choose the less effective option in terms of reducing output.

1. Introduction

A set-aside policy as a means of production control has been a feature of the Common Agricultural Policy (CAP) since 1988 when a voluntary scheme was introduced (Hope and Lingard, 1992; Fraser, 1991). But production control, particularly of cereals, remains a concern in the European Union (EU) into the 1990s and was a factor contributing to the May 1992 reform of the CAP. With this reform the set-aside policy was substantially modified along the lines of the US acreage reduction programme (Ervin, 1988). In particular, farmers are required to set-aside a proportion of their croppable land in order to receive compensatory payments for reductions in intervention prices associated with the reform. Moreover, since this reform there has been debate over the operation of the set-aside policy, with producers in particular continuing to argue for reductions in the set-aside proportion of land on the basis of historically low cereal stockpiles, and others arguing for the need to maintain or even strengthen supply control in order to meet commitments associated with the Uruguay Round of the GATT Agreement.

An additional feature of the reformed set-aside policy, which has been largely neglected in this debate and which distinguishes it from the US counterpart, is that farmers are given a choice between temporary and permanent set-aside. In general terms, farmers are able to choose between setting-aside a different area of land each year (rotational set-aside) or the same area (non-rotational set-aside). Associated with this choice is a differential rate of set-aside, with a higher rate applying to non-rotational set-aside in recognition of the "slippage" problem.

* Rob Fraser is Associate Professor of Agriculture and Resource Economics and Hild Rygnestad a PhD student, both in the Faculty of Agriculture, University of Western Australia. We are grateful for the helpful comments of the Editors and two anonymous referees on previous versions of this paper.

Journal of Agricultural Economics
47 (2) (1996) 255-260

Slippage refers to the situation whereby the proportionate reduction in output is less than the proportionate reduction in land under crop. Although this problem can arise for various reasons, the predominant cause is arguably heterogeneity of land quality, with farmers setting aside relatively poor-quality land and thereby increasing average yield (Hoag *et al.*, 1993; Brown, 1993).

The aim of this paper is to analyse the relationship between the choice feature of the May 1992 set-aside policy and the slippage problem due to heterogeneity of land quality. In particular, the paper considers the question of whether profit-maximising behaviour by farmers will result in them choosing the set-aside option which has the greater or the lesser impact on output.*

The structure of the paper is as follows. The first section develops a model of farmer choice between two set-aside options, rotational and non-rotational, based on a profit-maximising objective.† In addition, the model features both the optimal choice of a variable input to determine yield on land in production and scope for determining which land is set aside in the case of heterogeneous quality. As a consequence, not only can the total output associated with each option be determined, but also the relationship between choice and output can be assessed. To illustrate the use of the model, a numerical analysis is undertaken in the second section based on a set of values for the parameters of the model. For this illustration there is a clear tendency for farmers to choose the set-aside option which is least effective in reducing output across a broad range of combinations of land quality. Further research is needed to validate this finding.

2. The Model

The model assumes the farmer chooses the set-aside option, the quality of land in production and the variable input application rate on land in production with the objective of maximising the net present value of profits over a finite time period. The alternative of "opting-out" by not setting aside land and thereby foregoing the compensatory payments is not considered here (Froud *et al.*, 1996). With additional assumptions of constant costs and prices, constant returns to scale and no carry-over effects from year to year of variable input application, the optimal application rate for each year is also constant and can be determined for each hectare of land of given quality. Note that recent research suggests that any yield benefits associated with the rotation option are minimal (Garstang *et al.*, 1994).

Land quality is specified by use of the Mitscherlich response function (Paris, 1992):

$$w(N) = m(1 - de^{-bN})\tag{1}$$

where: w   = yield
        N   = variable input application rate
        m,d,b = parameters of the function.

---

* We are grateful to an anonymous referee for this "targeting" of our contribution.
† It is recognised that EU farmers also have a choice of "mixing" these two options. Although not considered here, some preliminary analysis suggests that, in the context of this model, such a choice is typically inferior in terms of profit to one of the "pure" options.

LAND HETEROGENEITY AND THE EFFECTIVENESS OF CAP SET-ASIDE   257

In the response function m indicates the quality of the land. The other parameters, d and b, determine the starting-point and the slope of the function respectively.

The revenue function for each year in the simple case of homogeneous land quality is given by:

$$R = L(1 - \alpha)wP + L\alpha w_a s + L(1 - \alpha)w_a k \qquad (2)$$

where: L = area of land (ha)

α = set-aside rate (depends on which option the farmer chooses)

w = actual yield (t/ha)

P = price for output (ECU/t)

w_a = reference yield (t/ha)

s = set-aside premium (ECU/t)

k = compensatory payment (ECU/t).

The cost function for each year for homogeneous land quality is given by:

$$C = L(1 - \alpha)VC_F + L(1 - \alpha)VC_H m + LFC \qquad (3)$$

where: VC_F = $C_F N$

C_F = cost of variable input (ECU/t)

VC_H = harvesting costs (ECU/ha)

FC = fixed costs (ECU/ha).

Subtracting equation (2) from equation (3) gives the yearly profit (π) for land of homogeneous quality. This is discounted and summed over the specified time horizon to give the net present value (NPV) of profit:

$$NPV = \sum_{t=1}^{T} (\pi/(1 + r)^{t-1}) \qquad (4)$$

where: T = time horizon

r = discount rate.

The optimal choice of variable input application rate (N^*) can be found by taking the derivative of (4) with respect to N. From (1), (2) and (3) this is given by:

$$N^* = -(1/b)\ln(C_F/Pmdb). \qquad (5)$$

In the simple case of homogeneous land quality, the farmer's optimal choice of set-aside option will be that which for the optimal level of N in (5) results in the higher value of (4). Note that in this case the higher set-aside rate applying to the non-rotational option guarantees that total output reduction over the time period will be greater than for the rotational option.

---

* The inclusion of m as a determinant of harvesting costs is designed to represent a simple positive relationship between yield and harvesting costs.

However, in the case of heterogeneous land quality, the farmer also takes into account the impact on the net present value of profits of setting aside land of different qualities. In particular, for the non-rotational option, a farmer will find it more profitable to set aside poorer quality land up to the rate required by the option because of its lower level of profit from production. For the rotational option, a farmer will find it more profitable to set aside poorer quality land at the beginning of the time period because of the discounting of profits in subsequent periods. Consequently, with heterogeneous land quality the rotational option will typically result in better quality land being taken out of production at some time, whereas for the non-rotational option the better quality land is always in production. This difference in production patterns acts to counter the differential output effect of the higher set-aside rate associated with the non-rotational option, and so the potential arises for output over the time period to be lower with the rotational option.

These conflicting impacts on total output reduction of the effect of the rotation requirements and the effect of the different set-aside rates for the two options in the context of heterogeneous land quality are best illustrated by a numerical application of the model. Such an application will also enable the relationship between the most profitable option and total output reduction to be revealed.

Table 1 Yield, Input, Cost-structure, Response Functions, NPV and Output Ratios for Three Land Qualities‡

	Unit	Average Land	Good Land	Poor Land
N*	t/ha	0.60	0.79	0.38
Yield, w(N*)†	t/ha	5.08	7.08	3.08
C_F	ECU/t	491.82	491.82	491.82
VC_F	ECU/ha	297.20	386.87	187.45
Harvesting costs	ECU/ha	150	180	120
FC	ECU/ha	230	230	230
Total costs	ECU/ha	677.20	796.87	537.45
m		10	12	8
d		0.90	0.90	0.90
b		1	1	1
NPV (R)/NPV (NR)*		1	1.03	0.74
Output (R)/Output (NR)		1.06	1.06	1.06

Notes: * R – Rotational set-aside option   NR – Non-rotational set-aside option.
† Yield response function: $w(N^*) = m.(1 - d.e^{-b.N^*})$.
‡ Other data used in the analysis P = 100 ECU/t; k = 45 ECU/t;
  s = 57 ECU/t; r = 8%;
  α(R) = 15%; α(NR) = 20%;
  L = 100; T = 6.

3. The Numerical Application

The details of the numerical application are summarised in Table 1. This application specifies three types of land quality and other parameter values so that the optimal yield on average quality land is exactly equal to the reference yield. As shown in the second last row of this table, this specification results in a farmer with homogeneous average-quality land being indifferent between the two set-aside options because earnings from production equal set-aside compensation. However, earnings on good land exceed set-aside compensation, and so for homogeneous good land the rotational option with its

Figure 1 **Combining Output with Farmer Choice of Set-Aside Option for Heterogeneous Land Quality**

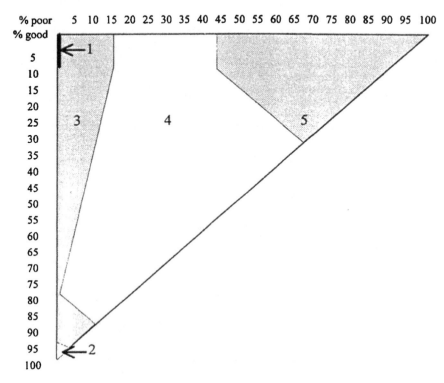

Note: The rest of the land is of average quality .
Zone 1 – Indifferent to choice and R gives higher total output
Zone 2 – R chosen and gives higher total output
Zone 3 – NR chosen and R gives higher total output
Zone 4 – NR chosen and gives higher total output
Zone 5 – NR chosen and R gives higher total output.

lower set-aside rate ($\alpha(R) = 15\%$) is preferred, while the opposite is true for homogeneous poor land. Since the last row confirms the observation of the previous section that with homogeneous land total output reduction is greater for the non-rotational option (because of its higher set-aside rate: $\alpha(NR) = 20\%$), it follows that the farmer's choice supports the effectiveness of the set-aside policy in the case of homogeneously poor land, but is contrary in the case of homogeneously good land.

Next consider the case of heterogeneous land quality. The profit and output implications of heterogeneity are collectively summarised in Figure 1. Zone 1 represents the farmer's indifference between the two options as long as the amount of good land is less than or equal to 10%, and there is no poor land.* Outside this zone, the relative profitability of permanently setting aside poor-quality land, or never setting aside good-quality land, typically dominates and

* Note that the 10% arises from the combination of a six-year time period and a 15% set-aside rate for the rotational option. Thus up to 10% of good-quality land need never be set-aside.

the non-rotational scheme is chosen. The exception to this is Zone 2 where the very large proportion of good land means that the relative profitability of only setting aside 15% of this land with the rotational option dominates the choice.

The conflict between the effects on total output reduction of the rotational requirements and the different set-aside rates for the two options is also represented in Figure 1. As observed in Section 1, for homogeneous land quality, total output reduction is greater for the non-rotational option because of its higher set-aside rate. Figure 1 shows that this effect dominates the effect of the rotational requirements for deviations from homogeneity to the extent represented by Zones 3 and 5 (and including Zones 1 and 2). However, in Zone 4 the impact on total output reduction of being required, with the rotational option, to set aside at some time average and/or good-quality land dominates the differential set-aside rate effect. Consequently, in Zone 4 total output is lower for the rotational option. Therefore, the collective profit and output implications of heterogeneous land quality represented in Figure 1 suggest that only for land quality combinations represented by Zones 3 and 5 (37% of the range of land quality combinations) does the farmer choose the more effective set-aside option in terms of reducing total output.

Finally, these Zones (3 and 5) increase in size if the types of land are less divergent in terms of quality (i.e. the m values closer together), and if the set-aside rates of the two options are more divergent.* These observations suggest that the extent to which the opportunity for choice between set-aside options exacerbates slippage is negatively related to the set-aside rate differential of the options, and is positively related to the extent to which a farmer's land is of heterogeneous quality. However, these conclusions are based on the relative profitability across a broad range of land quality combinations of the non-rotational option featured in this application of the model. If instead the rotationl option was generally the more profitable, then these relationships may not apply. It follows that, while this paper may have raised concerns about the impact of set-aside options on the slippage problem, there is a need for further research which combines the model developed here with empirical estimates of the farmer-specific information before firm conclusions can be reached.

References

Brown, C. G. (1993). CAP Reforms in Historical and International Perspective, *Agricultural Economics Discussion Paper Series 1/93*, Department of Agriculture, University of Queensland, St Lucia.

Ervin, D. E. (1988). Cropland Diversion (Set-Aside) in the US and UK. *Journal of Agricultural Economics*, 39(2): 183-196.

Fraser, R. W. (1991). Nice Work If You Can Get It: An Analysis of Optimal Set-Aside. *Oxford Agrarian Studies*, 19(1): 61-69.

Froud, J., Roberts, D. and Fraser, R. W. (1996). Participation in Set-Aside: What Determines the Opting-In Price? *Journal of Agricultural Economics*, 47(1): 89-98.

Garstang, J. R., Clark, W. S. and Dampney, P. M. R. (1994). Production Methods for Cereals Within the Reformed CAP. Home-Grown Cereals Authority Research Review No. 26.

Hoag, D. L., Babock, B. A. and Foster, W. E. (1993). Field-Level Measurement of Land Productivity and Programme Slippage. *American Journal of Agricultural Economics*, 75: 181-189.

Hope, J. and Lingard, J. (1992). The Influence of Risk Aversion on the Uptake of Set-Aside: A MOTAD and CRP Approach. *Journal of Agricultural Economics*, 43(3): 401-411.

Paris, Q. (1992). The Von Liebig Hypothesis. *American Journal of Agricultural Economics*, 74(4): 1019-1028.

---

* For example, increasing $\alpha(NR)$ to 25% results in Zones 3 and 5 collectively representing 89% of the range of land quality combinations, even though this example also shows a small increase in the size of Zone 2.

Journal of Agricultural Economics — Volume 50, Number 2 — May 1999 — Pages 328-335

Chapter 7

An Assessment of the Impact of Implementing the European Commission's *Agenda 2000* Cereal Proposals for Specialist Wheatgrowers in Denmark

Rob Fraser and Hild Rygnestad

*T*his paper undertakes an assessment of the impact of implementing the European Commission's Agenda 2000 *cereal proposals for specialist wheatgrowers in Denmark. The economic model of a representative farm developed in Rygnestad and Fraser (1996) is extended to include a model of nitrate leaching and then used to simulate the impact of implementing the proposals. The results of this simulation are compared and contrasted with those of the sectoral and regional impact studies reported in European Commission (1998b). In particular, the proposals are shown to have an environmentally-beneficial effect in terms of reduced nitrate leaching, with the magnitude of this effect dependent both on the quality of land and on the ex ante set-aside rate.*

1. Introduction

The reform of the Common Agricultural Policy (CAP) of May 1992 represented a significant move of this policy away from an emphasis on price support for producers and towards an emphasis on direct income support. Key features of that reform, with respect to the cereal sector, were a substantial reduction in the level of price support coupled with compensatory payments for this reduction based on area yield and contingent on participation in a set-aside programme aimed at some degree of production control.

The release by the European Commission (EC) of its *Agenda 2000* document, which was recently updated to a set of legislative proposals, represents a new set of proposals aimed at taking the CAP further towards a market-responsive income support policy (European Commission, 1997; 1998a). Key features of this set of proposals for the cereals sector are a 20 per cent reduction in price support to a "safety-net level", an off-setting increase in the level of the area-yield-based compensatory payment and, in reflection of the adjustment towards market prices, a setting of the set-aside rate at zero.

■ This research was completed while Hild Rygnestad was a PhD student and Rob Fraser an Associate Professor in Agricultural and Resource Economics at the University of Western Australia. Hild Rynestad is currently a Research Assistant at the Danish Institute of Agricultural and Fisheries Economics in Copenhagen. This research has been partially supported by the Australian Research Council. We are grateful to two anonymous referees and the Editor for helpful comments.

The aim of this paper is to analyse the impact of this set of proposals at the level of the individual producer, with the particular focus being on specialist wheatgrowers in Denmark. In previous research (Rygnestad and Fraser, 1996) we analysed the impact of the May 1992 reform on an individual cereal producer's economic welfare and production decisions, and highlighted the role of land quality in determining this impact. In this paper we extend our previous economic methodology to include a physical analysis of nitrogen application and leaching associated with optimal production decisions, an analysis which incorporates actual estimates of production relationships based on Danish scientific research. As a consequence, in this context we are able to provide a detailed assessment of the impact of each of the components of the *Agenda 2000* cereal proposals on a specialist wheatgrower's economic welfare, as well as the associated production responses. In addition, we are able to assess the impact of these responses on nitrate-leaching from the producer's activities. We demonstrate once again the role of land quality in determining not only the magnitude but also in some cases the direction of these various impacts. Moreover, we demonstrate the important role of the ex ante rate of set-aside in determining the impact of the implementation of the *Agenda 2000* cereal proposals. In so doing we are able to compare and contrast our results with the sectoral and regional findings of the recently published "CAP Reform Proposals: Impact Analysis" (European Commission, 1998b).

The plan of the paper is as follows. Section 2, sets out details of the modelling and data used in our analysis. Section 3 reports the results of our attempt to simulate the impact of the *Agenda 2000* cereal proposals. In particular, these results are divided into economic and physical impacts, and the roles of land quality and the *ex ante* set-aside rate in determining the results are discussed along with reference to the results of other impact studies. The paper ends with a brief conclusion which focuses on the extent to which our findings can be generalised to other countries and farming systems.

2. Modelling and Data

The economic model used in this paper is based on Rygnestad and Fraser (1996). The essential modifications are the use of yield response functions estimated from the results of Danish scientific field trials (NCCP, 1985-95), and the use of Danish cost and income structures for the 1996/97 growing season, including the appropriate subsidy income. Note that whereas the parameter values for the average land quality yield response function are estimated directly from the results of the field trials, the parameter values for the poor and good land quality functions are established by subjectively modifying these direct estimates.[1]

As an extension to the economic model, a model to predict the rate of nitrate leaching is used. This model has been estimated on the basis of Danish empirical field trials carried out during the 1980s (Simmelsgaard, 1991). It has been used in a number of

---

[1] The adjusted R^2 for this estimation was 0.66, with all parameter values significant at the 5 per cent level. The basis of subjectively modifying these direct estimates was by reference to the results from Danish field trials for low, average and high yielding soils. Note that, compared with Rygnestad and Fraser (1996), there is no choice between rotational and non-rotational set-aside and there is no yield increment or change in nitrogen application rate associated with land previously set-aside being brought back into production. These assumptions markedly simplify the analysis with only minor impacts on the results.

different studies of Danish agriculture (Skop, 1993; Schou and Vetter, 1994; Paaby *et al.*, 1996). The model, as described by Simmelsgaard (1991), quantifies nitrate leaching from agricultural land as a function of soil type, precipitation, crop rotation and the application of nitrogen from commercial fertilisers and animal manure. For the purpose of this analysis a reduced form of the model is used including winter wheat production in one climatic region, and only using nitrogen applied through commercial fertilisers.

The nitrate leaching rate, X, from a farm is taken to be the sum of leaching from productive (1 - a) and from set-aside land (a):

$$X = (1 - a) \times e^{0.7\left(\frac{N^* - 1}{n}\right)} + a\gamma \qquad (1)$$

where: X = nitrate leaching, rate, kg/ha

n = reference rate of nitrogen application, t/ha

N* = actual nitrogen application rate (= optimal rate from the economic model), t/ha

x = reference rate of nitrate leaching (N*/n = 1) from productive land, kg/ha

γ = nitrate leaching rate from set-aside land, kg/ha

a = set-aside rate, per cent.

According to the model, nitrate leaching, X, increases with a higher level of fertiliser use, N*, indicating an increased proportional loss of applied nitrogen through nitrate leaching. It should also be noticed that the model is dependent on land quality, with reference rates of nitrogen application, n, and leaching, x and γ, established for each quality. These three parameters, together with the 0.7 factor, are based on the empirical field trials already mentioned (Simmelsgaard, 1991).

The key equations of the models and full details of the data used in the analysis are provided in Table 1.[1]

3. Analysis of *Agenda 2000* Cereal Proposals

Based on the models and data outlined in the previous section, in this section we simulate the impact on a specialist wheatgrower with homogeneous quality land of implementing the *Agenda 2000* cereal proposals. In particular, we impose on the base case scenario a 20 per cent reduction in the price of wheat (from 110 ECU/t), an increase in the hectare premium to 66 ECU/tonne, and a reduction in the ex ante set-aside rate to zero. Note that this latter reduction is simulated to apply from three ex ante levels of set-aside: 17.5 per cent, 10 per cent and 5 per cent. Use of the 17.5 per cent level enables direct comparability of our results with those of the SPEL/EUMFSS and RAUMIS models in European Commission (1998b), while the lower levels reflect recent requirements.

[1] Any queries regarding the models, data or analysis can be clarified by contacting the authors directly.

Table 1   Cost-structure, Yield Response and Nitrate Leaching Functions for Three Land Qualities in the Base Case Scenario[4]

Cost Structure	Unit	Land Qualities		
		Poor Land	Average Land	Good Land
Fertiliser costs	ECU/ha	90	113	124
Other variable costs	ECU/ha	125	194	240
Fixed costs	ECU/ha	688	688	688
Total costs	ECU/ha	903	995	1052

Yield Response Function (Wheat)

Function parameters[2]	m	-	5.45	8.45	10.45
	d	-	0.51	0.53	0.55
	b	-	11.05	11.07	11.09
Optimal nitrogen application, N^{*1}	t/ha		0.17	0.21	0.23
Optimal yield, $y(N^*)^2$	t/ha		5.01	8.01	10.01

Nitrate Leaching Function Reference Rates

Wheat, x^3	kg/ha	45.00	39.00	35.00
Set-aside, γ^3	kg/ha	40.00	31.00	25.00
Nitrogen application, n	t/ha	0.18	0.19	0.20

Notes: [1] Optimal nitrogen: $N^* = -1/b \, \ell n \, [p_f/(p_w \, m \, d \, b)]$

   [2] Yield response function: $y(N^*) = m \, (1 - d \, e^{-bN^*})$

   [3] Average leaching values are extrapolated from information on poor and good land in Simmelsgaard (1991).

   [4] Other data used in the analysis:

Wheat price (p_w)	= 110 ECU/t;	N fertiliser price (p_f)	= 539 ECU/t;
Hectare premium	= 54.3 ECU/t;	Set-aside premium	= 68.8 ECU/t;
Reference yield	= 5.22 t/ha;	Time frame	= 6 years;
Discount rate	= 4 per cent;	Farm size	= 21 ha;
Exchange rate:	1 ECU = 9.35 DKR		

Sources: DIAFE, 1998; NCCP, 1985-95; Rygnestad and Fraser, 1996; Simmelsgaard, 1991; Statistics Denmark, 1998; Commission of the European Communities, 1997.

Accordingly, Table 2 contains details of the impact of the *Agenda 2000* cereal proposals on the Net Present Value (NPV) of profit for land of three qualities and for three *ex ante* levels of set-aside. Column(4) contains details of the collective impact of the proposals, while the other three columns contain details of the impact on individual components of income. These outcomes for a representative farm are much as would be expected by informed observers, and in general terms are consistent with the findings of the sectoral and regional impact studies reported in European Commission (1998b). In particular, the extent of increased net subsidy income (i.e., the increase in the hectare premium less the loss of set-aside premiums) is not sufficient to compensate for the net loss of production income (following the decrease in wheat price and despite extra production income from land previously set-aside). Moreover, these results generalise the SPEL/EU-MFSS and RAUMIS model results reported in European Commission (1998b) which are based exclusively on an *ex ante* set-aside rate of 17.5 per cent. Specifically, they show that

Table 2 Impact of Implementing the *Agenda 2000* Cereal Proposals on a Wheatgrower's NPV of Profit (ECU)[1]

			Change in NPV (ECU)		
		Net Subsidy Income (1)	Net Production Income		Total (4)
			(2)	(3)	
Ex Ante Set-Aside Rate	Land Quality		Land in Production	Land Set-Aside	
17.5 per cent	Poor	5,452.91	-10,280.91	4,527.20	-300.79
	Average	5,452.91	-16,507.56	7,963.89	-3,090.76
	Good	5,452.91	-20,658.81	10,331.97	-4,873.92
10 per cent	Poor	6,102.39	-11,215.54	2,586.97	-2,526.17
	Average	6,102.39	-18,008.25	4,550.79	-7,355.07
	Good	6,102.39	-22,536.88	5,903.98	-10,530.51
5 per cent	Poor	6,535.37	-11,838.62	1,293.49	-4,009.76
	Average	6,535.37	-19,008.70	2,275.40	-10,197.94
	Good	6,535.37	-23,788.93	2,951.99	-14,301.57

Note: [1] The values in this table are calculated on the basis of the revenue and cost equations detailed in Rygnestad and Fraser (1996) plus the data contained in Table 1.

the net loss of NPV is greater the lower is the *ex ante* set-aside rate due to the increased magnitude of the net loss of production income. In addition, these results enrich the sectoral and regional level results reported in European Commission (1998b) by demonstrating that the loss of NPV is greater on farms with higher quality land (again because of the increased magnitude of the net loss of production income).

Turning to the physical impacts of the implementation of the *Agenda 2000* cereal proposals, Table 3 contains details of the simulated responses for output, nitrogen use and nitrate leaching for all three ex ante rates of set-aside and types of land quality. In particular, column (1) shows the combined impact on total output both of increasing the amount of land in production and of decreasing the level of price support. For each situation it is clear that on balance total output increases, reflecting the dominance of the role of the amount of land in production in determining the output response. In this context, column (2) shows the specific impact of the decrease in price support on the optimal nitrogen application per hectare of land previously in production. These results suggest that the extent of reduced use of nitrogen is greatest on poor quality land, a finding which is also reflected in the output responses in column (1).

However column (3), which depicts total nitrogen use, represents a more complex set of results. Recalling that the impact of implementing the *Agenda 2000* cereal proposals on total nitrogen use is a balance of reduced nitrogen use on land previously in production, and of increased nitrogen use associated with the cropping of land previously set-aside, Table 3 shows that this balance depends on the *ex ante* rate of set-aside. In particular, for an *ex ante* set-aside rate of 17.5 per cent, the additional use of nitrogen on land previously set-aside is the dominant factor, while the reverse applies for an *ex ante* set-aside rate of 5 per cent. Moreover, the 10 per cent set-aside case represents a situation where the overall impact on nitrogen use also depends on the quality of land.

Table 3   Impact of Implementing the *Agenda 2000* Cereal Proposals on Output, Nitrogen Use and Leaching

Ex Ante Set-Aside Rate	Land Quality	Wheat Output (1)	N/ha (2)	Total N (3)	N Leaching (4)
		Percentage Change			
17.5 per cent	Poor	18.52	-12.14	6.50	-6.53
	Average	19.53	-9.63	9.54	-2.72
	Good	19.87	-8.72	10.64	-0.50
10 per cent	Poor	8.65	-12.14	-2.37	-6.97
	Average	9.57	-9.63	0.41	-4.69
	Good	9.88	-8.72	1.42	-3.38
5 per cent	Poor	2.93	-12.14	-7.51	-7.26
	Average	3.81	-9.63	-4.87	-5.96
	Good	4.10	-8.72	-3.92	-5.21

Finally in Table 3, column (4) contains details of the impact of the Agenda *2000* cereal proposals on the rate of nitrate leaching. Once again, the results in this column are a combination of two factors: decreased nitrate leaching associated with reduced nitrogen use on land previously in production; and increased nitrate leaching associated with additional nitrogen use on land previously set-aside. But, unlike the case of nitrogen use, these results also suggest a clear dominance of the former factor, even in the situation of a 17.5 per cent *ex ante* set-aside rate. This finding can be explained by reference to the leaching model which shows that, with increased nitrogen use, an increasing proportion of applied nitrogen is leached rather than being taken up by the crop. Consequently, the reduced nitrogen use on land previously in production has the dominant impact on total leaching, and this dominance is stronger both on poor quality land and for lower *ex ante* set-aside rates.

In general terms these physical impacts are also consistent with those reported in European Commission (1998b). In particular, the SPEL/EU-MFSS sectoral model used in that study predicts an increase in wheat production, while the RAUMIS regional model (of Germany) predicts an improvement in "nitrogen balance". Nevertheless, there are divergences between the various results both in terms of magnitude and direction. More specifically, the extent of output increase in Table 3 is considerably larger than that predicted by the SPEL/EU-MFSS model, ostensibly because of the exclusion of voluntary set-aside from our model. Note that the inclusion of this option in our model would both reduce the predicted magnitude of the output increase, and increase the predicted magnitude of the reduction in nitrate leaching. In addition, the RAUMIS model predicts a decline in wheat production which is inconsistent with the SPEL/EU-MFSS model results (and those in Table 3), but which is associated with the predicted improvement in "nitrogen balance" through decreased nitrogen application. In contrast, for an *ex ante* set-aside rate of 17.5 per cent, our model predicts reduced nitrate leaching not through decreased total nitrogen application, but by a shift in its allocation from land previously in production to land previously set-aside. Therefore, based on this comparison of results it can be concluded that the impact of the *Agenda 2000* cereal proposals on total nitrogen use is likely to be a poor indicator of the impact of these proposals on nitrate leaching. Specifically, the advantage of the leaching model included in our analysis is that it clarifies the relative significance for the rate of nitrate leaching of changes in the nature and scope of nitrogen application associated with the implementation of the *Agenda 2000* cereal proposals.[1]

4. Conclusion

The aim of this paper has been to undertake an assessment of the impact of implementing the EU's *Agenda 2000* cereal proposals at the level of the individual producer. This assessment involved first extending the economic model of Rygnestad and Fraser (1996) to include a model of nitrate leaching and developing a base case scenario focusing on specialist wheatgrowers in Denmark (section 2). We then simulated the impact of implementing the proposals both on a wheatgrower's NPV of profit, and on the associated physical magnitudes of output, nitrogen use and nitrate leaching (section 3). These impacts were evaluated for three levels of *ex ante* set-aside and three qualities of land.

Our use of a representative farm approach has produced for a 17.5 per cent *ex ante* set-aside rate findings of reduced income but increased wheat output which, after allowing for the exclusion of voluntary set-aside from our approach, are consistent with the results from the SPEL/EU-MFSS sectoral model reported in European Commission (1998b), while our finding of environmental benefits in terms of reduced nitrate leaching is consistent with the results from the RAUMIS regional model of Germany also reported in European Commission (1998b). Moreover, even though the output results from the SPEL/EU-MFSS and RAUMIS models are themselves inconsistent, we are able suggest a possible explanation for the inconsistency in terms of the reallocation of wheat output away from land previously in production towards land previously set-aside.

Finally, our results for specialist wheatgrowers in Denmark have highlighted the important roles both of the quality of land under wheat and of the policy variable, the *ex ante* set-aside rate, in determining the magnitude of the income and nitrate leaching effects of the implementation of the *Agenda 2000* cereal proposals. In this context, our results suggest that the recent change of the obligatory set-aside rate from 5 per cent to 10 per cent will have lessened both the negative income effects for these farmers of the implementation of the proposals, and the extent of the associated environmental benefits measured in terms of reduced nitrate leaching. Moreover, with the average to good quality wheatgrowing land in Denmark concentrated on the Islands, our findings suggest it is in this region that wheatgrowers will be most affected by the implementation of the *Agenda 2000* cereal proposals, and that improvements in the rate of nitrate leaching will be smallest.

Regarding the issue of extrapolating our results beyond specialist wheatgrowers in Denmark, we acknowledge that we are unable to do so in the context of other farming systems because we have only considered the subset of *Agenda 2000* proposals applicable

---

[1] Note that in our economic model there is no opportunity to substitute farm manure for commercial fertiliser. To the extent that this is feasible for specialist wheatgrowers, and the results from the RAUMIS model suggest a slight tendency for this substitution to occur at a regional level, the nitrate leaching improvements in Table 3 will be over-estimates.

directly to cereals. Such considerations clearly are the domain of the very large models featured in European Commission (1998b). However, we are confident that our results can be extended to specialist wheatgrowers in other European countries. In particular, we do not think that differences in plant growth due to land quality and climate between, say, Denmark and England would be sufficient to outweigh the importance of the wheatgrower's land quality and the *ex ante* set-aside rate in determining the impacts identified in Table 3 for output and nitrate leaching. For example, on the basis of the findings of Roberts *et al.* (1996) for specialist wheatgrowers in Eastern England that average wheat yields are approximately 6 tonnes/ha, we would rate typical land quality in this region of England as between poor and average in the context of Table 3, and estimate the likely physical impacts accordingly. It then remains to adjust these estimates for any associated up-take of voluntary set-aside.

References

Commission of the European Communities (1997). *The Agricultural Situation in the European Union: 1996 Report.* Brussels.

DIAFE (1998). *Økonomien i landbrugets driftsgrene 1996/97 (Economics of Agricultural Enterprises 1996/97).* The Danish Institute of Agricultural and Fisheries Economics, 81 Vol. b.

European Commission (1997). "Commission Publishes its Communication 'Agenda 2000 Cereal: For a Stronger and Wider Europe'", Agenda 2000 Cereal Press Release IP/97/660, Strasbourg/Brussels, 16 July.

European Commission (1998a). *Agenda 2000: The Legislative Proposals.* IP/98/258. Strasbourg/Brussels, 18 March.

European Commission (1998b). *CAP Reform Proposals: Impact Analyses.* Directorate-General for Agriculture (DG VI), Brussels.

NCCP (1985-95). *Oversigt over landsforsøgene. Forsøg og undersøgelser i de landøkonomiske foreninger. (Summary of agricultural experiments).* In Danish, Various years, Landsudvalget for Planteavl (The National Committee on Crop Production), Århus.

Paaby, H., Møller, F., Skop, E., Jensen, J. J., Hasler, B., Braun, H. and Asman, W. A. H. (1996). *The Costs of Reducing Nutrient Loads to Marine Recipients - Method, Model and Analysis.* Danish Environmental Research Institute, Report No. 165.

Roberts, D., Froud, J. and Fraser, R. (1996). Participation in Set-Aside: What Determines the Opting-In Price? *Journal of Agricultural Economics,* 47(1), 89-98.

Rygnestad, H. and Fraser, R. (1996). Land Heterogeneity and the Effectiveness of CAP Set-Aside, *Journal of Agricultural Economics,* 47(2), 255-260.

Schou, J. S. and Vetter, H. (1994). *Regulering af arealanvendelsen i vandindvindingsområder. (Regulation of farm-land use in water supply areas).* In Danish with English Summary, Danish Institute of Agricultural and Fisheries Economics, Report No. 79.

Simmelsgaard, S. E. (1991). *Estimering af funktioner for kvælstofudvaskning (Estimation of functions for nitrate leaching).* In Kvælstofgødning i landbruget - behov og udvaskning nu og i fremtiden (Nitrogen fertilisers in Danish Agriculture - present and future application for leaching). In Danish, Statens Jordbrugsøkonomiske Institut, Rapport No. 62, København.

Skop, E. (1993). *Calculation of Nitrate Leaching on a Regional Scale.* Danish Environmental Research Institute, Report No. 65.

Statistics Denmark (1998). *Priser på vigtige handelsgødninger. (Prices of important commercial fertilisers).* Statistiske efterretninger, 1998:16, p. 20.

Journal of Agricultural Economics — Volume 52, Number 2 — May 2001 — Pages 29-41

Chapter 8

Using Principal-Agent Theory to Deal with Output Slippage in the European Union Set-Aside Policy

Rob Fraser

(Manuscript received January 2000; Revision received October 2000; accepted December 2000)

*T*his paper proposes modifications to the existing EU set-aside policy which are designed to alleviate the problem of output slippage associated with heterogeneous land quality by using "incentive-compatible" mechanisms drawn from principal-agent theory. Specifically, it is suggested that there should be differential reference yields based on land quality to discourage the "adverse selection" of lower quality land for set-aside, and that the scope of set-aside monitoring should be expanded to include both the quantity and the quality of land set-aside so as to discourage "moral hazard" problems. The potential of these modifications is illustrated using a numerical analysis, which is also used to evaluate the role of a range of factors which determine the set-aside decision. Finally, an estimate of the "benefits" from reducing slippage required to justify the costs of including these modifications is provided.

1. Introduction

"Slippage" in a set-aside programme is defined as a situation where the percentage reduction in output is less than the percentage reduction in the area of land in production (Gardner, 1987). As demonstrated by Rygnestad and Fraser (1996) land heterogeneity plays a major role in determining slippage in the European Union's (EU) set-aside policy, with growers choosing to set-aside the less productive land on their farms so as to keep better land in production.[1] Moreover, this problem of "adverse selection"

■ Rob Fraser is Professor of Agricultural Economics, Imperial College, Wye, and Adjunct Professor of Agricultural and Resource Economics, University of Western Australia. E-mail: r.fraser@ic.ac.uk for correspondence. Thanks are due to Ben White, Uwe Latacz-Lohmann and Michael Burton for helpful discussions. I am also grateful for the helpful comments of two anonymous reviewers.

[1] Empirical estimates of the extend of slippage from this policy are difficult to obtain because of the role of other factors such as technological improvements in yield. However, the simulation results of Rygnestad and Fraser (1996) suggest slippage of up to 30 per cent from the proportion of land taken out of production is feasible. This is consistent with the initial EU approach taken to set-aside, with different rates applying to the rotational and non-rotational schemes. For example, in England the rates were 15 per cent and 18 per cent respectively.

provides the basis for the argument of Bourgeon *et al.* (1995) in favour of a voluntary set-aside policy in the EU as opposed to the existing mandatory policy. In particular, they demonstrate that a voluntary scheme designed to be "incentive compatible" in the tradition of principal-agent theory (see Laffont and Tirole, 1993) will see the aggregate area of land set-aside concentrated among the "less-efficient farms" but may still result in more effective output-reduction than a mandatory scheme which features a uniform set-aside area and payment for each farm.

The broad aim of this paper is to develop the contribution of Bourgeon *et al.* (1995) to debate over the EU's mandatory set-aside policy. However, whereas their approach was to use principal-agent theory to develop a voluntary alternative to the existing mandatory scheme, the approach taken here is to integrate incentive-compatible mechanisms into the mandatory scheme in a way that tackles the slippage problem.[2]

It should be emphasised that in this situation the objective of the principal is not to maximise a social welfare function which takes account of the various interests of producers, consumers and taxpayers. Rather the objective is to achieve output control from the use of a given rate of compulsory set-aside in the most cost-effective way. In this sense, the paper is focussed in a "second best" area of government policy, that of trying to expend a given budget most effectively.

More specifically, this paper suggests modifications to the existing set-aside scheme which have the effect of encouraging growers to choose to set-aside their more productive land. But in this case dealing with the problem of "adverse selection" creates the associated problem of "moral hazard", with the mechanism designed to give growers the incentive to set-aside their more productive land creating a new incentive to "cheat" and declare this the land which has been set-aside when in fact it is still in production.[3] Consequently, the suggested modifications to the existing set-aside scheme must include a broadening of the monitoring system to allow validation not only of the proportion, but also the quality of set-aside land.

The structure of the paper is as follows. Drawing on the model of the grower's set-aside decision developed in Rygnestad and Fraser (1996), Section 1 incorporates incentive-compatible features into the structure of the set-aside policy which deal with the joint problems of adverse selection and moral hazard. With these features, a grower with heterogeneous land quality is both encouraged to set-aside their more productive land, and discouraged from claiming to have done this while in fact doing the opposite. In order to illustrate the potential for these modifications to the existing set-aside policy to reduce the problem of slippage associated with heterogeneous land quality, Section 2 contains a numerical analysis of the theoretical formulation in Section 1. This analysis shows how the success of the suggested modifications is dependent on a range of factors, some of which are related to the specification of the modified set-aside policy, while others are out of the control of the policy-maker and relate to conditions both on and off-

---

[2] Note Bourgeon *et al.* (1995) did also suggest that, in the absence of an incentive-compatible voluntary scheme, the mandatory scheme should at least feature an "opt-out facility" (p 1504). However, as discussed in Froud *et al.* (1996), such a feature does exist in the mandatory scheme in the form of contingent compensatory payments.

[3] The joint problems of adverse selection and moral hazard in policy mechanism design have just begun to be analysed in the agri-environmental area. See White and Moxey (1999) and Latacz-Lohmann and Webster (1999). Note that Bourgeon *et al.* (1995) did not consider the issue of moral hazard.

farm. In particular, the overall cost-effectiveness of the changes is shown to depend on the level of world prices relative to EU prices.[4] The paper ends with a brief conclusion relating the existing EU set-aside policy to the theory of policy mechanism design.

2. Modifying the Set-Aside Policy

Based on Rygnestad and Fraser (1996), a specialist cereal grower in the EU receives income from three main sources: production income, compensatory payments and set-aside payments. However, both compensatory and set-aside payments are determined with respect to the relevant reference yield for the grower's region, and so these payments are uniform for a particular grower, regardless of the heterogeneity of their land. Consequently, for this grower it is only production income which varies according to the quality of land in production. It follows that when this grower chooses which land to set-aside, it will be that land which generates the lowest production income.[5] It is this choice which represents "adverse selection" within the context of the existing set-aside policy, and is responsible for the "slippage" associated with the policy in situations of heterogeneous land quality.

Given this feature of the existing set-aside policy, consider now the issue of how it could be modified to eliminate the "adverse selection". It is suggested here that in order to deal with slippage in situations of heterogeneous land quality, the payment for set-aside land needs to reflect the quality of that land, and needs to do so to an extent which counters the associated differential in production income. Specifically, for two types of land (g = good; b = bad):[6]

$$py_b + sr_g \geq py_g + sr_b \tag{1}$$

where:

p = price per unit of output
y_i = yield from land of type i (i = g,b)
s = set-aside premium per unit of reference yield
r_i = reference yield for land of type i.

Allowing for the situation of uncertain production income gives:

$$E(py_b) + sr_g \geq E(py_g) + sr_b \tag{2}$$

where:

$E(py_i)$ = expected production income from land of type i.

Note that if (2) is satisfied, then even a risk averse grower will choose to set-aside "good" land:

$$E(U(py_b + sr_g)) > E(U(py_g + sr_b)) \tag{3}$$

---

[4] Note that Bourgeon *et al.* (1995), make the point that this ratio also determines the overall rationale for a set-aside policy.

[5] Or in the case of rotational set-aside, this land will be set-aside first. See Rygnestad and Fraser (1996).

[6] Note that in the numerical analysis to follow three types of land (good, average and bad) are included in order to be consistent with the treatment of land heterogeneity in Rygnestad and Fraser (1996). However, the setting-aside of average land is always an inferior option in the context of adverse selection and moral hazard, and so it is omitted in this section in order to simplify the presentation.

because:

$$\text{Var}(py_g) > \text{Var}(py_b) \tag{4}$$

where:

$E(U(I))$ = expected utility of total income (I) $(U^{\cdot}(I) > O, U''(I) < O)$
$\text{Var}(py_i)$ = variance of production income from land of type i.

That is, the typically higher yield from "good" land means that the overall level of variability of production income will also be higher (given similar levels of seasonal variability), and so a risk averse grower will find both the expected level and variability of total income from setting-aside good land more attractive.[7]

However, although achieving this incentive-compatibility corrects the problem of "adverse selection" by encouraging growers to set-aside better quality land, in so doing it creates the problem of "moral hazard" whereby a grower states that "good" land is being set-aside whereas in fact it is the "bad" land that is set-aside:

$$E(py_g) + sr_g > E(py_b) + sr_g \tag{5}$$

Consequently, the monitoring of set-aside needs to be extended so that it is not just the quantity, but also the quality of set-aside land that is monitored. Given that monitoring typically involves only partial coverage of the grower population, but that if detected as "cheating" then the grower suffers a penalty, (5) needs to be adjusted so that "truth-telling" is worthwhile:[8]

$$E(py_g) + sr_g - qsr_g x < E(py_b) + sr_g \tag{6}$$

where:

q = probability of being monitored $(O \leq q \leq 1)$
x = penalty proportion, $(O \leq x)$.

Or in the case of a risk averse grower:

$$E(U(py_g + sr_g - qsr_g x))   < E(U(py_b + sr_g)) \tag{7}$$

Note that (6) may not hold, but (7) still holds for a risk averse grower because the greater variance of total income associated with attempting to "cheat" has a dominant impact on expected utility. This point is developed formally in the Appendix for the example of three land types for use in the numerical analysis of the next section.

Finally in this section, it should be recognised that the cost-effectiveness of these changes in terms of the EU budget relies on the benefits associated with reduced slippage exceeding the costs of higher set-aside payments and more detailed monitoring. For example, where these benefits take the form of reduced export restitution payments:

---

[7] I am grateful to an anonymous reviewer for pointing out to me that in the situation where yield is also uncertain, and there is a very strong negative covariance between price and yield, this inequality of variances may not hold.

[8] Note that because the expected penalty associated with cheating is linear in q and x, it is feasible for the principal to trade-off one instrument against the other. For example, the expected penalty can be maintained despite lowering the probability of detection if the fine from detection is raised proportionately. I am grateful to an anonymous reviewer for pointing this out. See also Polinsky and Shavell (1979).

Using Principal-Agent Theory to Deal with Output Slippage in the European Union Set-Aside Policy   *33*

$$(\bar{p} - \bar{p}_w)(y_g - y_b) > s(r_g - r_a) + Z \tag{8}$$

where:

$\bar{p}$ = expected grower price

$\bar{p}_w$ = expected world price

r_a = existing reference yield

Z = extra monitoring cost.

Equation (8) highlights the important role of expected world prices relative to EU prices in determining the cost-effectiveness of the proposed modifications to the existing set-aside policy. Moreover, in considering equations (2), (7) and (8) collectively, it can be seen that there are a range of policy-related, on-farm and off-farm factors which have a role in determining the effectiveness of the proposed modifications. Evaluating the role of these factors is the aim of the numerical analysis of the next section.

3. The Numerical Analysis

The principal purpose of this section is to illustrate, using a numerical analysis, the potential for the proposed "incentive-compatible" modifications to the existing EU set-aside policy to alleviate the slippage problem of this policy. In addition, the numerical analysis will be used to evaluate the role of the range of on-farm, off-farm and policy-related factors identified in equations (2), (7) and (8) as influencing a grower's set-aside decision.

Such an analysis requires a complete specification of the circumstances in which the grower is to make the decision of which land to set aside. In what follows, use is made of the off-farm and policy parameter values specified in Fraser and Rygnestad (1999). In addition, use is made of the details contained in Fraser and Rygnestad (1999) regarding the on-farm specification of the yield response functions for three qualities of land. Finally, the analysis is simplified by assuming the farm in question has equal proportions of the three land qualities (where average land is denoted by the subscript "a"), and that the compulsory set-aside proportion is one-third of all land. This elimination of the complications of differing proportions serves only to enhance the clarity of the analysis.

This approach provides the following parameter values as they relate to the existing set-aside policy.[9]

$$y_g = 10.00; \quad y_a = 8.01; \quad y_b = 5.03; \quad p = 110; \quad s = 70; \quad r_a = 8$$

and the coefficient of variation of price $(CV_p) = 0.35$.

---

[9] See Fraser (2000) regarding details of the coefficient of variation of price (CVp). Note that compensation payments have been suppressed as they are constant across land types. In addition, unreported numerical analysis shows that these "optimal" yields are relatively insensitive to the other parameter values in the grower's decision framework. Consequently, they will be fixed at these levels in what follows. Note the precise yeilds used for y_a and y_b facilitate the base case pattern of results in Table 2.

34 Rob Fraser

Add to this the following cost data based again on Fraser and Rygnestad (1999):

> cost/tonne on good land = 36
> cost/tonne on average land = 38
> cost/tonne on bad land = 42
> fixed costs = 688

Finally, assume the attitude to risk of the grower can be represented by the mean-variance formulation and the constant relative risk aversion function form:[10]

$$E(U(\pi)) = U(E(\pi)) + \tfrac{1}{2}U''(E(\pi)) \cdot Var(\pi) \tag{9}$$

where:

$E(\pi)$ = expected profit

$Var(\pi)$ = variance of profit

and

$$U(\pi) = \frac{\pi^{1-R}}{1-R} \tag{10}$$

where:

R = constant coefficient of relative risk aversion

$$= {-U''(\pi) \cdot \pi} \Big/ {U'(\pi)}$$

Table 1: Numerical Results Relating to Setting Aside Each Type of Land Given the Existing Set-Aside Policy

	Good	Average	Bad
		Land Quality Set-Aside	
	Good	*Average*	*Bad*
$E(\pi)^a$	790.58	953.83	1188.98
$Var(\pi)^b$	251935.8	334698.7	480969.6
$E(U(\pi))^c$	53.40	58.93	66.03
Total Output	13.04	15.03	18.01

Notes a: $E_g(\pi) = p(y_a + y_b) + sr_a - (c_a y_a + c_b y_b) - F$

where: c_i = cost/tonne on land type i
F = fixed cost
$E_i(\pi)$ = expected profit setting aside land type i
$E_a(\pi)$ and $E_b(\pi)$ contain appropriate adjustments

b: $Var_g(\pi) = (y_a + y_b)^2 Var(p)$
$Var_a(\pi) = (y_g + y_b)^2 Var(p)$
$Var_b(\pi) = (y_g + y_a)^2 Var(p)$

c: R = 0.5

[10] See Hanson and Ladd (1991) and Pope and Just (1991) for arguments supporting the assumptions regarding the mean-variance approximation and the form of the utility function.

Using Principal-Agent Theory to Deal with Output Slippage in the European Union Set-Aside Policy   35

Note this coefficient is set at 0.5 for the numerical analysis, although unreported analysis shows its value does not affect the general pattern of results.

On this basis, Table 1 contains details of the numerical results relating to the expected profit, variance of profit and expected utility of profit from setting aside good, average and bad land respectively, given the existing features of the EU set-aside policy. Table 1 shows the expected finding that, given the existing formulation of the EU set-aside policy, the best decision for the grower is to set-aside the poor land, but that this "adverse selection" results in the largest total output from the farm.

Next, consider the modification of the existing set-aside policy to a form proposed in Section 1 as being "incentive-compatible". In particular, introduce the following differential reference yields for good, average and poor set-aside land:

$$r_g = 10$$
$$r_a = 7.6$$
$$r_b = 4.3.$$

In addition, let the features of the monitoring system be as follows:

$$q = 0.5$$
$$x = 1$$

These values imply that setting aside good land is associated with full compensation, but that setting aside other types gives less than full compensation, while a "cheating" grower

Table 2: Base Case Results for the Incentive-Compatible Set Aside Policy

	Land Quality Set-Aside		
	Good	Average	Bad
Truth-telling			
$E_T(\pi)$	930.58	925.83	929.98
$Var_T(\pi)$	251935.8	334698.7	480969.6
$E(U_T(\pi))$	58.79	57.88	58.04
Cheating			
$E_C(\pi)$[a]			978.98
$Var_C(\pi)$[b]			603469.6
$E(U_C(\pi))$			57.65

Notes a: $E_C(\pi) = (1-q)(sr_g + p(y_g + y_a)) + q(s(1-x)r_g + p(y_g + y_a)) - c_a y_a - c_g y_g - F$

   b: $Var_C(\pi)$ as given by $Var_C(I)$ in the Appendix (A7)

---

[11] One anonymous reviewer has pointed out that to specify $q = 0.5$ is certainly too high for EU conditions. Recalling the point made previously that the principal can trade-off q and x to maintain a constant expected penalty, it is clear that in the numerical analysis a "more realistic" value of q could be used in association with the value of $x > 1$ (e.g. the expected penalty is equivalent for $q = 0.5$ and $x = 1$, and for $q = 0.1$ and $x = 5$). However, as can be seen in the Appendix, modifying these values also changes the variance of income from cheating, leading to complex impacts on producer behaviour which are beyond the scope of this paper. Nevertheless, the impact of a 10 per cent lower value of q is considered in the sensitivity analysis which follows.

has a 50 per cent chance of being detected, and suffers the penalty of full withdrawal of set-aside payments if caught.[11] Using these "Base Case" parameter values for the modified set-aside policy gives the results contained in Table 2.   This table shows that the introduction of differential reference yields as specified results in the "truth-telling" grower finding it beneficial to set-aside good land ahead of the other types, and that this "truth-telling" is more beneficial than "cheating" by claiming to have set-aside the good land, but instead to have set-aside the bad land. Note also that although the expected profit from "cheating" exceeds that for all cases of "truth-telling", the greater variance of profit in the case of "cheating" means that overall the risk averse grower prefers not to "cheat".   However, this excess of expected profit from "cheating" over "truth-telling" means that a less risk averse grower may find the increased risk from "cheating" worthwhile. In particular, for $R \leq 0.25$:

$$E(U_T(\pi)) < E(U_C(\pi))$$

Finally in relation to the Base Case, the cost-effectiveness of the modifications as specified by equation (8) can be evaluated by setting a cost of enhanced monitoring (to check land quality as well as quantity) and then determining the level of expected world price required for (8) to hold. For example, if the extra cost of monitoring is approximately 1 per cent of the expected profit of each farm (i.e. 9.3), then (8) holds if:

$$\bar{p}_w \leq 80.$$

Alternatively, if the extra cost of monitoring is twice this level, then (8) holds if:

$$\bar{p}_w \leq 78.$$

Consider next the role of off-farm factors relating to the grower's price distribution in determining the success of the proposed modifications to the existing set-aside policy. The top panel of Table 3 shows that if the expected grower price ($\bar{p}$) falls from 110 to

Table 3: Evaluating the Role of the Grower's Price Distribution

	Land Quality Set-Aside		
	Good	*Average*	*Poor*
$\bar{p} = 100^a$			
$E_T(\pi)$	800.21	775.56	749.84
$E_C(\pi)$			798.84
$CV_p = 0.2^b$			
$E(U_T(\pi))$	60.29		
$E(U_C(\pi))$			60.30

Notes a: Base Case: $\bar{p} = 110$
        b: Base Case: $CV_p = 0.35$

Using Principal-Agent Theory to Deal with Output Slippage in the European Union Set-Aside Policy   37

100, then not only does this accentuate the desirability of setting-aside good land, but also it reduces the expected profit from "cheating" to a level where, regardless of the attitude to risk of the grower, "truth-telling" is always preferable. Note, however, that in this case the modifications are only cost-effective (for $Z = 1\%$ of $E_T(\pi)$) if:[12]

$$\bar{p}_w \leq 70.$$

In contrast, if the variability of grower prices is reduced (to $CV_p = 0.2$), then the associated reduction in the riskiness of production income means that the expected utility of "cheating" exceeds that from "truth-telling" for $R = 0.5$. Consequently, for this level of price variability only growers with attitudes to risk in excess of $R = 0.5$ would find "truth-telling" worthwhile. It follows that decreases in the expected level and variability of grower prices have opposite impacts on the effectiveness of the proposed modifications, with lower expected prices enhancing this effectiveness by discouraging "adverse selection", and lower variability of prices diminishing it by encouraging "moral hazard".

Finally in this section consider the role of a range of policy-related factors in determining the effectiveness of the modifications. Of the four components of the modified set-aside policy (s, r_i, q and x), decreasing the probability of detection (q) and the size of penalty (x) have the predictable consequence of increasing the attraction of "cheating". In particular:

$$E(U_T(\pi)) < E(U_C(\pi))$$

for:

$\quad q \leq 0.45 \quad$ (Base Case: q = 0.5)

and for:

$\quad x \leq 0.92 \quad$ (Base Case: x = 1.0).

In addition, decreasing the set-aside payment has a proportionately greater effect where good land is set-aside as

$$r_g > r_a > r_b$$

For example, for s = 69 (Base Case s = 70):

$\quad E_T(\pi) \quad$ (good land set-aside) = 920.58

while:

$\quad E_T(\pi) \quad$ (bad land set-aside) = 925.68

Consequently, lower values of q, x and s all diminish the effectiveness of the proposed modifications, with decreases in q and x encouraging "moral hazard" and decreases in s encouraging "adverse selection".

The remaining feature of the modified set-aside policy is the set of reference yields on

---

[12] This choice of $Z = 1\%$ of $E_T(\pi)$ is based on estimates of the cost of income tax audits and may be inappropriate in other situations. As shown previously, note from equation (8) that if Z was instead 2 per cent then, given the associated parameter values, the cost-effective $\bar{p}_w$ would be 2 units lower.

which set-aside payments are based. Reductions in all three of these values need not alter the "truth-telling" preference for setting-aside good land.   However, the relative importance of production income is increased in this situation and, as a consequence, the expected utility from "cheating" increases relative to "truth-telling". The top and bottom panels of Table 4 illustrate this effect, with the top panel showing that a decrease in the set of reference yields from: $r_g = 10$; $r_a = 7.6$; $r_b = 4.3$ to $r_g = 9.2$; $r_a = 6.8$; $r_b = 3.4$ is consistent with a continued "truth-telling" preference for setting-aside good land, and for "truth-telling" over "cheating". However, a further decrease to: $r_g = 9.1$; $r_a = 6.7$; $r_b = 3.4$, although still not encouraging "adverse selection" (ie the setting-aside of poor land rather than good land if truth-telling), is sufficient to lead to a preference for "cheating". It follows that lowering the value of the set of reference yields need not encourage "adverse selection", but clearly does encourage "moral hazard".   Note also that these lower reference yields encourage the cost-effectiveness of the modified set-aside policy, with the benefits of reduced slippage exceeding the costs for the settings in Table 4 for:[13]

$$\bar{p}_w \leq 91$$

compared with:

$$\bar{p}_w \leq 80$$

for the Base Case.

Table 4: Evaluating the Role of the Set of Reference Yields

		Land Quality Set-Aside	
	Good	Average	Poor
$r_g = 9.2$; $r_a = 6.8$; $r_b = 3.4$[a]			
$E_T(\pi)$	874.58	869.83	866.98
$E(U_T(\pi))$	56.71		
$E(U_C(\pi))$			56.69
$r_g = 9.1$; $r_a = 6.7$; $r_b = 3.4$			
$E_T(\pi)$	867.58	862.82	866.98
$E(U_T(\pi))$	56.44		
$E(U_C(\pi))$			56.57

Note a: Base Case: $r_g = 10$; $r_a = 7.6$; $r_b = 4.3$

4. CONCLUSION

This paper has proposed modifications to the existing EU set-aside policy which are designed to alleviate the problem of output slippage associated with heterogeneous land

---

[13] This result applies for $r_g = 9.2$. For $r_g = 9.1$, the requirement is: $\bar{p}_w \leq 92$.

quality in a way which is cost-effective for the EU budget. Drawing on the core concepts of principal-agent theory, these "incentive-compatible" modifications involve:

(i)   establishing differential reference yields to reflect the heterogeneity of land quality

(ii) broadening the scope of monitoring to include not just the quantity but also the quality of set-aside land.

Establishing differential reference yields means that where higher quality land is set-aside, the set-aside payment is also higher. As a consequence, an incentive is created for the grower to choose to set-aside higher quality land. As shown in Section 1, if sufficient this incentive can overcome the tendency for "adverse selection" of lower quality land which is a feature of the existing set-aside policy. However, creating this incentive also creates an incentive to "cheat" and claim to be setting-aside good land while actually keeping it in production. As a consequence, to counter this problem of "moral hazard" the policy's monitoring programme needs to be extended to check both the quantity and the quality of set-aside land.

In Section 2 a numerical analysis of these modifications was undertaken to illustrate their potential to alleviate the slippage problem. In addition, this numerical analysis enabled the evaluation of the role of a range of on-farm, off-farm and policy-related factors in determining the grower's set-aside decision. It was shown that, if the proportion of production income in total income decreases due to a fall in expected grower prices or an increase in set-aside payments, then "adverse selection" is discouraged. However, lower levels of risk aversion among growers and a decrease in the riskiness of either production income or of being detected "cheating" encourage "moral hazard". Finally, it was shown that the cost-effectiveness of these modifications is dependent on the excess of EU grower prices over world prices. Moreover, although the general level of differential reference yields can be lowered to reduce the cost of implementing the modifications (Table 4), these results suggest that the margin between EU and world prices needs to be in excess of 20 per cent for the benefits of alleviating slippage to justify the costs of using "incentive-compatible" mechanisms in the set-aside policy.

References

Bourgeon, J-M., Jayet, P-A. and Picard, P. (1995) "An Incentive Approach to Land Set-aside Programs", *European Economic Review* 39:1487-1509.

Fraser, R.W. (2000) "Risk and Producer Compensation in the *Agenda 2000* Cereal Reforms: a Note", *Journal of Agricultural Economics* 51(3) : 468-72.

Fraser, R.W. and Rygnestad, H.L. (1999). "An Assessment of the Impact of Implementing the European Commission's *Agenda 2000* Cereal Proposals for Specialist Wheatgrowers in Denmark", *Journal of Agricultural Economics* 50(2):328-35.

Froud, J., Roberts, D. and Fraser, R.W. (1996). "Participation in Set-aside: What Determines the Opting-in Price", *Journal of Agricultural Economics* 47(1):89-98.

Gardner, B.L. (1987). *The Economics of Agricultural Policies*, Macmillan Publishing Company, New York.

Hanson, S.D. and Ladd, G.W. (1991). "Robustness of the Mean-variance Model with Truncated Probability Distributions", *American Journal of Agricultural Economics* 73(2):436-45.

Laffont, J-J. and Tirole, J. (1993). *A Theory of Incentives in Procurement and Regulation*, MIT Press, Massachusetts.

Latacz-Lohmann, V. and Webster, P. (1999). "Moral Hazard in Agri-environmental Schemes", mimeo, Wye College, University of London.

Mood, A.M., Graybill, F.A. and Boes, D.C. (1974). *An Introduction to the Theory of Statistics*, 3rd Edn, McGraw-Hill, Tokyo.

Polinsky, M. and Shavell, S. (1979). "The Optimal Trade-off between the Probability and Magnitude of Fines", *American Economic Review* 69(5):880-91.

Pope, R.D. and Just, R.E. (1991). "On Testing the Structure of Risk Preferences in Agricultural Supply Analysis", *American Journal of Agricultural Economics* 73(3):743-8.

Rygnestad, H.L. and Fraser, R.W. (1996). "Land Heterogeneity and the Effectiveness of CAP Set-aside", *Journal of Agricultural Economics* 47(2):255-60.

White, B. and Moxey, A. (1999). "An Approach to Designing Agri-environmental Policy with Hidden Information and Hidden Action", mimeo, University of Newcastle-upon-Tyne.

APPENDIX: Variance of Income from "Cheating"

It is assumed that the grower has three land quality types, good, average and bad, in equal proportions, and that the compulsory set-aside rate is one-third of total land. It is also assumed that there is price uncertainty, but no yield uncertainty.

On this basis, total income (I) from "cheating" and setting-aside bad land while claiming to set-aside good land is:

$$I = sr_g + p(y_g + y_a) \quad \text{if not detected} \tag{A1}$$

$$I = sr_g + p(y_g + y_a) - sr_g x \quad \text{if detected} \tag{A2}$$

where:

y_a = yield from average land.

With a probability of detection of q, expected income from cheating ($E_C(I)$) is given by:

$$E_C(I) = (1 - q)(sr_g + \overline{p}(y_g + y_a)) + q(s(1-x)r_g + \overline{p}(y_g + y_a)) \tag{A3}$$

In addition, the variance of income from cheating ($Var_C(I)$) is given by:[14]

$$Var_C(I) = \int p \, (1-q)(sr_g + p(y_g g + y_a) - E_C(I))^2 f(p)dp$$

$$+ \int pq(s(1-x)r_g + p(y_g + y_a) - E_C(I))^2 f(p)dp \tag{A4}$$

Consider the first term on the right-hand-side of (A4). Substituting for $E_C(I)$ using (A3) and rearranging gives:

$$(1-q)(y_g + y_a)^2 Var(p) + (1-q)(q(sr_g - s(1-x)r_g))^2 \tag{A5}$$

A similar process for the second term gives:

$$q(y_g + y_a)^2 Var(p) \quad + \quad q((1-q)(s(1-x)r_g - sr_g))^2 \tag{A6}$$

where:

Var(p) = variance of the grower price.

Combining (A5) and (A6) gives:

$$Var_C(I) = (y_g + y_a)^2 Var(p) + ((1-q)q^2 + q(1-q)^2)(sr_g x)^2 \tag{A7}$$

[14] See Mood *et al.* (1974), p.185.

Note that the second term on the right-hand-side of (A7) is unambiguously positive.
Consequently, since:

$$y_g > y_b$$

It follows that:

$$\text{Var}_C(I) > \text{Var}_T(I) \qquad (A8)$$

where:

$$\text{Var}_T(I) = \text{variance of income from "truth-telling"}$$
$$= (y_a + y_b)\text{Var}(p)$$

Therefore, as stated in Section 1, even if equation (6) does not hold (expected income from "truth-telling" does not exceed expected income from "cheating"), a risk averse grower may still prefer "truth-telling" because of the overall dominance of the higher variability of total income from "cheating" in the decision. It follows that the attitude to risk of the grower will play a role in determining the success of the proposed modifications. This role is evaluated in the numerical analysis of Section 2.

PART B

ENVIRONMENTAL STEWARDSHIP AS AN AGRICULTURAL LAND USE POLICY IN THE EUROPEAN UNION

Introduction to Part B

During the 1990s there was a growing awareness within the EU not just of the problem of production surpluses which had led to the May 1992 CAP reforms, but also of the negative environmental effects of agricultural land use intensification and extensification, which ultimately led to the Agenda 2000 CAP reforms and the creation of "Pillar 2" support for the protection and enhanced provision of environmental goods and services as part of the CAP's agricultural land use policy.

In relation to the intensification of agricultural land use, Chapter 7 has already identified the nitrate leaching problem associated with the use of fertiliser to increase cereal yields — a problem which was instrumental in the creation of both Nitrate Sensitive Zones and Environmentally Sensitive Areas in the UK. In relation to the extensification of agricultural land use, there was growing social concern about the destruction of habitats (e.g. hedgerows and native woodland) in order to increase the area of land under cereal production — a concern which led to the creation of the Countryside Stewardship Scheme, itself a precursor to what is now known as the Environmental Stewardship Scheme (see for example Latacz-Lohmann and Van der Hamsvoort (1998) and associated references).

Moreover, the creation of "contracts" between farmers and government agencies in relation to the participation of farmers in these various schemes led to a rise in academic interest in using principal-agent theory to inform the design of such schemes as part of the CAP's agricultural land use policy — see for example Choe and Fraser (1999); Moxey, White and Ozanne (1999); Ozanne, Hogan and Colman (2001); and White (2002) (see also Wu and Babcock (1996) in relation to the US Conservation Reserve Programme). Chapter 9 provides a taxonomy of the particular research focus of such papers (and others) — which typically included one or both of the problems of adverse selection and moral hazard, consideration of a range of policy instruments (such as payments for participation and penalties for non-compliance), and a consideration of the role of the attitude to risk of farmers, both in the face of uncertain production income and in the context of non-compliance behaviour. Chapter 9 also concludes that risk aversion among farmers provides an opportunity both to encourage participation in such schemes by offering certain payments for participation (in contrast to uncertain production income) and to deter non-compliance by increasing the riskiness of cheating behaviour.

After the resolution of the Agenda 2000 CAP reforms it became clear that such land use-based contracts between farmers and government agencies were here to stay (in the EU). As a consequence, academic interest in applications of principal-agent theory to contract design both grew and spread to reflect the expanding remit of Pillar 2 support for the CAP's agricultural land use policy in relation to the protection and enhanced provision of environmental goods and services.

One such area of interest focussed on the core issue of heterogeneous land quality in agriculture, which was shown in Part A to be an important cause of "slippage" in using set-aside as a production control policy. For example, Lankoski and Ollikainen (2003) showed in the context of designing contracts to deal with environmental externalities that it was in society's best interests to "target" such polices to take account of heterogeneous land quality. Chapter 10 develops this concept of policy "targeting" further, and shows how it can be used to manage the behaviour of farmers so as to reduce the moral hazard problem in relation to their compliance behaviour (see also Lankoski, Lichtenberg and Ollikainen (2010) for subsequent analysis of the policy "targeting" research reported in Chapter 10).

Moreover, in the same way that "slippage" in a set-aside policy has its origins in the adverse selection by farmers of lower yielding land to take out of production, so the concern about adverse selection arose in relation to the behaviour of farmers participating voluntarily in environmental stewardship schemes. In particular, would participating farmers choose to put land into environmental stewardship which delivered worthwhile improvements in environmental goods and services? And could the participation of farmers in environmental stewardship schemes be managed so as to reduce the problem of adverse selection?

These questions are investigated in a theoretical context in Chapter 11, and then evaluated empirically in Chapters 12 and 13. More specifically, Chapter 11 builds on the earlier work of Wu and Babcock (1996), Moxey, White and Ozanne (1999) and Feng (2007) to assess what seems to be a fundamental inconsistency in the specification of such schemes: that farmers receive payments based on the foregone agricultural income from their participating land, while the benefits for society from funding these payments is determined by the environmental goods and services provided by such land. In addition, the associated "incentive compatibility" problems may be exacerbated by the presence both of heterogeneous agricultural land quality for production and of environmental land quality for social benefits. Chapter 11 concludes that the relationship between the quality of land for agricultural production compared with its quality for generating environmental benefits is an empirical question, but nevertheless, scope remains for the "principal" to manage participation in the scheme to improve its cost-effectiveness.

This management of participation issue is considered in more detail in Chapter 12 in the context of an empirical application to the Higher Level

Stewardship Scheme in England. Participation by agents (farmers) in this scheme is voluntary, but participants are chosen by the principal (Natural England) using a self-determined scoring mechanism. Moreover, this self-determination creates an opportunity for the principal to manage participation so as to maximise its delivery of environmental benefits from a given budget available to provide payments for participating land. On this basis Chapter 12 provides empirical evidence that participating land is prioritised (by Natural England) based on: (i) it qualifying for lower payments per hectare (i.e. more participating hectares for a given budget) and (ii) its proximity to cities (i.e. more recreation benefits per participating hectare).

Chapter 13 then considers empirically the relationship between the quality of participating land for generating agricultural income as compared to environmental benefit. It finds evidence to confirm that farmers are typically submitting their lower yielding land for participation (i.e. as with "compliance" set-aside), but that there is biological evidence that this land typically also provides relatively high environmental benefits per hectare because it is often adjacent (usually as buffer strips/field margins) to important habitat areas such as waterways and hedgerows. As a consequence, and as foreshadowed by the research reported in Chapter 7, the presence of such a negative correlation between agricultural land quality and its provision of environmental benefits results in effect in the "auspicious selection" by farmers of land for participation in environmental stewardship schemes.

During the first decade after the implementation of the Agenda 2000 CAP reforms research also continued on the relationship between moral hazard, compliance behaviour and the design of agri-environmental schemes. Such research typically investigated the scheme's design features (e.g. size of penalty, probability of detection) which would reduce or eliminate non-compliance behaviour, depending on whether farmers are risk neutral or risk averse. See for example: Hart and Latacz-Lohmann (2005), Ozanne and White (2007), Yano and Blandford (2009), and Yano and Blandford (2011). And although these papers provided the impetus for the research reported in Chapter 14, the research in this chapter is novel in that it breaks away from the static (i.e. atemporal) framework of the previous literature to consider the role of compliance behaviour in relation to contract duration in a multi-period setting. More specifically, in developing such an intertemporal model of compliance behaviour, this theoretical research demonstrates that a risk averse farmer has an unambiguous preference for cheating early rather than late in their contract period. As a consequence, it is further demonstrated that the principal can increase compliance and therefore improve the cost-effectiveness of the scheme by concentrating monitoring resources on farmers who are early in their contract period.

Moreover, this concern about compliance behaviour in a dynamic policy context leads into the research reported in Chapter 15, because arguably one of the most volatile components of the production circumstances of EU farmers over the last two decades has been the policy context.[1] This has included major reforms to the CAP in 1992 and 2000, along with their associated "implementation processes" and "transition periods", as well as numerous smaller CAP "adjustments" (e.g. the abolishing of set-aside in 2008). However, despite this apparent policy volatility, Chapter 15 identifies two core themes among the plethora of policy changes: (i) reduced price support for agricultural production in favour of direct payments as "uncoupled" farm income support and (ii) a shift of farmer income support from agriculture-based payments ("Pillar 1") to environment-based payments ("Pillar 2"). As a consequence, EU farmers are now exposed to far greater market price risk than previously, but also have the opportunity to derive substantial "safe" income from participation in environmental stewardship, and in so doing shift their land use from agricultural production to the production of environmental goods and services. And given their increased exposure to market price risk, such diversification of land use is an attractive risk management response — hence the popularity of environmental stewardship options such as field margins ("buffer strips") (see Natural England, 2011).

But recent discussion of the form of the CAP after 2013 (and "towards 2020") has included proposals to strengthen risk management tools by directing CAP support towards market-based risk management instruments such as forward pricing, futures markets and price insurance, thereby reducing the riskiness of income from agricultural production (see for example: European Commission, 2010). Given this proposal, the research reported in Chapter 15 draws attention to a potential negative consequence of such a change in CAP support — an associated increase in cheating behaviour by farmers in the context of environmental stewardship as they re-balance their reduced production income risk by taking the additional risk of non-compliance. However, given this potential negative policy impact, Chapter 15 also suggests appropriate agricultural land use policy design solutions so as to neutralise this impact.

Part B concludes with my Presidential Address from the Annual Conference of the Agricultural Economics Society in 2013 (Chapter 16). This Address represents a synthesis of much of the research undertaken previously into the moral hazard problem in agri-environmental policy. It shows that we are currently well aware of the range of potential causes of non-compliance behaviour among farmers, and of the existence of such behaviour among farmers, but as yet we have no empirical evidence regarding which of these potential causes are actually significant contributors to this non-compliance behaviour. As a consequence, Chapter 16 sets out an "agenda" of empirical research required for the development of an evidence-based policy response to non-compliance behaviour in the context of agricultural land use.

---

[1] Note that the research reported in Chapter 15 has previously only been available as a conference paper.

References

Choe, C. and Fraser, I. (1999) Compliance monitoring and agri-environmental policy, *Journal of Agricultural Economics* 50(3): 468–487.

European Commission (2010) *The Common Agricultural Policy (CAP) towards 2020 — Meeting the food, natural resources and territorial challenges of the future.* [Online] Available at: http://ec.europa.eu/agriculture/cap-post-2013/communication/index_en.htm (Accessed 18th November 2011).

Feng, H. (2007) Green payments and dual policy goals, *Journal of Environmental Economics and Management* 54(2): 323–335.

Hart, R. and Latacz-Lohmann, U. (2005) Combating moral hazard in agri-environmental schemes: A multiple agent approach, *European Review of Agricultural Economics* 32(1): 75–91.

Lankoski, J. and Ollikainen, M. (2003) Agri-environmental externalities: A framework for designing targeted policies, *European Review of Agricultural Economics* 30(1): 51–75.

Lankoski, J., Lichtenberg, E. and Ollikainen, M. (2010) Agri-environment program compliance in a heterogeneous landscape, *Environmental and Resource Economics* 47(1): 1–22.

Latacz-Lohmann, U. and Van der Hamsvoort, C. (1998) Auctions as a means of creating a market for public goods from agriculture, *Journal of Agricultural Economics* 49(3): 334–345.

Moxey, A., White, B. and Ozanne, A. (1999) Efficient contract design for agri-environment policy, *Journal of Agricultural Economics* 50(2): 187–202.

Natural England (2011) *Environmental Stewardship.* [Online] Available at: http://www.naturalengland.gov.uk/ourwork/farming/funding/es/default.aspx (Accessed 16th May 2011).

Ozanne, A., Hogan, A. and Colman, D. (2001) Moral hazard, risk aversion and compliance monitoring in agri-environmental policy, *European Review of Agricultural Economics* 28(3): 329–347.

Ozanne, A. and White, B. (2007) Equivalence of input quotas and input charges under asymmetric information in agri-environmental schemes, *Journal of Agricultural Economics* 58(2): 260–268.

White, B. (2002) Designing voluntary agri-environment policy with hidden information and hidden action: A note, *Journal of Agricultural Economics* 53(2): 353–360.

Wu, J. and Babcock, B. (1996) Contract design for the purchase of environmental goods form agriculture, *American Journal of Agricultural Economics* 78: 935–945.

Yano, Y. and Blandford, D. (2009) Use of compliance rewards in agri-environmental schemes, *Journal of Agricultural Economics* 60(3): 530–545.

Yano, Y. and Blandford, D. (2011) Agri-environmental policy and moral hazard under multiple sources of uncertainty, *European Review of Agricultural Economics* 38(1): 141–155.

Journal of Agricultural Economics — Volume 53, Number 3 — November 2002 — Pages 475-487

Chapter 9

Moral Hazard and Risk Management in Agri-environmental Policy

Rob Fraser[1]

(Original received May 2001; revision received March 2002; accepted May 2002)

This paper develops the key finding of Ozanne, Hogan and Colman (2001) that risk aversion among farmers ameliorates the moral hazard problem in relation to agri-environmental policy compliance. It is shown that risk averse farmers who face uncertainty in their production income are more likely to comply with such a policy as a means of risk management. In addition, it is shown that a principal who has control over both the level of monitoring and the size of penalty, if detected, can reduce non-compliance by adjustments to these instruments which increase the variance of farmers' income but leave the expected penalty unchanged. It is concluded that risk management by both principals and agents has the potential to diminish the moral hazard problem, especially given proposed developments in agri-environmental policy in the European Union.

1. Introduction

Agri-environmental policy mechanism design has recently become a popular topic among economists working on European Union agricultural policy. Arising from the mainstream economics area of principal-agent theory with imperfect information, a series of studies has addressed the two issues of adverse selection and moral hazard in the context of the Common Agricultural Policy (CAP): Bourgeon, Jayet and Picard (1995); Latacz-Lohmann (1998, 1999); Choe and Fraser (1998, 1999); Moxey, White and Ozanne (1999); Fraser (2001); Hogan (2001); Ozanne, Hogan and Colman (2001).

Between them, these papers have addressed a range of features of policy mechanism design:

i)   the context of the agri-environmental policy: nitrate leaching (Latacz-Lohmann; Moxey, White and Ozanne; Ozanne, Hogan and Colman; Hogan); environmentally sensitive areas (Choe and Fraser); and set-aside (Bourgeon, Jayet and Picard; Fraser)

[1] Rob Fraser is Professor of Agricultural Economics at Imperial College at Wye and Adjunct Professor of Agricultural and Resource Economics at the University of Western Australia. E-mail **r.fraser@ic.ac.uk** for correspondence. The author is grateful for the helpful comments of two anonymous referees on a previous version of this paper.

ii)   whether the principal is dealing with adverse selection only (Bourgeon, Jayet and Picard; Moxey, White and Ozanne), moral hazard only (Ozanne, Hogan and Colman) or both adverse selection and moral hazard (Latacz-Lohmann; Choe and Fraser; Hogan; Fraser)

iii)   in the situation where moral hazard is included, whether farmers are risk neutral (Latacz-Lohmann) or risk averse (Choe and Fraser; Ozanne, Hogan and Colman; Fraser; Hogan)

iv)   in the situation where moral hazard is included, whether monitoring uncertainty is due to imperfect monitoring (Choe and Fraser), or incomplete monitoring[2] (Latacz-Lohmann; Ozanne, Hogan and Colman; Fraser; Hogan)

v)   in the situation where moral hazard is included, where the principal has as an instrument of policy choice the level of monitoring only (Ozanne, Hogan and Colman; Hogan), or both the level of monitoring and the level of penalty/reward (Choe and Fraser; Latacz-Lohmann; Fraser).

The key result to come out of the most recent paper, that by Ozanne, Hogan and Colman (2001, p.343), is that previous studies, particularly those which overlook the issue of risk aversion among farmers, "may have exaggerated the moral hazard problem". More specifically, they show that, at levels of risk aversion which are high relative to estimates in the literature, the principal's problem collapses to one of adverse selection only.

The aim of this paper is to develop further the insight of Ozanne, Hogan and Colman (2001) regarding the importance or otherwise of the moral hazard problem in agri-environmental policy. The general approach is to apply existing theoretical contributions from the principal-agent literature for the benefit of agri-environmental policy mechanism design. In so doing the paper will develop the roles of risk aversion and risk management among agents as factors encouraging compliance and therefore influencing policy design. More specifically, it is shown that full recognition of the income risk faced by farmers, where this income comprises not just policy payments but also production income, diminishes the attraction of non-compliance among even moderately risk averse farmers and encourages compliance as a risk management strategy. Bearing in mind that the implementation of the Agenda 2000 cereal reforms will substantially increase the riskiness of production income for growers, this observation is of considerable relevance to current

---

[2] Imperfect monitoring means the risk associated with monitoring stems from the principal's potential failure to accurately assess the agent's behaviour whereas incomplete monitoring means this risk stems from the principal's monitoring of only a proportion of the population of agents.

policy design concerns. Second, as a further application of existing principal-agent theory, the paper explores the trade-off between the penalty for non-compliance and the level of monitoring used by the principal. Drawing on the mainstream economics contributions of Polinsky and Shavell (1979) and Kaplow and Shavell (1994) which explored this trade-off in determining the behaviour of both risk neutral and risk averse agents, the paper focuses exclusively on the risk aversion of agents and in this context develops the concept of a mean-penalty preserving increase in non-compliance risk. This concept is then used to show how the moral hazard problem among risk averse farmers can be diminished without any change in expected penalties. In effect, this development identifies the exploitation of the risk aversion of agents as a device for the principal to encourage compliance as a risk management strategy for agents. The mechanism used in applying this concept is a shift in the balance of compliance instruments away from the level of monitoring and towards the size of penalty, which, given current proposals in the UK to introduce unlimited fines for non-compliance, seems also to be a finding of considerable relevance to current policy design concerns (Ozanne, Hogan and Colman, 2001).

The structure of the paper is as follows. Section 2 develops the model of Fraser (2001), which uses the context of set-aside as a framework for analysing the moral hazard problem, to incorporate the two extensions proposed above. In particular, this development shows both the joint dependence of income variance on production and policy compliance payments, and the joint role of the non-compliance penalty and the level of monitoring in determining this income variance. Using this extended framework, Section 3 undertakes a numerical analysis which illustrates the extent to which the moral hazard problem can be diminished among risk averse farmers by an increase in the level of production income uncertainty and by a mean-penalty preserving adjustment of the compliance instruments. The paper ends with a brief conclusion that addresses policy implications.

2. The Model

The model developed in Fraser (2001) is one of set-aside choice by a farmer with heterogeneous land quality, facing an uncertain price for production. From the principal's point of view, adverse selection in terms of output control occurs if the farmer chooses to set aside lower quality land rather than higher quality land, and the problem of moral hazard arises through the principal combating this adverse selection by offering set-aside payments differentiated by land quality, thereby creating the incentive for the farmer to "cheat" by claiming to have set aside higher quality land while actually having set aside lower quality land.[3] Note that, as specified in Fraser (2001), the objective of the principal is cost minimisation based on trading off the costs of export restitutions against the costs of output control. In what follows it is assumed that output control is financially viable. Note also from Fraser (2001) that for the agent it is assumed that participation in the set-aside programme is worthwhile. Since non-participation would involve foregoing compensatory payments, and since such payments are estimated as approximately 20 per cent of total income according to Fraser and Rygnestad (1999), this assumption seems reasonable.

More specifically it is assumed that the farmer has three land types, good, average and poor, in equal proportions, and that the compulsory set-aside rate is one-third of total land. It is also assumed that although there is price uncertainty, there is no yield uncertainty. These assumptions are made for the purpose of analytical simplification; however the implications of their relaxation are discussed in the conclusion. Given this specification, there are three forms of behaving truthfully: declaring to have set aside good, average or poor land and actually having done so; and six forms of cheating: declaring to have set aside one type of land and actually having set aside either of the other two types.[4] In what follows it will be assumed that the reference yields chosen by the principal for set-aside land of different qualities are such that, of the three forms of behaving truthfully, setting aside good land is the preferred choice. In addition, it will be assumed that of the six forms of cheating, setting aside poor land and declaring to have set aside good land is the preferred choice. As a consequence, the focus of the agent's decision problem is on a comparison of the alternatives of declaring to have set aside good land, and actually doing so ("behaving truthfully"), with making the same declaration but actually setting aside poor land ("cheating"). Note that the numerical analysis of the next section is based on parameter values which implement these assumptions.

On this basis, total income (I) from "cheating" and setting-aside poor land while claiming to set-aside good land is:

$$I = sr_g + p(y_g + y_a) \qquad \qquad \text{if not detected} \qquad \qquad (1)$$

$$I = sr_g + p(y_g + y_a) - sr_g x \qquad \qquad \text{if detected} \qquad \qquad (2)$$

where: y_a = yield from average land; y_g = yield from good land; p = uncertain price per unit of output; s = set-aside premium per unit of reference yield;

---

[3] I am grateful to an anonymous referee for pointing out that an alternative approach to "cheating" would involve not setting aside any land. This re-specification would increase the attraction of cheating, but otherwise would produce findings consistent with what follows regarding risk management.

[4] I am grateful to an anonymous referee for clarifying the full structure of the agent's decision problem.

r_g = reference yield for good land; x = parameter determining the size of penalty.

With a probability of detection of q, expected income from cheating ($E_c(I)$) is given by:

$$E_c(I) = (1-q)\big[sr_g + \overline{p}(y_g + y_a)\big] + q\big[s(1-x)r_g + \overline{p}(y_g + y_a)\big] \tag{3}$$

where $\overline{p}$ = expected price.

In addition, the variance of income from cheating ($\mathrm{Var}_c(I)$) is given by:

$$\mathrm{Var}_c(I) = \int (1-q)\big[sr_g + p(y_g + y_a) - E_c(I)\big]^2 f(p)\,dp$$
$$+ \int q\big[s(1-x)r_g + p(y_g + y_a) - E_c(I)\big]^2 f(p)\,dp \tag{4}$$

where $f(p)$ = probability distribution governing price.

Consider the first term on the right-hand-side of (4). Substituting for $E_c(I)$ using (3) and rearranging gives:

$$(1-q)(y_g + y_a)^2 \mathrm{Var}(p) + (1-q)\big[q(sr_g - s(1-x)r_g)\big]^2 \tag{5}$$

A similar process for the second term gives:

$$q(y_g + y_a)^2 \mathrm{Var}(p) + q\big[(1-q)(s(1-x)r_g - sr_g)\big]^2 \tag{6}$$

where: $\mathrm{Var}(p)$ = variance of price.

Combining (5) and (6) gives:

$$\mathrm{Var}_c(I) = (y_g + y_a)^2 \mathrm{Var}(p) + ((1-q)q^2 + q(1-q)^2)(sr_g x)^2 \tag{7}$$

Equation (7) shows that the variance of income from cheating is the sum of the variance of production income and the variance of income associated with the penalty if detected.[5]

Including the cost of producing on land of different qualities, expected profit from cheating ($E_c(\pi)$) is given by:

---

[5] Note that although the other forms of cheating involve a reduction in expected income, they may also involve lower levels of income variation. Therefore the potential exists for these other forms of cheating to be preferred by the agent. I am grateful to both anonymous referees for pointing this out.

480 Rob Fraser

$$E_c(\pi) = (\bar{p} - d_g)y_g + (\bar{p} - d_a)y_a - sr_g - qsr_g x - F \tag{8}$$

where d_g = cost/tonne on good land

d_a = cost/tonne on average land

F = total fixed costs net of compensatory payments,[6]

while the variance of profit from cheating ($\text{Var}_c(\pi)$) is as specified in equation (7) because there is no uncertainty of costs.

Alternatively, total income from behaving truthfully and setting aside good land is given by:

$$I = sr_g + p(y_a + y_p) \tag{9}$$

where y_p = yield from poor land.

In this case expected income from behaving truthfully ($E_T(I)$) is given by:

$$E_T(I) = \bar{p}(y_a + y_p) + sr_g \tag{10}$$

and the variance of income from behaving truthfully ($V_T(I)$) is given by:

$$\text{Var}_T(I) = (y_a + y_p)^2 \text{Var}(p) \tag{11}$$

Including the cost of producing on land of different qualities, expected profit from behaving truthfully ($E_T(\pi)$) is given by:

$$E_T(\pi) = (\bar{p} - d_p)y_p + (\bar{p} - d_a)y_a - sr_g - F \tag{12}$$

where d_p = cost/tonne on poor land, while the variance of profit from behaving truthfully ($\text{Var}_T(\pi)$) is as specified in equation (11).[7]

A comparison of (8) and (12) shows that:

$$E_c(\pi) - E_T(\pi) = (\bar{p} - d_g)y_g - (\bar{p} - d_p)y_p - qxsr_g \tag{13}$$

while a comparison of (7) and (11) shows that:

$$\text{Var}_c(\pi) - \text{Var}_T(\pi) = \text{Var}(p)\left[(y_g + y_a)^2 - (y_a + y_p)^2\right]$$
$$+ \left[(1-q)q^2 + q(1-q)^2\right](sr_g x)^2 \tag{14}$$

---

[6] Note that compensatory payments are independent of the quality of set-aside land.
[7] Note that although setting aside good land has been assumed to be the preferred form of behaving truthfully in this analysis, as long as the expected profit from this behaviour exceeds that of the other truthful forms, then this assumption holds because the other forms have by definition greater income variation.

If the farmer is risk neutral, the decision of cheating or not depends on whether equation (13) exceeds or is less than zero. Moreover, this balance clearly depends on the production-based expected net rewards to cheating (the first two terms on the right-hand-side) relative to the policy-based expected costs of being caught (the third term). However if the farmer is risk averse, then equation (14) also needs to be considered. Since both terms on the right-hand-side of (14) are positive, the more risk averse the farmer, the more important the value of this expression will be in determining the choice of whether or not to cheat. This observation relates to the finding of Ozanne, Hogan and Colman (2001) that moral hazard is less of a problem the more risk averse the farmers. As a corollary, it can be observed that this situation also applies the more uncertain the production income: the size of (14) is positively related to $\text{Var}(p)$.

Finally in this section consider the role of the policy-determined expected level and variance of the penalty from being caught. The expected penalty from being caught ($E(C)$) is given in (13) as:

$$E(C) = qxsr_g \tag{15}$$

while the contribution of the prospect of paying a penalty to the variance of income ($\text{Var}(C)$) is given from (14) as:

$$\text{Var}(C) = \left[(1-q)q^2 + q(1-q)^2\right](sr_g x)^2 \tag{16}$$

An examination of (15) confirms the observation of Latacz-Lohmann (1998, p7) that for a risk neutral farmer "the probability of detection and the size of sanction are perfect substitutes with respect to reducing non-compliance". However, an examination of (16) shows that this perfect substitutability breaks down in the case of risk aversion. As noted by Kaplow and Shavell (1994, p8) "risk-bearing costs are not linear" in the two non-compliance parameters. In particular:

$$\frac{\text{Var}(C)}{q} = (1-2q)(sr_g x)^2 \tag{17}$$

while

$$\frac{\text{Var}(C)}{x} = 2(sr_g)^2((1-q)q^2 + q(1-q)^2)x \tag{18}$$

Equation (17) shows that:

$$\frac{\text{Var}(C)}{q} \begin{array}{c} > \\ < \end{array} 0 \text{ as } q \begin{array}{c} < \frac{1}{2} \\ > \end{array} \tag{19}$$

while (18) shows that $\dfrac{\text{Var}(C)}{x}$ is unambiguously positive.

It follows that if: $$q > \frac{1}{2}$$

then it is possible for q to be decreased and x increased such that the expected penalty from being detected is unchanged, yet the variance of this penalty is unambiguously increased. In other words, in this situation it is possible to diminish the moral hazard problem among risk averse farmers without any change in the expected penalty from cheating. That this option is likely to feature a decrease in monitoring costs because of the associated decrease in the probability of detection only serves to enhance its appeal.

In the alternative situation of: $$q < \frac{1}{2}$$

off-setting adjustments in q and x which are mean-penalty preserving have conflicting impacts on $\text{Var}(C)$ according to (17) and (18). However, the non-linearity of $\text{Var}(C)$ in these parameters suggests adjustments in q and x which are off-setting with respect to $\text{E}(C)$ are unlikely to be so with respect to $\text{Var}(C)$. And while casual assessment of (17) and (18) suggests the impact of changes in x are likely to dominate those in q, particularly for values of q close to 0.5, a numerical analysis is needed to evaluate this analytical ambiguity.

Nevertheless, it may be concluded from the analysis of this section that moral hazard associated with policy non-compliance is likely to be less of a problem among risk averse farmers the more uncertain their production income because of associated risk management behaviour by these farmers. In addition, the analysis suggests that, for a principal with control over the magnitude of both the probability of detection and the size of penalty, the potential exists to diminish the problem of moral hazard among risk averse farmers without any change in the expected penalty from detection by manipulating these monitoring parameters to encourage risk management behaviour. These analytical findings are illustrated numerically in the next section.

3. Numerical Analysis
In order to undertake a numerical analysis which illustrates the findings of the previous section, use is made of the numerical framework outlined in Fraser (2001).

This approach provides the following parameter values:

$$y_g = 10.00; y_a = 8.01; y_p = 5.03; \overline{p} = 110; s = 70; d_g = 38; d_p = 42; F = 688$$

plus

$$r_g = 10; q = 0.5; x = 1$$

as a Base Case. Note that although this value of q could be considered high, and the value of x low, relative to actual values in current UK agri-environmental schemes, the role of these parameter values is explored in the sensitivity analysis later in this section.

Finally, assume the attitude to risk of the farmer can be represented by the mean-variance framework and the constant relative risk aversion functional form:[8]

$$E(U(\pi)) = U(E(\pi)) + \frac{1}{2}U''(E(\pi))\text{Var}(\pi) \qquad (20)$$

where $\quad U(\pi) = \dfrac{\pi^{1-R}}{1-R} \qquad\qquad\qquad (21)$

and $\quad R =$ constant coefficient of relative risk aversion

$$= -U''(\pi)\frac{\pi}{U'}(\pi)$$

where $\quad U''(\pi)$ is the 2nd derivative of the utility function $(U(\pi))$.
Note that $U''(\pi) < 0$

On this basis, Table 1 contains details of the numerical results regarding the levels of expected utility from cheating and truth-telling for a range of attitudes to risk and of coefficients of variation of price (CV_p).[9] Table 1 shows that, using the Base Case parameter values, a risk neutral (i.e. $R=0$) farmer will choose to cheat regardless of the variability of production income. But for a risk averse farmer the additional variability of profit introduced by cheating is a disadvantage which must be balanced against the expected gains from cheating. Nevertheless, Table 1 shows that in the case where there is no uncertainty of production income, the expected gains from cheating always dominate, and even the most risk averse farmer (i.e. $R=0.75$) chooses to cheat.

Table 1: Impact of Changes in the Uncertainty of Production Income on $E(U(\pi))$

	CV_p					
	0		0.2		0.35^a	
	$E_T(U(\pi))$	$E_c(U(\pi))$	$E_T(U(\pi))$	$E_c(U(\pi))$	$E_T(U(\pi))$	$E_c(U(\pi))$
R						
0	930.76	978.72	930.76	978.72	930.76	978.72
0.25	224.68	230.52	222.68	226.93	218.55	219.53
0.5	61.02	61.57	60.29	60.29	58.80	57.64
0.75	22.09	22.11	21.90	21.76	21.49	21.05

Note: $\quad ^a\ E_T(U(\pi)) = E_c(U(\pi))$ for $R = 0.28$

---

[8] See Hanson and Ladd (1991) and Pope and Just (1991) for arguments supporting these assumptions.
[9] See Hazell, Jaramillo and Williamson (1990) for evidence supporting this range of variation in world wheat prices. Note that Bardsley and Harris (1987) estimate a risk aversion coefficient for wheatgrowers in Australia of 0.7, while Newbery and Stiglitz (1981) suggest levels between 0.5 and 1.2 are consistent with most empirical estimates. Note also that unreported numerical analysis shows all the agent's incentive-compatibility constraints are satisfied for these parameter values. In particular, the assumptions of Section 2 regarding the preferred forms of cheating and behaving truthfully are validated.

The situation changes, however, once uncertainty of production income is allowed for. For example, in the case of $CV_p = 0.2$, such as could be argued to represent the situation before the implementation of the Agenda 2000 reforms, Table 1 shows that the most risk averse farmer chooses not to cheat, while the farmer with $R = 0.5$ is indifferent between cheating and behaving truthfully. Moreover, with increased exposure to world price uncertainty, as represented by the case of $CV_p = 0.35$ further numerical analysis shows that all farmers with $R > 0.28$ would choose not to cheat. Consequently, Table 1 is a clear illustration of the finding in Section 1 that moral hazard associated with policy non-compliance can be expected to be less of a problem among risk averse farmers once European Union markets become more completely exposed to world price fluctuations. This feature of the results is a manifestation of the general principle that farmers who are exposed to substantial risk will look for opportunities for risk management, including in this case choosing to reduce income risk by being policy compliant.

Next consider the second finding of Section 2 that a principal with control over the magnitude of both the probability of detection and the size of penalty may also be able to "manage" the risk faced by farmers considering cheating and do so without altering the expected penalty from detection. In this context, Table 2 contains details of a range of (q,x) combinations which are mean-penalty preserving and, for each combination, the associated variance of penalty. The bottom three combinations illustrate the analytical finding of Section 1 that, for $q > 0.5$, mean-penalty preserving adjustments in q and x will affect $Var(C)$ monotonically, with $Var(C)$ inversely related to q and positively related to x. Moreover, the top three combinations suggest that changes in x are the dominant factor determining the overall impact of mean-penalty preserving adjustments in q and x, with $Var(C)$ clearly positively related to x across the full range in Table 2. It follows that a principal has the potential to deter cheating among risk averse farmers without any increase in expected penalty across this full range.

Table 2: Impact of Mean-Penalty Preserving Changes in q and x on Var(C)

	E(C)	Var(C)
q,x		
0.1, 5	350	1102500
0.25, 2	350	367500
0.5, 1	350	122500
0.75, 0.67	350	40833
0.9, 0.56	350	13611

To illustrate this potential, consider the results presented in Table 3 which show the impact on the expected utility from cheating of a range of mean-penalty preserving increases in x (decreases in q).[10] The top panel of Table 3 is based on $CV_p = 0.2$ and repeats the results in Table 1 that for the Base Case settings farmers with risk aversion coefficients of less than 0.5 would choose to cheat. However, it is also shown that with a small increase in x to 1.1 ($q = 0.45$), a risk averse farmer with $R = 0.5$ would clearly choose not to cheat. Even though the expected penalty from detection is unchanged, the increase in the variance of income associated with the increase in x is sufficient to deter cheating. Since, on the basis of current agri-environmental policy practice in the UK, such values are actually more plausible, this finding suggests that already only those farmers with attitudes to risk represented by $R < 0.5$ are inclined to cheat.[11] Moreover, this panel of results shows that if x were increased to 2 ($q = 0.25$) even a farmer with $R = 0.25$ would choose not to cheat. Finally, note that in a situation with a higher level of variability in production income ($CV_p = 0.35$), an increase in x only to 1.2 is sufficient to deter a farmer with $R = 0.25$ from cheating. It follows that once European Union farmers become more exposed to world price uncertainty, the moral hazard problem will be confined to only the least risk averse of farmers.

Table 3: Impact of Mean-Penalty Preserving Changes in q and x on $E_c(U(\pi))$

	$E_T(U(\pi))$	$E_c(U(\pi))$			
		$x = 1$	$x = 1.1$	$x = 1.2$	$x = 2$
		$(q = 0.5)$	$(q = 0.45)$	$(q = 0.42)$	$(q = 0.25)$
$CV_p = 0.2$					
$R = 0.25$	222.68	226.93	226.37	225.80	221.33
$R = 0.5$	60.29	60.29	60.09	59.89	58.29
$CV_p = 0.35$					
$R = 0.25$	218.55	219.53	218.98	218.41	213.94
$R = 0.5$	58.80	57.64	57.44	57.24	55.64

4. Conclusion

The aim of this paper has been to develop further the key finding of Ozanne, Hogan and Colman (2001) that risk aversion among farmers ameliorates the moral hazard problem in relation to agri-environmental policy compliance. Extending the model of Fraser (2001), it was shown in Section 1 that risk averse farmers who face uncertainty in their production income are more likely to

---

[10] Note that these changes in parameter values do not alter the agent's preferred form of cheating.
[11] See Ozanne, Hogan and Colman (2001) and Choe and Fraser (1999) regarding current UK practice. I am grateful to an anonymous referee for this clarification.

comply with the requirements of an agri-environmental policy. In addition, drawing on the mainstream economics contributions of Polinsky and Shavell (1979) and Kaplow and Shavell (1994), it was shown that a principal who has control over both the level of monitoring and the size of penalty if detected not complying has the potential to reduce non-compliance among risk averse farmers by adjustments to these instruments which increase the variance of farmers' income, but leave the expected penalty for non-compliance unchanged. These findings were illustrated in Section 2 using a numerical analysis. Overall, it was shown that, for risk averse producers facing substantial production income uncertainty, choosing to comply with their agri-environmental policy is a form of risk management which has the effect of diminishing the moral hazard problem. For the principal, mean-penalty preserving adjustments of the instruments of non-compliance are a form of risk management which similarly diminishes the problem of moral hazard among risk averse farmers.

These findings are thought to be of considerable relevance in the context of European Union agri-environmental policy. First, the implementation of the Agenda 2000 reforms will see a substantial increase in the exposure of cereal growers to world price uncertainty and, as a consequence, to income risk. In this situation risk management strategies will become a more prominent concern for farm managers, and the opportunity to reduce risk by complying with an agri-environmental policy will therefore become more attractive. Note in this context that the model used in this paper has under-represented the importance of production income risk relative to non-compliance risk both by assuming the agri-environmental policy (set-aside) applies to one-third of land, rather than the 10 per cent of the Agenda 2000 agreement, and by ignoring yield uncertainty as a component of production income risk. Given the results in Table 1 it follows that, if the increase in exposure of farmers to world price variability with the implementation of the Agenda 2000 reforms were not as large as suggested (i.e. CV_p from 0.2 to 0.35), but this under-representation were allowed for, then the dominance of production-related risk in total income risk would still result in the risk management strategy of policy compliance being popular even among farmers with relatively low levels of risk aversion.

Second, as noted by Ozanne, Hogan and Colman (2001, p334) proposals "currently before the UK Parliament will, if passed, introduce unlimited fines for failure to comply with SSSI management agreements". In this situation, UK policy-makers will have the opportunity to implement their own risk management strategy as outlined above and thereby reduce the attraction of non-compliance to risk averse farmers without any increase in expected penalties, and with the expectation of savings from reduced monitoring costs.

It may be concluded that the elevation of risk management as a desirable strategy for risk averse farm managers will diminish the problem of non-compliance for agri-environmental policy makers.

References

Bardsley, P. and Harris, M. (1987). An Approach to the Econometric Estimation of Attitudes to Risk in Agriculture, *Australian Journal of Agricultural Economics* 31(2):112-26.

Bourgeon, J-P., Jayet, P-A. and Picard, P. (1995). An Incentive Approach to Land Set-aside Programmes, *European Economic Review* 39(4):1487-509.

Choe, C. and Fraser, I. (1998). A Note on Imperfect Monitoring of Agri-Environmental Policy, *Journal of Agricultural Economics* 49(2):250-58.

Choe, C. and Fraser, I. (1999). Compliance Monitoring and Agri-Environmental Policy, *Journal of Agricultural Economics* 50(3):468-87.

Fraser, R.W. (2001). Using Principal-agent Theory to Deal with Output Slippage in the European Union Set-aside Policy, *Journal of Agricultural Economics* 52(2):29-41

Fraser, R.W. and Rygnestad, H.L. (1999). An Assessment of the Impact of Implementing the European Commission's *Agenda 2000* Cereal Proposals for Specialist Wheatgrowers in Denmark, *Journal of Agricultural Economics* 50(2):328-35.

Hanson, S.D. and Ladd, G.W. (1991). Robustness of the Mean-variance Model with Truncated Probability Distributions, *American Journal of Agricultural Economics* 73(2):436-45.

Hazell, P.B.R., Jaramillo, M. and Williamson, A. (1990). The Relationship Between World Price Instability and the Price Farmers Receive in Developing Countries, *Journal of Agricultural Economics* 41(2):227-41.

Hogan, T. (2001). Information Asymmetry and Agri-Environmental Policy, PhD Thesis, University of Manchester.

Kaplow, L. and Shavell, S. (1994). Accuracy in the Determination of Liability, *Journal of Law and Economics* 37(11):1-15.

Latacz-Lohmann, U. (1998). Moral Hazard in Agri-Environmental Schemes, Paper presented to the Agricultural Economics Society Annual Conference, University of Reading, March.

Latacz-Lohmann, U. (1999). A Theoretical Analysis of Environmental Cross-compliance Within the Common Agricultural Policy, Paper presented to the Agricultural Economics Society Annual Conference, University of Belfast, March.

Moxey, A., White, B. and Ozanne, A. 1999. Efficient Contract Design for Agri-Environment Policy, *Journal of Agricultural Economics* 50(2):187-202.

Newbery, D.M.G. and Stiglitz, J.E. (1981). *The Theory of Commodity Price Stabilization*, Clarendon Press, Oxford.

Ozanne, A., Hogan, T., and Colman, D. (2001). Moral Hazard, Risk Aversion and Compliance Monitoring and Agri-Environmental Policy" *European Review of Agricultural Economics.* 28(3): 329-347.

Polinsky, M. and Shavell, S. (1979). The Optimal Trade-off Between the Probability and Magnitude of Fines, *American Economic Review* 69(5):880-891.

Pope, R.D. and Just, R.E. (1991). On Testing the Structure of Risk Preferences in Agricultural Supply Analysis, *American Journal of Agricultural Economics* 73(3):743-8.

Journal of Agricultural Economics — Volume 55, Number 3 — November 2004 — Pages 525-540

© *Agricultural Economics Society*

Chapter 10

On the Use of Targeting to Reduce Moral Hazard in Agri-environmental Schemes

Rob Fraser[1]

(Original submitted May 2003, revision received February 2004, accepted August 2004)

This paper investigates the role of targeting in the context of agri-environmental schemes involving monitoring and penalties. By separating participants into a target and a non-target group the aim of targeting is to reduce the moral hazard problem. The paper analyses three approaches to targeting which have different implications for the level of monitoring resources and the focus is on reducing the extent of cheating by participants in the non-target group. By complementing the adoption of targeting with appropriate adjustments to the monitoring/penalty parameters, it is shown how such an approach can exploit the risk aversion of participants to completely eliminate cheating by those participants in the non-target group. The implementation of such a system of targeting is discussed in the context of existing agri-environmental policies.

1. Introduction

The issue of policy mechanism design to address the problems of adverse selection and moral hazard has become popular in the recent literature relating to agri-environmental policy (Choe and Fraser, 1999; Fraser, 2001, 2002; Latacz-Lohmann, 1998; Moxey, White and Ozanne, 1999; Ozanne, Hogan and Colman, 2001). Both the incentive-compatible and the monitoring/penalties approaches have featured in this literature (see Moxey *et al.*, and Latacz-Lohmann respectively). However, in practical terms it is unlikely that the former approach will supplant the latter approach currently applied in agri-environmental policy contexts. Moreover, as is often the case is relation to existing policy, current practice has a tendency to move ahead of the literature.[2]

A relevant example of this in the monitoring/penalties area of regulatory policy is the use of "targeting" as a device for enhancing the efficiency of the resources applied to monitoring the implementation of a policy (*i.e.* addressing the moral hazard problem). In this situation the monitoring authority will announce in advance of the monitoring process commencing that a sub-group of participants will be "targeted" – implying that their probability of being monitored is higher than participants outside the sub-group.

---

1 Rob Fraser is Professor of Agricultural Economics, Imperial College London and Adjunct Professor of Agricultural and Resource Economics, University of Western Australia. Email r.fraser@imperial.ac.uk for correspondence. The author is grateful to two anonymous referees and the Managing Editor for their helpful suggestions for improving the previous version.

2 For example, price-cap regulation – See Breautigam and Panzar, 1993.

In the literature research has been reported exploring the adjustment of monitoring/penalty parameters to improve policy effectiveness (see, for example, Polinsky and Shavell, 1979) however, relatively little research appears to have been done in the area of targeting. More specifically, Greenberg (1984) and Landsberger and Meilijson (1982) developed the idea of targeting confirmed tax "cheats" using a class of models involving "state-dependent enforcement strategies" (Heyes, 2000, p116).[3] This idea was further developed in the mainstream law and economics literature with a continued focus on repeat offenders and how to deal with them (*e.g.* Polinsky and Rubinfeld, 1991). It was also subsequently adapted to the area of environmental compliance by Harrington (1988), motivated by his aim of explaining the "paradox" of the US EPA's handling of compliance violators. This research, and extensions of it (*e.g.* Russell, 1990; Harford and Harrington, 1991; Heyes and Rickman, 1999; and Raymond, 1999) have maintained a focus on the behaviour of those agents already in the target group, and on the use of penalties and other compliance regulations to influence their behaviour.[4] For a more thorough review, including a discussion of the "forgiveness" feature of Harrington-type models, see Heyes (2000) but note that in this published literature agents are always specified as risk neutral, and that little attention has been given to the behaviour of those agents in the non-target group.

In this context agri-environmental policy seems particularly well-suited to the application of targeting as agri-environmental schemes often have a clear geographical basis or relate to the provision of specific environmental features, and so it should be straight forward to target participants based on well-defined characteristics. Given this potential for applying the targeting approach to agri-environmental policy monitoring, the question arises as to the usefulness of this approach in alleviating the moral hazard problem. The aim of this paper is to investigate this question, with a particular focus on the role of risk aversion in determining the behaviour of those participants in the non-target group as the main contribution of the paper to the literature.[5]

The structure of the paper is as follows. Section 2 develops a model of a risk averse agent participating in an "agri-environmental " policy which requires an action on the part of the agent subject to monitoring by the principal. The agent receives a payment for undertaking this action, which itself involves an income reduction. Consequently, the opportunity exists for the agent to "cheat" by claiming to undertake the action, but actually not do so, thereby receiving the payment, but not experiencing the income reduction associated with the action. Therefore, a

---

[3] I am grateful to an anonymous referee for pointing this out to me.

[4] A recent exception in this literature is the contribution of Heyes (2002), which considers the idea of targeting using a "trigger" based on the size of the agent's claims/benefit from the principal.

[5] Note that, also in contrast with this literature, the members of the target and non-target groups will change from period to period as monitoring resources are focussed on a different environment-related "characteristic" of the agents. The only exception to this in what follows is that, if a non-target group agent is caught "cheating", then they default into the target group in the next period. Again I am grateful to an anonymous reference for pointing this out to me.

On the Use of Targeting to Reduce Moral Hazard in Agri-environmental Schemes 527

monitoring/penalties system is used by the principal in an attempt to prevent the loss of effectiveness of the policy brought about by such "cheating". It is into this specification that the additional monitoring feature of targeting can be inserted, and its potential usefulness investigated.

It should be emphasised at this point that an essential component of the targeting approach is repeated monitoring, whereby either the target group can be changed, or alternatively participants can be moved from the non-target group to the target group. Therefore, in Section 1 the decision framework of the agent is specified with an inter-temporal format so as to enable the targeting feature to be introduced. Within this framework three versions of the targeting approach will be considered. The first version is "resource-neutral" in that overall monitoring resources are unchanged with the introduction of targeting, and so an increase in the probability of detection in the target group is achieved by a reduction in the resources applied to detection in the non-target group, thereby decreasing the probability of detection in this group. The second version is "non-resource-neutral" in that overall monitoring resources are increased in order both to maintain the probability of detection in the non-target group at the level applying prior to the introduction of targeting, and to increase the probability of detection for those in the target group. The third version restores "resource-neutrality", but draws on the concept of a "mean-penalty-preserving" adjustment of the monitoring/penalty parameters (*i.e.* probability of detection and size of penalty) developed in Fraser (2002) as a means of exploiting the risk aversion of agents to influence their behaviour. These three versions are considered in order to more fully evaluate the potential for targeting to alleviate the moral hazard problem.

In Section 3 this model is analysed numerically and it is shown that although "resource-neutral" targeting can reduce the extent of cheating by those participants in the non-target group previously cheating, it cannot eliminate this propensity, and it may also encourage cheating by those in the non-target group previously behaving truthfully. It is then shown that with "non-resource-neutral" targeting as specified, the problem of participants deciding to turn to cheating can be avoided. However, using this approach it continues not to be possible to fully eliminate cheating among those participants in the non-target group cheating prior to the introduction of targeting. Nevertheless, it shown that the introduction of the third version of targeting, "resource-neutral" with a "mean-penalty-preserving" adjustment of the monitoring/penalty parameters for those participants in the non-target group, is capable of eliminating all cheating.

Finally it is argued in the Concluding Comments that although targeting has the potential to alleviate the moral hazard problem in existing agri-environmental schemes, it will operate most effectively if coupled with appropriate adjustments to the monitoring/penalty parameters for those participants in the non-target group.

2.   The Model

As stated in the Introduction, this section develops a model of an agent participating in an "agri-environmental" policy that requires an income-foregoing action on the part of the agent in return for a payment. In addition, the principal used a monitoring/penalty scheme to discourage moral hazard: taking the payment but not undertaking the action. Finally, in order to analyse the targeting approach outlined in the Introduction it is necessary to specify an inter-temporal feature to the agent's decision framework.

In what follows the agent's income in each period if behaving truthfully (I_T) is known with certainty:

$$I_T = B - y + x \tag{1}$$

where:

$$x > y$$

B = income if not participating

y = income forgone by participating

x = payment for participating

Alternatively, if the agent chooses to cheat in each period then income (I_C) sis uncertain:

$$I_C = B + x \qquad \text{if not caught} \tag{2}$$

$$= B + (1 - \delta)x \qquad \text{if caught}$$

where:

δ = penalty parameter ≥ 1

Specifying the probability of detection in the absence of targeting as p, means that the expected utility from cheating in a period *(EU(I_C))* is given by:

$$EU(I_C) = (1 - p)U(B + x) + pU(B + (1 - \delta)x) \tag{3}$$

where:

$U(I)$ = utility of income $(U'(I) > 0, U''(I) < 0)$

compared with the utility from behaving truthfully $(U(I_T))$ in a period:

$$U(I_T) = U(B - y + x) \tag{4}$$

On the Use of Targeting to Reduce Moral Hazard in Agri-environmental Schemes 529

Therefore, for a two-period decision problem, the present value of expected utility from cheating in both periods ($PVEU(I_{C12})$) is given by:

$$PVEU(I_{C12}) = EU(I_C) + EU(I_C)/(1+r) \qquad (5)$$

where:

r = discount rate,

while for behaving truthfully in both periods:

$$PVU(I_{T12}) = U(I_T) + U(I_T)/(1+r) \qquad (6)$$

On this basis the agent will choose to behave truthfully or cheat in both periods depending on:

$$PVU(I_{T12}) \gtrless PVEU(I_{C12}) \qquad (7)$$

Note that in this situation the "mixed" strategy of cheating in one period and behaving truthfully in the other will always be dominated by a "pure" strategy of cheating or behaving truthfully in both periods. This follows from the observation that, for example, if:

$$EU(I_C) > U(I_T) \qquad (8)$$

then:

$$PVEU(I_{C12}) > EU(I_C) + U(I_T)/(1+r) > U(I_T) + EU(I_C)/(1+r) > PVU(I_T) \qquad (9)$$

with the reverse applying if:

$$U(I_T) > EU(I_C) \qquad (10)$$

Next consider the introduction of targeting. For the first version of "resource-neutral" targeting outlined in the Introduction, the higher probability of detection of those in the target group (p_H) is achieved by shifting monitoring resources away from those in the non-target group, thus lowering this group's probability of detection (p_L). It follows that:

$$p_H > p > p_L \qquad (11)$$

On the basis that the agent in question is not in the target group initially, but that if caught in the first period moves into the target group for the second period, the present value of expected utility from cheating in both periods is given by [6]

$$PVEU(I_{C12}) = (1 - p_L)U(B + x) + p_L U(B + (1-\delta)x) +$$
$$+ (p_L(p_H U(B + (1-\delta)x) + (1 - p_H)U(B + x)) + \qquad (12)$$
$$+ (1 - p_L)(p_L U(B + (1-\delta)x) + (1 - p_L)U(B + x)))/(1+r)$$

---

[6] Note that the analysis of targeting for agents who start in the target group is a straightforward problem to consider and is omitted in what follows. Note also that the target group will generally be a minority of participants.

In addition, the present value of expected utility from behaving truthfully in the first period and cheating in the second $(PVEU(I_{T1C2}))$ is given by[7]:

$$PVEU(I_{T1C2}) = U(I_T) + (p_L U(B + (1-\delta)x) + (1-p_L)U(B+x))/(1+r) \qquad (13)$$

In this situation the impact of the targeting on the present value of expected utility from cheating in both periods may be positive or negative depending on the values of p_L and p_H. In particular, because $p_L < p$ the first term on the right-hand side of (12) is clearly higher that the first term on the right-hand-side of (5). However, the impact on the second term on the right-hand-side of (12) may be positive or negative. Nevertheless, the aim of the principal will be for the overall impact of introducing targeting to be a decrease in (12) relative to (5), so that an agent who, in the absence of targeting, was cheating in both periods would, with the introduction of targeting, find that (12) was smaller than (6) (the present value of behaving truthfully in both periods). Note that the numerical analysis in the next section will illustrate how the principal's objective can be achieved. However, it can be seen from (13) that if in the absence of targeting cheating is preferred ((5) exceeds (6)), then with the introduction of targeting, because $p_L < p$, it follows that:

$$PVEU(I_{T1C2}) > PVU(I_{T12}) \qquad (14)$$

As a consequence, although as will be illustrated in the next section, it is possible for the introduction of "resource-neutral" targeting to deter agents who were previously cheating in both periods from doing so, it is unambiguously the case that these agents will still find that the mixed strategy of cheating in one period is preferred to behaving truthfully in both periods. Therefore, "resource-neutral" targeting can prevent "full-time" cheating, but not "part-time" cheating. Moreover, in this context, it should be recognised that for an agent who in the absence of targeting chooses to behave truthfully in both periods (*i.e.* (6)) exceeds (5)), because $p_L < p$, the potential arises for:

$$pU(B + (1-\delta)x) + (1-p)U(B+x) < U(B-y+x) \qquad (15)$$

but:

$$p_L U(B + (1-\delta)x) + (1-p_L)U(B+x) > U(B-y+x) \qquad (16)$$

in which case:

$$PVEU(I_{T1C2}) > PVU(I_{T12}) \qquad (17)$$

In other words, the lower probability of detection associated with being in the non-target group may be sufficient to entice a previously truthful agent to adopt the mixed strategy of cheating in one period. In the numerical analysis of the next section, this potential for the introduction of "resource-neutral" targeting to induce

---

[7]   Note that the alternative mixed strategy of cheating in the first period and behaving truthfully in the second yields similar findings and so for simplicity is ignored in what follows.

"part-time" cheating among those previously behaving truthfully at all times is illustrated.

Therefore, it would seem that the "resource-neutral" form of targeting features two major failings in its attempt to deter non-target group participants from cheating: it does not discourage cheating completely by those previously cheating all the time; and it may encourage those previously behaving truthfully all the time to begin cheating some of the time.

In an attempt to improve the performance of targeting, consider the second version, "non-resource-neutral" targeting, proposed in the Introduction. In this case the principal devotes additional monitoring resources to the targeting activity in order to maintain the probability of detection in the non-target group at the level prevailing prior to the introduction of targeting:

$$p_L = p \tag{18}$$

It follows simply from (18) that if (15) holds, then the sign of (16) would be reversed, and so it is clearly the case that this form of targeting will not suffer from the failing of "resource-neutral" targeting of enticing those agents previously behaving truthfully to start cheating. However, for those previously cheating (*i.e.* (5) exceeds (6)), although the introduction of targeting may result in (12) being less than (6), so that behaving truthfully all the time is preferred to cheating all the time, it will still be the case that (14) holds, and the mixed strategy of cheating some of the time is preferred to behaving truthfully all the time. Note this follows from observing that for these agents:

$$EU(I_C) > U(I_T)$$

prior to targeting, so that with $p = p_L$ it will still hold subsequent to the introduction of targeting for those in the non-target group, and so (13) will exceed (6). As a consequence, even the more expensive ""non-resource-neutral" targeting will be unable to deter those agents previously cheating all the time from continuing to cheat some of the time.

Therefore, in a final attempt to improve the performance of targeting, consider the third version proposed in the Introduction: that of "resource-neutral" targeting accompanied by appropriate "mean-penalty-preserving" adjustments in the monitoring/penalty parameters of the non-target group (*i.e.* p_L and x) as outlined in Fraser (2002). Note at the outset that the aim of this version of targeting is to eliminate cheating completely, without either expending more resources on monitoring, or increasing the perception among non-target group participants of the expected penalty associated with cheating. In other words, this version of targeting features neither more expensive monitoring, nor an adjustment in the expected cost of cheating among participants in the non-target group. More specifically, it must hold that the increased probability of detection in the target group is resourced by a decreased probability of detection in the non-target group:

532 Rob Fraser

$$p_L < p < p_H \tag{19}$$

and that the expected cost of cheating among agents in the non-target group is unchanged:

$$p\delta x = p_L \delta_T x \tag{20}$$

where $\delta_T =$ new penalty parameter associated with targeting.

On this basis, the present value of expected utility from cheating all the time in the presence of targeting is given by:

$$
\begin{aligned}
PVEU(I_{C12}) &= p_L U\big(B + (1 - \delta_T)x\big) + (1 - p_L)U(B + x) + \\
&\quad + \big(p_L(p_H U(B + (1 - \delta_T)x) + (1 - p_H)U(B + x)) + \\
&\quad + (1 - p_L)\big(p_L U(B + (1 - \delta_T)x) + (1 - p_L)U(B + x))\big)/(1 + r)
\end{aligned} \tag{21}
$$

while the present value of expected utility from behaving truthfully in the first period and cheating in the second is given by:

$$PVEU(I_{T1C2}) > U(I_T) + \big(p_L U(B + (1 - \delta_T)x) + (1 - p_L)U(B + x)\big)/(1 + r) \tag{22}$$

It will be shown using the numerical analysis of the next section how the principal can select the parameters p_H, p_L and δ_T so as to be consistent with the requirements of (19) and (20) regarding monitoring expense and the expected cost of cheating, and yet transform a situation prior to targeting of:

$$PVEU(I_{C12}) > PVEU(I_{T1C2}) > PVU(I_{T12}) \tag{23}$$

to one with the introduction of targeting of:

$$PVU(I_{T12}) > PVEU(I_{T1C2}) > PVEU(I_{C12}) \tag{24}$$

and in so doing eliminate cheating completely by those participants in the non-target group. Based on Fraser (2002), it will also be shown how the key to this achievement is the adjustment of the monitoring/penalty parameters so as to increase the riskiness of cheating without affecting the expected penalty. In this way, the risk aversion of the agent is used to discourage cheating, rather than the size of the expected penalty.

3.   Numerical Analysis

In order to undertake a numerical analysis of the model developed in the previous section it is necessary to specify both a particular form for the agent's utility function, and a set of parameter values to act as a Base Case. In what follows the utility function is specified to take the constant relative risk aversion form[8]:

$$U(I) = \frac{I^{1-R}}{1 - R} \tag{25}$$

---

[8]   See Pope and Just (1991) for empirical evidence to support this assumption.

On the Use of Targeting to Reduce Moral Hazard in Agri-environmental Schemes 533

where R = constant coefficient of relative risk aversion

$$= -U''(I) \times \frac{I}{U'(I)}$$

In addition, the following parameter values are chosen for a Base Case:

$B = 20$	$y = 10$	$x = 18$
$\delta = 1$	$r = 0$	$p = 0.5$
$R = 0.5, 0.75$	$p_L = 0.4$	$p_H = 0.8$

Note from Fraser (2002) that the Base Case value of δ might be considered low relative to actual values in current agri-environmental schemes (as there is no penalty above the return of the fraudulently-claim payment), however, the role of this parameter is explored in subsequent sensitivity analysis. Other parameters with point values in the Base Case are largely illustrative, and typically affect only the magnitudes of results, not their relativities (see below).

On this basis Table 1 contains details of the Base Case results before and after the introduction of "resource-neutral" targeting for a participant in the non- target group.

Table 1: Base Case Results Before and After the
Introduction of Resource-Neutral Targeting

	R	
	0.5	0.75
No Targeting		
$PVU(I_{T12})$	21.17	18.41
$PVEU(I_{C12})$	21.27	18.39
$PVEU(I_{T1C2})$	21.22	18.40
Targeting		
$PVU(I_{T12})$	21.17	18.41
$PVEU(I_{C12})$	20.41	18.45
$PVEU(I_{T1C2})$	21.56	18.54

Note in this context that it has been assumed that the target group comprises 25% of participants so that an increase to 0.8 (*i.e.* $p_H = 0.8$) in the probability of detection for this group can be achieved by a reduction in the probability of detection of the non-target group to 0.4 (*i.e* $p_L = 0.4$). The results in Table 1 have been presented for non-target group participants with two levels of risk aversion ($R = 0.5, 0.75$) in order to create a Base Case situation where, in the absence of targeting, one type of agent ($R = 0.5$) chooses to cheat all the time, while the other ($R = 0.75$) chooses to behave truthfully all the time. In addition, as shown in Table 1, following the introduction of targeting the agent previously cheating all the time ($R = 0.5$) now finds that the mixed strategy of cheating some of the time becomes the preferred choice. It should be noted at this point that in this example targeting also increases $PVEU(I_{C12})$, but not by as much as $PVEU(I_{T1C2})$ is increased. Unreported numerical results show that if the target group is smaller (less than 20% of all participants), so that the probability of detection is greater for this group ($p_H > 0.9$) then the impact of targeting is to reduce $PVEU(I_{C12})$ below the level of $PVU(I_{T12})$ for non-target group participants. Nevertheless, even in this case the mixed strategy of cheating some of the time dominates all others. Therefore, Table 1 clearly illustrates the finding of the previous section that resource-neutral targeting will deter non-target group agents previously cheating all the time from this behaviour, but it will not deter them from cheating some of the time. Moreover, as is shown in Table 1 for the more risk averse agent ($R = 0.75$), targeting may encourage non-target group participants previously behaving truthfully all the time to commence cheating some of the time ($PVEU(I_{T1C2}) > PVU(I_{T12})$)[9].

Consequently, as suggested in Section 2, a modification to this targeting approach is required if these incentive failings are to be remedied. The first modification suggested in Section 2 was for extra monitoring resources to be spent with targeting to ensure that the increased probability of detection in the target group could be achieved without a reduction in the probability of detection among the non-target group. In this numerical analysis this modification is equivalent to introducing targeting with $p_H = 0.8$ and $p_L = p = 0.5$ Table 2 contains details of the impact of this modification on the Base Case results. The results in Table 2 show that, as indicated in Section 2, such a modification would be able to prevent targeting enticing those non-target group agents previously behaving truthfully all the time ($R = 0.75$) to begin cheating some of the time. However, for those non-target group agents previously cheating all the time ($R = 0.5$), with targeting it remains the case that cheating some of the time is preferred.

---

[9] Once again, if the target group is smaller and p_H higher then this type of agent would still prefer behaving truthfully all the time to cheating all the time, but both are dominated by the mixed strategy.

On the Use of Targeting to Reduce Moral Hazard in Agri-environmental Schemes 535

Table 2: Comparison of Resource-Neutral and Non-Resource-Neutral Targeting

	R	
	0.5	0.75
Resource-Neutral		
$p_L = 0.4$; $p_H = 0.8$		
$PVU(I_{T12})$	21.17	18.41
$PVEU(I_{C12})$	21.41	18.45
$PVEU(I_{T1C2})$	21.56	18.54
Non-Resource-Neutral		
$p_L = 0.5$; $p_H = 0.8$		
$PVU(I_{T12})$	21.17	18.41
$PVEU(I_{C12})$	20.77	18.17
$PVEU(I_{T1C2})$	21.22	18.40

On this basis, an alternative modification was proposed in the Introduction which remains resource-neutral, but which features a mean-penalty preserving adjustment of the monitoring/penalty parameters for the non-target group, and which aims to deter those in the non-target group who were previously cheating all the time from doing so at all in the presence of targeting. More specifically, consider an increase in δ from 1 to $(\delta_T = 1.25)$ which leaves the expected cost of cheating unchanged for those in the non-target group:[10]

$$\delta p x = \delta_T p_L x = 9 \tag{26}$$

Table 3 contains details of the impact of this modification to resource-neutral targeting on the Base Case results. The results in this table illustrate the potential for the proposed modification to targeting to achieve a complete elimination of cheating among non-target group participants and in particular among those participants who prior to targeting were cheating all the time, and who with the previous two approaches to targeting still preferred to cheat some of the time $(R = 0.5)$. Moreover, as indicated in Section 2, this elimination of the cheating incentive is not achieved by increasing either the resources expended on monitoring or the expected cost of cheating. Rather it is based on increasing the riskiness of cheating combined with the aversion to this increase stemming from the agent's attitude to risk. More specifically, the increase in the riskiness of cheating associated with the increase in δ (and the decrease of p to p_L) reduces the expected utility from cheating not only all the time (see equation (12)) but even some of the time (see equation (13)), and so for a sufficient increase in this risk combined with the risk aversion of the agent, the choice of behaving truthfully all the time can be made the preferred option.

---

[10] This expected cost is 9 in the Base Case as $\delta = 1$, $x = 18$ and $p = 0.5$

536 Rob Fraser

Finally, in this section consider the sensitivity of the findings in Table 3 to the adjusted size of the penalty parameter (∂)[11].

Table 3: Comparison of Resource-Neutral and
Penalty-adjusted Resource-Neutral Targeting

	R	
	0.5	0.75
Resource-Neutral $p_L = 0.4$; $\delta = 1$		
$PVU(I_{T12})$	21.17	18.41
$PVEU(I_{C12})$	21.41	18.45
$PVEU(I_{T1C2})$	21.56	18.54
Non-Resource-Neutral $p_L = 0.4$; $\delta = 1.25$		
$PVU(I_{T12})$	21.17	18.41
$PVEU(I_{C12})$	20.38	17.95
$PVEU(I_{T1C2})$	21.13	18.34

In particular, it could be argued that an increase in this penalty from the simple return of the fraudulently claimed payment ($\delta = 1$) to an additional 25% penalty ($\delta = 1.25$) is larger than permitted legally in some contexts. The implications of such a restriction are demonstrated in Table 4, where the increase in δ is restricted to an additional 10% penalty ($\delta = 1.1$). In this case it can be seen that although the associated increase in the riskiness of cheating is sufficient to deter the more risk averse agent ($R = 0.75$) from the cheating at all, it is not sufficient to discourage the less risk averse agent ($R = 0.5$) from cheating some of the time. It follows that if such a legal restriction actually applies, then a system of targeting may be prevented from eliminating cheating among less risk averse agents in the non-target group.

---

[11] I am grateful to an anonymous referee for suggesting this sensitivity analysis. Note that consideration of restrictions on the size of penalty has been a common feature of the literature in this area (*e.g.* Harrington, 1988; Harford and Harrington, 1991; Raymond, 1999). Other sensitivity analysis of parameters such as the rate of interest and the probability of being monitored are unreported as they revealed no contrary findings.

On the Use of Targeting to Reduce Moral Hazard in Agri-environmental Schemes 537

Table 4: Sensitivity of Results to the Adjusted Size of Penalty (δ)

	R	
	0.5	0.75
Resource-Neutral		
$P_L = 0.4$; $\delta = 1$		
$PVU(I_{T12})$	21.17	18.41
$PVEU(I_{C12})$	21.41	18.45
$PVEU(I_{T1C2})$	21.56	18.54
Penalty-Adjusted Resource-Neutral		
$P_L = 0.44^a$; $\delta = 1.1$		
$PVU(I_{T12})$	21.17	18.41
$PVEU(I_{C12})$	20.91	18.21
$PVEU(I_{T1C2})$	21.22	18.39

Note a: $p_H = 0.67$

4.   Concluding Comments

The concept of targeting in the context of monitoring/penalty systems involves separating the system's participants into a (larger) non-target and a (smaller) target group and increasing the probability of detection of those in the target group. The aim of this paper has been to explore the potential for targeting to be used to alleviate the moral hazard problem in the context of agri-environmental schemes because it is relatively straightforward to separate participants in such schemes based on well-defined environmental characteristics. The particular focus of the paper has been on the scope for using targeting to reduce the frequency of cheating among those participants in the non-target group, rather than the more common case of those targeted participants.

In Section 2 of the paper an intertemporal model of a risk averse agent participating in an agri-environmental scheme was developed. Participation required the agent to take action to forego income in return for a payment, thereby creating the incentive to cheat by receiving the payment but not taking the action. Hence, the principal uses a monitoring/penalty system to discourage cheating. Within this model context three alternative approaches to targeting were analysed. First, a resource-neutral approach was considered whereby the extra monitoring resources needed to increase the probability of detection in the target group were taken from those used for monitoring the non-target group, thereby decreasing the probability of detection in the non-target group. It was shown in Section 2, and subsequently illustrated in the numerical analysis of Section 3, that this approach can reduce the frequency of but not eliminate cheating among those in the non-target group who cheated all the time in the absence of targeting. Moreover, because this approach reduces the probability of detection for those in the non-target group it was shown that those in this group, who in the absence of targeting did not cheat at all, may as a consequence of this form of targeting be enticed to cheat some of the time.

Consequently, two alternative forms of targeting were considered in an attempt to eliminate these weaknesses in the first approach. The non-resource–neutral alternative involved increasing expenditure on monitoring resources in order to restore the probability of detection within the non-target group. It was shown in the numerical analysis of Section 3 how this approach could eliminate the propensity within the first approach to entice those previously not cheating at all to begin cheating some of the time in the presence of targeting. However, it was also demonstrated in Section 1 that this approach could not eliminate the preference of those previously cheating all the time to still cheat some of the time even in the presence of targeting. Therefore, the concept of a mean-penalty preserving increase in the riskiness of cheating developed in Fraser (2002) was incorporated to create a third form of targeting. This form was specified neither to expend more monitoring resources (resource-neutral), nor to increase the expected cost of cheating for those in the non-target group (mean-penalty preserving), but by appropriate adjustments in the monitoring/penalty parameters this approach was able to eliminate completely cheating by those participants in the non-target group. In particular, it was shown using the numerical analysis of Section 3 that, if the scope for adjusting the penalty is unrestricted, then by increasing the riskiness of cheating, the attraction of so doing to risk averse agents was able to be reduced to the point where behaving truthfully all the time was the preferred option.

On this basis it is argued that targeting has the potential to alleviate the moral hazard problem in existing agri-environmental schemes, particularly if coupled with appropriate adjustments to the monitoring/penalty parameters that deter risk aware agents in the non-target group from cheating.

For example, consider the English agri-environmental policy of "Environmentally Sensitive Areas". As explained by Fraser and Hone (2002): "A region could be designated an *Environmentally Sensitive Area* when it was considered to be of national environmental significance and was under threat from agricultural intensification, but it could be conserved via the adoption or continuation of particular farming technologies." (p229). In addition: "*Environmentally Sensitive Areas* operate by offering all farmers within a designated geographical area a standard payment for undertaking prescribed agricultural activities that will yield environmental benefits." (p229), although: "participation in the programs is voluntary" (p230). In order to implement a system of targeting as developed in the previous sections within the practice of the Environmentally Sensitive Areas policy note from Fraser and Hone (2002) that: "There are currently 22 designated Environmentally Sensitive Areas in England" (p230). Using these clear geographical regions, the first step would be to create a number of sub-groups of participants of roughly equal size. Based on the example of the numerical analysis this might be four sub-groups of 25%, with one geographically-defined sub-group designated for targeting in the first monitoring period, and the remaining sub-groups (75% of participants) not targeted. Note that in subsequent monitoring periods the target sub-group would rotate around the four geographically-defined sub-groups, with the exception of participants caught cheating in previous monitoring periods who would remain targeted, at least for some number of periods. The second step would be to adjust upwards the penalty associated with being caught cheating in order to increase the riskiness of cheating and thereby exploit the risk aversion of participants to reduce or eliminate cheating among non-targeted participants. Note from the results of the numerical analysis that if there are restrictions on the extent to which this penalty can be increased then less risk averse participants in the non-target group may not be deterred from cheating by the associated (restricted) increase in the riskiness of cheating. Finally, the effectiveness of the targeting system can be evaluated after several monitoring periods by comparing recent with historical levels of detected non-compliance. [12]

References

Breautigam, R.R. and Panzar, J.C. (1993) Effects of the change from rate-of-return to price-cap regulation, *American Economic Review* (Papers and Proceedings) 83(2):191-98.

Choe, C. and Fraser, I. (1999) Compliance monitoring and agri-environmental policy, *Journal of Agricultural Economics* 50(3):468-87.

Fraser R.W. (2001) Using principal-agent theory to deal with output slippage in the European Union set-aside policy, *Journal of Agricultural Economics* 52(2):29-41.

Fraser R.W. (2002) Moral hazard and risk management in agri-environmental policy, *Journal of Agricultural Economics* 53(3):475-87.

Fraser, I. and Hone, P. (2002) Development and implementation of agri-environmental policy: English experience and lessons for Australia, *Australian Journal of Environmental Management* 9(4):228-242.

Greenberg, J. (1984) Avoiding tax avoidance: a repeated game-theoretic approach, *Journal of Economic Theory* 32(1):1-13.

Harford, J.D. and Harrington, W. (1991) A reconsideration of enforcement leverage when penalties are restricted, *Journal of Public Economics* 45(3):391-95.

Harrington, W. (1988) Enforcement leverage when penalties are restricted, *Journal of Public Economics* 37(1):29-53.

Heyes, A.G. and Rickman, N. (1999) Regulatory dealing - revisiting the Harrington paradox, *Journal of Public Economics* 72(3):361-78.

Heyes, A. G. (2000) Implementing environmental regulation: enforcement and compliance, *Journal of Regulatory Economics* 17(2): 107-29.

Heyes, A. G. (2002) A theory of filtered enforcement, *Journal of Environmental Economics and Management* 43(1):34-46.

Landsberger, M. and Meilijson, I. (1982) Incentive-generating state dependent penalty systems: the case of income tax evasion, *Journal of Public Economics* 19(3):333-52.

---

[12] Note that a similar approach could be taken to adjusting the English "Countryside Stewardship Scheme", but with the focus of targeting on the environmental features provided by farmers rather than on geographical regions.

540 Rob Fraser

Latacz-Lohmann, U. (1998) Moral hazard in agri-environmental schemes, Paper presented to the Annual Conference of the Agricultural Economics Society, University of Reading, March.

Moxey, A., White, B. and Ozanne, A. (1999), Efficient contract design for agri-environmental policy, *Journal of Agricultural Economics* **50**(2):187-202.

Ozanne, A., Hogan, T. and Colman, D. (2001) Moral hazard, risk aversion and compliance monitoring and agri-environmental policy, *European Review of Agricultural Economics* **28**(3):329-347.

Polinsky, A.M. and Shavell, S. (1979) The optimal trade-off between the probability and magnitude of fines, *American Economic Review* **69**(5):880-91.

Polinsky, A.M. and Rubinfeld, D. (1991) A model of optimal fines for repeat offenders, *Journal of Public Economics* **46**(4):291-306.

Pope, R.D. and Just, R.E. (1991) On testing the structure of risk preferences in agricultural supply analysis, *American Journal of Agricultural Economics* **73**(3):743-8.

Raymond, M. (1999) Enforcement leverage when penalties are restricted: a reconsideration under asymmetric information, *Journal of Public Economics* **73**(2):289-95.

Russell, C.S. (1990) Game models for structuring monitoring and enforcement systems, *Natural Resource Modelling* **4**(2):143-173.

Journal of Agricultural Economics, Vol. 60, No. 1, 2009, 190–201
doi: 10.1111/j.1477-9552.2008.00183.x

Chapter 11

Land Heterogeneity, Agricultural Income Forgone and Environmental Benefit: An Assessment of Incentive Compatibility Problems in Environmental Stewardship Schemes

Rob Fraser[1]

(Original submitted April 2008, revision received September 2008, accepted September 2008.)

Abstract

This paper examines the issue of incentive compatibility within environmental stewardship schemes, where incentive payments to farmers to provide environmental goods and services are based on foregone agricultural income. The particular focus of the paper is land heterogeneity, either of agricultural or environmental value, leading to divergence between the actual and socially optimal level of provision of environmental goods and services. Given land heterogeneity, such goods and services are likely to be systematically over- or under-provided in response to a flat rate payment for income foregone.

Keywords: *land heterogeneity; agricultural income forgone; incentive compatibility; environmental stewardship.*

JEL classifications: *D82, L51, Q18, Q58.*

1. Introduction

The European Union's Common Agricultural Policy (CAP) has an established history of compensating farmers for policy changes which have reduced their production income. For example, the May 1992 CAP Reform introduced the concept of Direct Payments, which were designed to compensate farmers both for reduced price support and for foregone production income on set-aside land (see Fraser, 1993; Froud *et al.*, 1996). More recently, agricultural policy developments in the European Union have encouraged farmers to provide environmental goods and

---

[1] Professor of Agricultural Economics, University of Kent and Adjunct Professor of Agricultural and Resource Economics, University of Western Australia. E-mail: r.fraser@kent.ac.uk.
I am particularly grateful to the Editor in Chief, as well as to two anonymous referees for their helpful comments on previous versions.

services. An example of this type of policy was the UK's Countryside Stewardship Scheme, which has recently evolved into the Environmental Stewardship Scheme (DEFRA, 2007a).

A general problem for such schemes is that of asymmetric information (Fraser and Fraser, 2005), which can itself be broken into the specific components of adverse selection and moral hazard. A range of studies have analysed the implications for agri-environmental policy design (e.g. Wu and Babcock, 1996; Moxey *et al.*, 1999; Fraser, 2002). However, a key difference between these two components is that moral hazard encourages illegal or extra-contractual behaviour by scheme participants, while adverse selection does not involve illegal behaviour, but is centred on incentive compatibility. DEFRA (2007a) states that the Environmental Stewardship Scheme 'generate(s) financial incentives for farmers to provide the public goods they would not otherwise deliver' (p. 6), where these 'payments are based on income foregone' (p. 13). In this case, scheme participation encourages farmers to participate based on income foregone, rather than on the benefits participation is supposed to deliver to the wider public. From the policy design perspective, this basis for payment to farmers raises the question of whether it properly corrects the market failure in relation to the provision of environmental goods and services, and in so doing delivers 'the socially optimal level of those goods and services' (p. 6). For example, Harvey (2003) points out that 'the suppliers are not explicitly rewarded for their provision and hence cannot be expected to supply them in appropriate quantities' (p. 714).

In this context Rygnestad and Fraser (1996) demonstrated a relevant problem of incentive compatibility in policy design as it related to the operation of the CAP's set-aside policy in situations of heterogeneous land quality. In particular, with set-aside premiums established with reference to average levels of production income foregone, heterogeneous land quality means that it is in farmers' best interests to set aside the lowest quality land in terms of production income, which results in policy 'slippage' in terms of output control. Other research which has identified heterogeneity of land as an important consideration in agri-environmental policy design includes Campbell (2007) and Hanley *et al.* (2007), who point out that 'Supply prices would be expected to vary across farmers, because of differences in opportunity costs' (p. 434), while 'Willingness to pay for a given public good such as moorland landscapes could also be expected to vary spatially' (p. 435).[2]

The aim of this paper is to show that the relationship between land heterogeneity and incentive compatibility is also a problem for the design of agri-environmental schemes, such as the UK's Environmental Stewardship Scheme, where payments to farmers for providing environmental goods and services are based on average levels of agricultural income foregone, rather than on society's willingness to pay for these environmental goods and services. In particular, it will be shown that, if land is heterogeneous, both in terms of agricultural value and in terms of environmental value, then foregone income payment leads to a systematic misallocation of

---

[2] In this context of land heterogeneity Oñate *et al.* (2006) also found evidence of 'differences in gross margins among modelled representative farms, related to the homogeneity of the area' and affecting the consequences of implementing an agri-environmental scheme (p. 257). Johnston and Duke (2007) also found evidence of 'significant preference heterogeneity' in relation to land-related policy attributes among respondents surveyed about agricultural land preservation (p. 1108).

taxpayer funding, both within and between landscape regions. Note that we only consider income-foregone payments here. We do not consider other incentives, financial and otherwise, for farmers to adopt environmentally friendly practices (see, e.g. Pannell *et al.*, 2006; Knowler and Bradshaw, 2007). This important point is considered in the section 4.

The structure of the paper is as follows. Section 2 examines the problem of 'local' land heterogeneity, demonstrating: (i) that a uniform incentive payment system based on average production income foregone within a region of similar environmental value and agricultural land-use results in actual levels of provision of environmental goods and services which are strongly sensitive to the levels of these payments; (ii) that such payments systematically encourage under- or over-provision of environmental goods and services between farms relative to the socially optimal levels within the region. Section 3 then examines the problem of land heterogeneity between regions, either in the level of agricultural income or in the size of environmental benefits. Once again it is shown that, with incentive payments based on agricultural income foregone, taxpayer funding will be systematically misallocated between regions. In particular, there will be:

(i) excess provision of environmental goods and services in regions of relatively high agricultural income and/or low environmental benefits from such goods and services;
(ii) inadequate provision of environmental goods and services in regions of relatively low agricultural income and/or high environmental benefits from such goods and services.

Moreover, such misallocation may be so extreme that the overall level of social benefit is less than the cost of taxpayer funding, resulting not only in a re-distribution of income, but also in a dead weight loss to society from the policy's operation.

2. Local Land Heterogeneity

This section examines the problem for policy design of 'local' land heterogeneity, i.e. within a single region of similar environmental value and similar agricultural land use. From the policy perspective 'local' can also indicate a region where the payments for providing the same environmental goods and services are uniform across the region. However, even within such a region, land productivity will vary both within and between farms. For example, in the study of Danish cereal farms by Rygnestad and Fraser (1996), crop land was broadly characterized as being poor, average or good, with maximum yields varying in each case from 5.45 to 8.45 to 10.45 tonnes/ha. Moreover, each farm was characterised by the proportion of each of these land types which it comprised. As a consequence, each farmer would respond to the introduction of compulsory set-aside by setting aside their lowest quality land, whilst farms with an overall higher quality of land would experience the largest decreases in production income.

Given such land heterogeneity on-farm, the marginal cost of diverting land to environmental purposes increases as more land is diverted. This marginal cost is represented in Figure 1 by the line MC_E^0 (assuming continuous variation in land productivity over the farm). In this situation, if the established incentive payment per hectare in the region for converting land from agricultural production to the

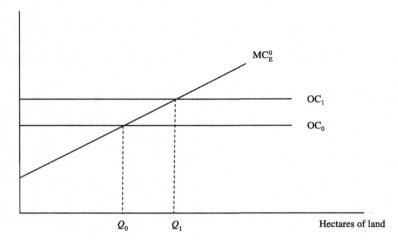

Figure 1. Marginal cost of providing environmental goods and services

provision of environmental goods and services is given by OC_0, then the farmer will choose to convert the Q_0 hectares for which the marginal cost (agricultural income foregone) is less than (or equal to) this incentive payment. As can be readily seen from this representation, the lower the quality of the land on a farm, the lower the marginal (or opportunity) cost of diverting land to environmental purposes, and the greater the area of land which will be diverted for any given payment. On the other hand, the more homogenous is the land on the farm, the flatter is the marginal cost, and the more sensitive is diverted area to the level of payment.

The socially optimal diverted area for this farm is defined by the social (willingness-to-pay) demand curve for environmental goods and services. This is represented by the line D_S in Figure 2, which otherwise replicates Figure 1. Figure 2 is drawn to represent an ideal outcome, where the farmer's actual choice of area to convert (Q_A) is exactly equal to the socially optimal area to convert (Q_S) – i.e. where the marginal social willingness to pay for conversion is exactly equal to the farmer's marginal cost of conversion, and where both are equal to the established incentive payment for converting land. This situation is unique, demonstrating that payment based on income foregone is not necessarily inconsistent with a socially optimal outcome.[3] More specifically, in this situation the combined value of consumer surplus:

$$\square OQ_A CE$$

and producer surplus:

$$\triangle ABC$$

less the amount of government (taxpayer) funding to farmers to achieve the area converted:

---

[3] My thanks go to an anonymous referee for pointing out this special case to me.

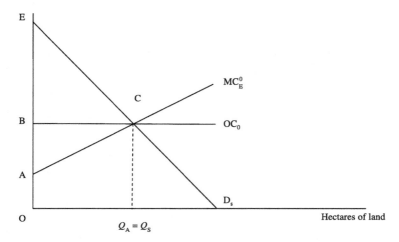

Figure 2. Comparison of actual and socially optimal area of converted land

$$\square OQ_A CB$$

is maximised as:

$$\triangle ACE.$$

In particular, for smaller converted areas (than $Q_A = Q_S$) this net benefit is lower since the loss of combined consumer and producer surplus exceeds the savings in government spending, compared with the optimum, while for larger converted areas (than $Q_A = Q_S$) the gain in combined consumer and producer surplus is less than the amount of extra government spending.

However, this fortunate coincidence of a fixed income foregone payment and a socially optimal conversion of land will only happen if: (i) all farms in this region are identical in terms of their spread of land quality (i.e. all farms have the same MC_E curve); (ii) the social demand for environmental provision is common to all land in the region; (iii) the uniform payment is established at exactly the appropriate level to balance the common marginal cost with the common social benefit. Otherwise, it is clear that land heterogeneity will result in any uniform payment delivering a socially sub-optimal provision of converted land on any particular farm in the region.[4] This situation is represented in Figure 3, where both the incentive payment per hectare of converted land and the social demand curve for each hectare of converted land are unchanged from those in Figure 2 (i.e. OC_0 and D_S), but above-average and below-average marginal cost of conversion farms

---

[4] Because existing agri-environmental policies such as the ESS are based on uniform incentive payments within regions, no consideration is given here to specific farm-based incentive payments. However, a scheme featuring specific farm-based payments would be worth investigating if the demand for environmental provision in a region could be substituted between farms, for example such that low-quality farm land specialised in this provision, thereby improving overall social benefit.

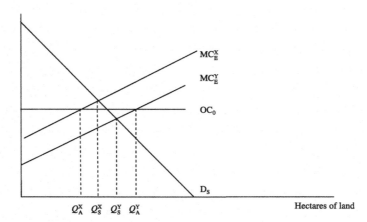

Figure 3. Comparison of actual and socially optimal area of converted land between farms
X and Y

are represented by MC_E^X and MC_E^Y, respectively. As is clear from Figure 3, between-farm land heterogeneity results in different levels of converted land being chosen by the two farmers (i.e. Q_A^X compared with Q_A^Y). In addition, even though the social demand curve for converted land is the same for farms X and Y, their differing marginal costs of conversion implies a different socially optimal area of converted land on each farm, with area on farm Y exceeding that for farm X (i.e. $Q_S^Y > Q_S^X$) to reflect farm Y's lower marginal cost of conversion. More importantly, a uniform conversion incentive payment per hectare for the two farms in this case results in under- or over-provision of environmental goods and services by farmers relative to the social optimum for their farm. Specifically, for farms in the region which have above-average quality of agricultural land for the region (such as X), farmers will systematically choose to convert less than the socially optimal area of converted land for their farms (i.e. the marginal social willingness to pay for land to be converted exceeds the marginal cost of doing so). The obverse applies to farmers with below-average quality of agricultural land for the region (such as Y). Even though the environmental value of land is the same across the region, a uniform payment means that the provision of environmental goods and services will be concentrated in parts of the region where the agricultural value of land is below average. Moreover, this intra-regional misallocation of funds will occur even when the total funding to the region for the provision of environmental goods and services within the region is similar to the socially desirable level.[5]

---

[5] If environmental value was much higher than given by D_S, then at some level both types of farms would feature inadequate provision. Similarly, for environmental value much lower than D_S, at some level both types of farms would feature excess provision. Even so, the provision of environmental goods and services will be concentrated in parts of the region where the agricultural value of land is below average.

Rob Fraser

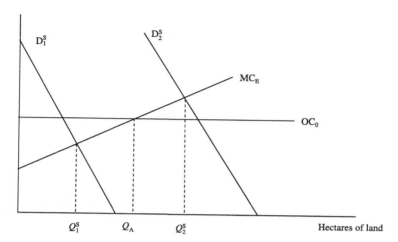

Figure 4. Two regions with different environmental value

3. Land Heterogeneity Between Regions

A similar problem arises because of heterogeneity in the social value of environmental care, as is likely to be the case between two different regions. To begin, and to keep the analysis as simple as possible, consider two such regions, with different social valuations of the care provision, but with farms assumed to be identical as far as their opportunity costs of conservation, amenity, recreation and environmental (care) provision is concerned (albeit with heterogeneous land within the farm, and hence upward sloping MC curves).

3.1. Heterogeneity in environmental value

In this case the two regions are specified to be equivalent in terms of agricultural productivity, such that the incentive payment per hectare for converting land to the provision of environmental goods and services is identical for the two regions. However, the two regions are heterogeneous in terms of the marginal social value of their environmental landscape, with one region featuring greater marginal social willingness to pay for environmental goods and services per hectare than the other for each hectare of converted land. This situation is represented in Figure 4, showing that the actual proportion of land chosen to be converted to the provision of environmental goods and services is the same for both regions (Q_A), consistent with their identical agricultural productivity and incentive payments to convert land. However, it can also be seen that the environmental land heterogeneity between the two regions results in a systematic misallocation of the provision of environmental goods and services between the two regions. In particular, a flat rate payment results in excess provision of environmental goods and services in the region of low environmental value, and

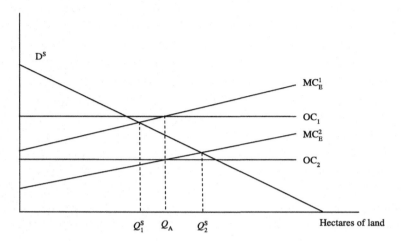

Figure 5. Two regions with different agricultural value

inadequate provision of environmental goods and services in the region of high environmental value.[6]

3.2. Heterogeneity in agricultural value

At the other extreme, consider two regions with the same environmental value (demand for environmental care), but with different agricultural productivities (marginal costs of provision) (Figure 5). An example of this type of situation in the UK would be an arable region and a hill-farming region, where the agricultural income per hectare is higher in the arable region than in the hill-farming region, but where the total environmental value of the two regions is similar, perhaps because the hill-farming region features higher environmental value per individual user, but is more distant from a population centre than the arable region. In this case, payment rates established with reference to income foregone will result in different payments in each region, which may (or may not) result in the same amounts of land diverted (converted) to environmental provision. But the common demand (willingness to pay) for care means that the socially optimal amount of converted land in the region of low agricultural value exceeds that for the region of high agricultural value (i.e. $Q_2^S > Q_1^S$). In this case, an incentive payments scheme based on agricultural income foregone for environmental values which are identical, results in a systematic misallocation of the provision of environmental goods and services between the two regions, with a particular bias towards excess provision in the region of

---

[6] Note as in the previous section that for extremely divergent levels of incentive payments and marginal social willingness-to-pay environmental goods and services could be under- or over-provided in both regions. However, the extent of under- or over-provision would still differ markedly between the two regions, and a bias remain towards under-provision in the region of higher environmental value and over-provision in the region of lower environmental value.

high agricultural value, and inadequate provision in the region of low agricultural value.

3.3. Heterogeneity in both agricultural and environmental value

In practice, both the opportunity costs of providing care and the social valuations of the environmental provision differ between and within regions. It is highly unlikely that the cost of provision is systematically reflective of the social value of environmental care. For example, Fraser and Rygnestad (1999) showed for Danish cereal growing that croppable land with relatively low agricultural productivity was also the land that offered the highest potential benefits from set-aside in terms of reduced nitrate leaching. Moreover, in the UK (and other EU countries), the so-called 'less favoured areas' in terms of agricultural income per hectare, are also increasingly being referred to as areas of 'high nature value' (European Environment Agency, EEA, 2004). As a consequence, the following numerical illustration is based on a negative correlation between agricultural and environmental value – low agricultural value being associated with high environmental value, and *vice versa*.

A numerical illustration allows quantification of both total government spending and total consumer and producer surplus generated by such spending on the operation of an incentive payment system for the conversion of agricultural land to the provision of environmental goods and services.

Based on the framework of the previous subsections, let the low agricultural/high environmental value region have the following specification (where this region is denoted by 'H'):

$$D_H = 120 - q$$
$$MC_H = 15 + 0.5q$$
$$OC_H = 30.$$

While for the high agricultural/low environmental value region (denoted by 'L'):

$$D_L = 60 - q$$
$$MC_L = 50 + 0.25q$$
$$OC_L = 70.$$

Table 1 shows the numerical results. As expected from the findings of sections 2.1 and 2.2, and given the specified negative correlation between agricultural and environmental value, there is excess provision of environmental goods and services in region L, and inadequate provision in region H. Moreover, given the chosen parameter values, there is larger governmental spending than is socially optimal, and the combined value of consumer and producer surplus is less than that achieved with the socially optimal provision of environmental goods and services. But the most significant quantitative finding is that, while the combined value of consumer and producer surplus exceeds governmental spending in the case of the socially optimal provision (a ratio of 1.95 : 1), the actual provision leads to a deadweight welfare loss with total governmental spending exceeding the combined gains in consumer and producer surplus (a ratio of 0.92 : 1). In this case, the operation of the incentive payments scheme based on agricultural income foregone results in an overall reduction in social welfare.

Table 1

Results of the numerical illustration

	Region L	Region H	Total
Area converted			
Actual	80	30	110
Optimal	8	70	78
Governmental spending			
Actual	5600	900	6500
Optimal	416	3500	3916
Consumer surplus			
Actual	1800	3150	4950
Optimal	448	5950	6398
Producer surplus			
Actual	800	225	1025
Optimal	8	1225	1233
Consumer and producer surplus			
Actual	2600	3375	5975
Optimal	456	7175	7631

4. Conclusion

It is clear from this analysis that any flat rate payment scheme for environmental care will generate suboptimal provision when either or both the opportunity costs of provision and the social values of the environment are heterogeneous. Furthermore, the more different are the costs and values of environmental provision between different areas (within or between regions), the greater is the misallocation likely to be, to the extent that the total costs of any flat rate scheme can exceed the benefits. The focus here has been on payments based on income foregone (the opportunity costs of providing environmental care). In particular, such a system will encourage over-provision of environmental goods and services (relative to the socially optimal level) on farms with relatively low average quality of agricultural land (section 2). In addition (section 3) such a system will encourage:

(i) over-provision of environmental goods and services (relative to the socially optimal level) in regions of relatively high agricultural income and/or low environmental benefits from such goods and services;

(ii) under-provision of environmental goods and services (relative to the socially optimal level) in regions of relatively low agricultural income and/or high environmental benefits from such goods and services.

Moreover, in a situation where the regions involved feature a negative correlation between agricultural and environmental value, it was shown that the misallocation of funding for the provision of environmental goods and services between regions may be so great as to result in an overall reduction in social welfare from the operation of the scheme.

In essence, as argued by Harvey (2003), the policy design problem is to "properly" reflect the public or social values of the (environmental goods and services) back to the landowners' because 'only then can we expect market forces ... to encourage land users to operate at the socially optimal level' (p. 714).

200   *Rob Fraser*

In this context it is interesting to note that although the UK's Environmental Stewardship Scheme states that it uses agricultural income foregone as the basis for determining incentive payments for the provision of environmental goods and services, that scheme does actually contain an exception to this 'rule'. Specifically, within the component of this scheme called 'higher level stewardship' one of the identified environmental services is 'educational access', which provides 'schools and colleges' with the opportunity to visit farms and have farmers 'explain the links between farming, conservation and food production' (DEFRA, 2007b, p. 94). In this case, the incentive payments to farmers is 'per visit', and in applying to participate in the provision of 'educational access' farmers are 'expected to provide evidence of this demand' (DEFRA, 2007b, p. 94). Consequently, in making their decision regarding whether to provide this environmental service farmers must take account of the social benefit associated with its provision in so far as this will determine the 'demand' for 'educational access'. Perhaps this approach might be made more common across the other environmental services?

However, as argued by Pannell *et al.* (2006) 'adoption of conservation practices is complex and multifaceted' (p. 1421) and as suggested by Knowler and Bradshaw (2007) 'efforts to promote conservation agriculture will have to be tailored to reflect the particular conditions of individual locales' (p. 25). Therefore, while dealing with the joint problems of land heterogeneity and incentive compatibility, agri-environmental policy design should also be sensitive to broader considerations of farmer participation where this participation is voluntary. On the other hand, the transactions and implementation costs associated with such 'well-designed' policy instruments delivered by government on our behalf might well exceed the benefits. If so, the appropriate conclusion is not necessarily that the current system of cost-based flat rate payments is second best, but rather that we should be seeking different processes to allow the beneficiaries of environmental care to connect more closely with those able to provide these services (Harvey, 2003).

References

Campbell, D. 'Willingness to pay for rural landscape improvements: Combining mixed logit and random-effects models', *Journal of Agricultural Economics*, Vol. 58, (2007) pp. 467–483.

DEFRA. Environmental Stewardship Evaluation Plan (2007a). Available at: http://www.defra.gov.uk/erdp/pdfs/es/ES-EvaluationPlan-jul06.pdf.

DEFRA. Higher Level Stewardship Handbook (2007b). Available at: http://www.defra.gov.uk/erdp/pdfs/es/hls-handbook.pdf.

European Environment Agency. *High Nature Value Farmland – Characteristics, Trends and Policy Challenges*, EEA Report No. 1, 2004.

Fraser, R. W. 'Set-aside premiums and the May 1992 CAP reforms', *Journal of Agricultural Economics*, Vol. 44, (1993) pp. 410–417.

Fraser, R. W. 'Moral hazard and risk management in agri-environmental policy', *Journal of Agricultural Economics*, Vol. 53, (2002) pp. 475–487.

Fraser, R. W. and Fraser, I. M. 'The implications of information asymmetries for agri-environmental policies', Paper presented to the OECD Workshop on Information Deficiencies in Agri-Environmental Policies, June (2005). Available at: http://www.oecd.org/agr/meet/idap.

Fraser, R. W. and Rygnestad, H. L. 'An assessment of the impact of implementing the European Commission's *Agenda 2000* cereal proposals for specialist wheat growers in Denmark', *Journal of Agricultural Economics*, Vol. 50, (1999) pp. 328–335.

Froud, J., Roberts, D. and Fraser, R. W. 'Participation in set-aside: What determines the opting-in price?' *Journal of Agricultural Economics*, Vol. 47, (1996) pp. 89–108.

Hanley, N., Colombo, S., Mason, P. and Johns, H. 'The reform of support mechanisms for upland farming: Paying for public goods in the severely disadvantaged areas of England', *Journal of Agricultural Economics*, Vol. 58, (2007) pp. 433–453.

Harvey, D. R. 'Agri-environmental relationships and multi-functionality', *The World Economy*, Vol. 26, (2003) pp. 705–725.

Johnston, R. and Duke, J. 'Willingness to pay for agricultural land preservation and policy process attributes: Does the method matter?' *American Journal of Agricultural Economics*, Vol. 89, (2007) pp. 1098–1115.

Knowler, D. and Bradshaw, B. 'Farmers' adoption of conservation agriculture: A review and synthesis of recent research', *Food Policy*, Vol. 32, (2007) pp. 25–48.

Moxey, A., White, B. and Ozanne, A. 'Efficient contract design for agri-environmental policy', *Journal of Agricultural Economics*, Vol. 50, (1999) pp. 187–202.

Oñate, J., Atance, I., Bardaji, I. and Lluisa, D. 'Modelling the effect of alternative CAP policies for the Spanish high-nature value cereal-steppe farming systems', *Agricultural Systems*, Vol. 94, (2006) pp. 247–260.

Pannell, D., Marshall, G., Barr, N., Curtis, A., Vanclay, F. and Wilkinson, R. 'Understanding and promoting adoption of conservation practices by rural landholders', *Australian Journal of Experimental Economics*, Vol. 46, (2006) pp. 1407–1424.

Rygnestad, H. L. and Fraser, R. W. 'Land heterogeneity and the effectiveness of CAP set-aside', *Journal of Agricultural Economics*, Vol. 47, (1996) pp. 255–260.

Wu, J. and Babcock, B. A. 'Contract design for the purchase of environmental goods from agriculture', *American Journal of Agricultural Economics*, Vol. 78, (1996) pp. 935–945.

Journal of Agricultural Economics, Vol. 61, No. 2, 2010, 369–380
doi: 10.1111/j.1477-9552.2010.00240.x

Chapter 12

Adverse Selection in the Environmental Stewardship Scheme: Does the Higher Level Stewardship Scheme Design Reduce Adverse Selection?

Emmanuelle Quillérou and Rob Fraser[1]

(Original submitted April 2009, revision received September 2009, accepted January 2010.)

Abstract

The Environmental Stewardship Scheme provides payments to farmers for the provision of environmental services based on foregone agricultural income. This creates a potential incentive compatibility problem which, combined with information asymmetry about farm land potential, can lead to adverse selection of land into the Scheme and therefore a less cost-effective provision of environmental goods and services. However, the Higher Level Stewardship (HLS) Scheme design includes some features that potentially reduce adverse selection. This paper studies the adverse selection problem of the HLS using a principal-agent framework at the regional level. It is found that, at the regional level, the enrolment of more land from lower payment regions for a given budget constraint has reduced the adverse selection problem through contracting a greater overall area and thus higher overall environmental benefit. In addition, for landscape regions with the same payment rate (i.e. of the same agricultural value), differential weighting of the public demand for environmental goods and services provided by agriculture (measured by weighting an environmental benefit function by the distance to main cities) appears to be reflected in the regulator's allocation of contracts, thereby also reducing the adverse selection problem.

Keywords: *Adverse selection; agri-environment; contract; environmental stewardship; principal agent.*

JEL classifications: *D78, D82, H44, Q18, Q58.*

[1] Emmanuelle Quillérou is the contact author (emmanuelle_quillerou@yahoo.fr). The authors are, respectively, in the Kent Business School and in the School of Economics at the University of Kent, Canterbury CT2 7NZ, UK, where Rob Fraser is Professor of Agricultural Economics, and also Adjunct Professor of Agricultural and Resource Economics, University of Western Australia. The authors are particularly grateful to Dr Iain Fraser, the Associate Editor and two anonymous referees for helpful comments on previous versions. We also thank Natural England Agri-Environment Team for the provision of data on the agri-environmental schemes, without which this study would not have been possible.

370   *Emmanuelle Quillérou and Rob Fraser*

1. Introduction

From 1992, the European Common Agricultural Policy's successive reforms have
shifted away from production support by including a parallel agri-environmental
policy reflecting the multifunctionality of agriculture. This agri-environmental policy
offers payments to farmers for providing environmental goods and services. The
main agri-environmental scheme in England since 2005 has been the Environmental
Stewardship Scheme, which builds on the baseline cross-compliance requirements
(Defra, 2005a). It is a nationally set two-tier scheme, corresponding to two levels of
increasing environmental commitment: the Entry Level Stewardship/Organic Entry
Level Stewardship (ELS/OELS) tier with more general requirements (and higher
participation), and the Higher Level Stewardship (HLS) tier with more specific environmental requirements and a higher level of environmental commitment (and consequently more limited participation). The ELS tier (along with the OELS, its
equivalent for organic agriculture) is based on a whole-farm approach and open to
all farmers and landowners, within five-year contracts (Defra, 2005a). It relies on
self-selection by farmers of environmental options from a given 'menu', each option
corresponding to a given number of points reflecting the agricultural income foregone (which is nationally estimated) (Defra, 2005a). ELS (OELS) agreements are
guaranteed providing farmers meet a 30-point (60-point) target per hectare for a
corresponding payment of £30/ha (£60/ha) (Defra, 2005a).

The second tier or HLS targets more complex types of management and capital
work plans (Defra, 2005a,b). Like the ELS, farmers still self-select land management options within a set 'menu' and for fixed per-unit payments for each option.
However, entry is at the discretion of Natural England (the operating authority),
which competitively selects applications using a scoring and threshold mechanism.
This is derived from the previous Countryside Stewardship Scheme, and assesses
the environmental value provided so as to select contracts providing 'good *value for
money*' (Defra, 2005a,b). Scoring of applications is spatially differentiated, based on
159 Joint Character Areas, i.e. areas of the English countryside with similar landscape character, each with a specific association of wildlife and natural features
(Defra, 2005b). Each Joint Character Area has a corresponding set of environmental key and secondary targets (detailed in specific 'targeting statements') for the
management of a variety of features, against which farm applications are scored,
with priority given to Sites of Special Scientific Interest (SSSIs) and Scheduled Mon-
uments (Defra, 2005b). Scored applications are then pooled for all Joint Character
Areas within the same administrative region (roughly corresponding to the government office regions). The threshold entry decision criterion or cut-off score is then
set for all Joint Character Areas within the same administrative region, in relation
to the available regional budget, so that all applications with a score above the
(budget-determined) regional threshold score are retained for contracting.

The Environmental Stewardship Scheme aims at delivering environmental benefits
but is based on incentive payments typically calculated as an average of the agricultural income foregone by farmers (or opportunity cost, OC) and not as the environmental benefit derived from the land entered into the Scheme. As agricultural
income and environmental benefit are not necessarily (spatially) positively correlated
(OECD, 2004, Fraser, 2009), the discrepancy between farmer incentives to enter the
Environmental Stewardship Scheme based on their individual OC of agricultural
production and the government agencies' (Defra and Natural England) objective of

paying farmers for an environmental benefit potentially leads to an incentive compatibility problem (Fraser and Fraser, 2006). In combination with information asymmetries regarding farmer's OC of environmental service provision and land quality, this incentive incompatibility can lead to adverse selection of land for entry into the schemes which therefore reduces the cost effectiveness of the Scheme and results in a socially sub-optimal provision of environmental goods and services (Fraser, 2009). In particular, the potential for adverse selection into the Scheme would be expressed as the lowest agricultural quality land being entered into the Scheme by farmers rather than the highest environmental quality land as targeted by the government. The quasi-market payment for agri-environment provision is thus unlikely to be optimal (compared with a full information situation), and the combination of incentive incompatibilities and information asymmetries is likely to lead to systematic misallocation of taxpayer funding, both within and between landscape regions.

However, while all Environmental Stewardship tiers are likely to be subject to incentive incompatibility, as will be explained in this paper, this problem is potentially reduced in the case of the HLS both because it includes explicit selection based on environmental benefit criteria and because this selection is subject to a budget constraint. In particular, although farmers with the lowest agricultural OC have the greatest incentive to apply for the Scheme, the selection mechanism means that only farmers assessed as providing higher environmental benefit are admitted into the Scheme, thereby potentially reducing the adverse selection problem and increasing the cost effectiveness of the Scheme. In addition, the operation of the HLS subject to a budget constraint on total payments to farmers encourages the selection of 'low-cost' farmers which, where they are providing similar environmental benefits to 'high-cost' farmers, will also improve the overall cost effectiveness of the Scheme. Therefore, this paper focuses on the features of the HLS policy design that operate to decrease the potential for adverse selection, thereby improving the cost effectiveness of the Scheme.[2]

Most of the literature on adverse selection is based on theoretical analysis of contract design mechanisms to reduce incentive incompatibilities (Wu and Babcock, 1996; Moxey *et al.*, 1999; Feng, 2007), but very few studies have actually empirically examined this information problem for agri-environmental contracts. In this paper, the HLS contract design is taken as given, and instead emphasis is placed on the HLS contract allocation mechanism. In addition, this paper evaluates both theoretically and empirically the potential for reducing adverse selection, and therefore improving cost effectiveness, by explicit government selection from applicants based on environmental benefits and subject to a budget constraint on total payments to farmers. The next section develops a principal-agent model to assess the potential for adverse selection reduction in the HLS at the regional level (compared with a spatially uniform national policy), followed by empirical evidence of whether adverse selection has been reduced. The paper ends with a summary and conclusions.

---

[2] Although the HLS can be seen as a budget-constrained auction, based on an environmental score, this theoretical analogy is not developed here. For more detailed discussions of auction systems, see Latacz-Lohmann and Schilizzi (2005) and Connor *et al.* (2008). In addition, a payments-by-results approach has been discussed as a theoretical alternative to the current specification of the HLS but is not considered here (see Schwarz *et al.*, 2008).

2. Methodology

The analysis is based on a theoretical principal-agent model of optimal farmer participation relative to the social optimum, in relation to land heterogeneity both within and between 'regions', as developed by Fraser (2009). A principal-agent model is developed to analyse HLS contract allocation by the principal (Natural England), in relation to the potential effects of the adverse selection of farmers into the HLS, as well as the combination of policy mechanisms aimed at reducing adverse selection at the regional level and subject to the budget constraint. The reference point for assessing adverse selection reduction will be taken as a nationally uniform scheme (nationally uniform payment rate and environmental benefit per hectare). The focus is restricted to those HLS options involving entering land into the Scheme, as these most directly compete with agricultural production. The following analysis is specified as a between-region comparison, 'regions' here referring to the Joint Character Areas (areas of relatively homogenous environmental features and landscape), and which are within the same budget area.

Under this framework, farmers are considered as profit maximisers in relation to supplying environmental goods and services, which consequently leads to their selection of lower agricultural value land for HLS entry (i.e. with the highest net returns to entering the Scheme in relation to fixed payments based on average agricultural foregone income). The principal (Natural England) is assumed to maximise social welfare (i.e. the environmental benefit, EB) across regions subject to a budget constraint:

$$\max_{Q} \text{EB}_{\text{HLS}} = \sum_{r} w_r \times \text{eb} \times q_r \qquad (1)$$

subject to the budget constraint: $\sum_{i,j,r} q_{i,j,r} p_{j,r} \leq$ Total Budget with EB_{HLS} the total environmental benefit from HLS Scheme allocation for government (Natural England); w_r the regional weight reflecting relative regional environmental values; eb the environmental benefit per hectare entered into HLS, a decreasing function of q_r (the function is assumed the same across regions); Q the total quantity of environmental service over England (sum of q_r for all regions r); q_r the quantity of environmental service in region r; $q_{i,j,r}$ the quantity of environmental service for contract i, option j and in region r; $p_{r,j}$ the regional payment rate for option j in region r (national average foregone agricultural income adjusted for regional variations).

It is assumed that eb is a decreasing function of the quantity of land offered for entry into HLS: the more the hectares entered into HLS, the lower the environmental benefit per hectare. For modelling purposes, the environmental benefit function is assumed the same within a given region (with the same landscape character) and across regions with its value depending only on the quantity of land entered into the Scheme (the consequences of relaxing this regional assumption are considered later in this analysis). However, the weighted environmental benefit per hectare for a given region ($w_r \times$ eb) varies across regions. By construction, $w_r \times$ eb also is a decreasing function of the quantity of land entered into HLS. This formalisation can be interpreted as capturing a uniform environmental non-use landscape value (i.e. scarcity and uniqueness of the environmental good) through the quantity of land entered into the Scheme, whereas the relative weighting can be interpreted as reflecting differential environmental use value of the land entered into the Scheme across regions. As such, the principal can be seen as attempting to capture the full

Does the HLS Scheme Design Reduce Adverse Selection? 373

social benefit from environmental goods and services provided by land entered into the Scheme (see Brunstad *et al.*, 1999; Fleischer and Tsur, 2000; Hanley *et al.*, 2003, 2007; Bateman *et al.*, 2006).

Under the stated assumptions and the budget constraint, the social welfare (EB)-maximising first-order condition under the budget constraint, after rearranging the terms, becomes

$$\sum_r (w_r \times \text{eb} \times q_r) \frac{\partial \ln(q_r)}{\partial Q} - \lambda \sum_{i,j,r} q_{i,j,r} p_{j,r} \frac{\partial \ln(q_{i,j,r})}{\partial Q}$$

$$= \left[\lambda \sum_{i,j,r} q_{i,j,r} p_{j,r} \frac{\partial \ln(p_{j,r})}{\partial Q} \right] - \left[\sum_r w_r \times \text{eb} \times q_r \frac{\partial \ln(w_r \times \text{eb})}{\partial Q} \right] \quad (2)$$

From equation (2), the marginal net environmental benefit for the principal from the land entered into HLS (left-hand side) can be decomposed into the net benefit obtained by varying the payment rates regionally (first term on the right-hand side) plus the net benefit obtained from the regional variation of environmental benefit per hectare between regions (second term on the right-hand side). The terms on the right-hand side of equation (2) are equal to zero for a nationally uniform scheme (nationally uniform payment rates and environmental benefits per hectare respectively). The marginal net environmental benefit for the principal from the land entered into HLS for a spatially differentiated Scheme consequently represents the cost-effectiveness gains from a reduction in adverse selection compared with a nationally uniform scheme (i.e. no explicit selection of contracts).

Following equation (2), the principal's objective function can be decomposed into two parts:

- selection of Q by varying q_r between regions for different regional payment rates $p_{r,j}$ for a given constant weighted environmental benefit per hectare (constant w_r).
- selection of Q by varying the weighted environmental benefit per hectare between regions $w_r \times \text{eb}$ for a given constant payment rate ($p_{r,j}$).

Differentiating the welfare-maximising first-order condition (equation 2) with respect to the regional payment rate $p_{r,j}$ for a given weighted environmental benefit per hectare (w_r constant across regions) leads, after rearranging, to

$$\frac{\partial \ln q_r}{\partial \ln p_{j,r}} = -1 < 0 \quad (3)$$

From equation (3), the total quantity of land Q entered into the HLS-maximising environmental benefit is such that, for each extra hectare of land entered into the Scheme, the proportion of land entered in each region is equal to the opposite of the proportional change in payment rates for the region (given the same weighted environmental benefit per hectare). This is equivalent to Hypothesis 1.

Hypothesis 1: For the same given HLS budget (and equal regional weights), the quantity admitted into HLS will be greater in regions with lower payment rates (reflecting lower foregone agricultural incomes).

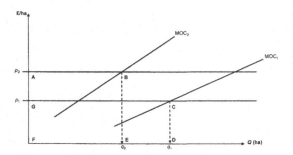

Figure 1. Comparison of land areas offered for entry between regions 1 and 2 with different marginal opportunity costs (MOC) and payment rates (p), for the same budget (ABEF = GCDF)

This implies that, for the same environmental benefit derived from each hectare of land entered into the Scheme (i.e. assuming equal regional weights), for a given budget (ABEF = GCDF in Figure 1) there is an overall associated higher total environmental benefit (Figure 1: $eb(q_2) > eb(q_1)$ by definition of eb as a decreasing function of q) because more hectares can be contracted overall by contracting in lower payment regions (region 1 in Figure 1). This has the effect of improving cost effectiveness through the mechanism of the budget constraint. Note, however, that if environmental non-use value and the agricultural OC correlate negatively (as suggested by Robinson and Sutherland, 2002; Hendrickx *et al.*, 2007), regions with lower payment rates (reflecting lower foregone agricultural incomes) would also be those of high environmental non-use value. The increased entry of land in these regions would thus further increase the total environmental benefit (as illustrated in Fraser, 2009, Table 1).[3]

If one region displays a higher environmental benefit per hectare (i.e. the total willingness to pay per hectare is higher), the objective function can be adjusted to weight one region more highly (i.e. w_r now varying across regions). Differentiating the welfare-maximising first-order condition (equation 2) with respect to the weighted environmental benefit per hectare $w_r \times eb$ for given regional payment rates per option ($p_{r,j}$ constant across regions) leads, after rearranging, to

$$\frac{\partial \ln(q_r)}{\partial \ln(w_r \times eb)} = 1 > 0. \tag{4}$$

From equation (4), the total quantity of land Q entered into the HLS-maximising environmental benefit is such that, for each extra hectare of land entered into the Scheme, the proportion of land entered in each region is equal to the proportion of (weighted) environmental benefit per hectare for that region (constant payment rates). This is equivalent to Hypothesis 2.

---

[3] The assumption of a uniform environmental benefit function can also be formally relaxed using the model in this paper. Consistent with the results in Fraser (2009), for the same given HLS budget the quantity of land contracted will be higher in the regions with higher environmental benefit per hectare for the same regional fixed payment rates per hectare (i.e. similar agricultural value). This modelling is available upon request.

Hypothesis 2: For differing regional weights, the quantity of land contracted will be higher in the regions with higher weighted environmental benefit for the same regional fixed payment rates per hectare (i.e. similar agricultural foregone incomes).

This implies that (for the same budget) regions with a higher weighted environmental benefit per hectare (region 1 in Figure 2) are likely to display a higher rate of land admitted into the HLS (from Figure 2: the entry of q in region 1 is more likely to be chosen by the principal over the entry of q in region 2, for the same budget, as it will lead to a greater weighted environmental benefit per hectare). This again has the effect of improving the cost effectiveness of the Scheme, as the principal is choosing mainly farmers from the region with higher environmental benefit per hectare, thus achieving a higher total environmental benefit given the budget constraint.

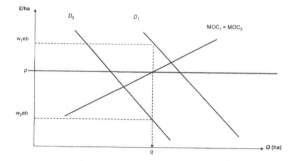

Figure 2. Comparison of the weighted environmental value of the land offered for entry between regions 1 and 2, for the same marginal opportunity costs (MOC)

In the empirical evaluation, the differential regional weights have been proxied by distances to some of the main cities (with distance inversely related to environmental value in the principal's objective function), implying that the principal allocates for a given budget proportionately more contracts in regions closer to cities (i.e. with a higher environmental benefit per hectare) than in regions with similar agricultural OC but farther from cities. For examples of this use (or recreation) value interpretation of distance, see Fleischer and Tsur (2000), Hanley *et al.* (2003) and Bateman *et al.* (2006). The use of distance as a proxy for the environmental use value of agricultural land in HLS is also consistent with the explicit aim of the HLS to promote 'public access and understanding of the countryside' (Thomson and Whitby, 1976; Defra, 2005b, p. 6; Boatman *et al.*, 2008).

In summary, this general conceptualisation of the principal's contract allocation problem characterises the principal as choosing from applicants to the HLS based on an attempt to capture both environmental non-use value of the land entered (through the quantity of land entered), and environmental use value (through the distance to cities).[4]

---

[4] We are grateful to our anonymous reviewers and the Associate Editor for pointing out this use and non-use value interpretation to us.

3. Empirical Evidence

From the above analysis, evidence that adverse selection is being reduced, and cost effectiveness thereby increased, would be a statistically significant link between the number of hectares entered into HLS in a given region and the associated regional payment rates (Hypothesis 1), and with the distance to the main cities (Hypothesis 2).

Contract data for all Environmental Stewardship tiers were provided by Natural England for nine landscape regions (Joint Character Areas) in the budget region of Yorkshire and the Humber, with some contract characteristics detailed at the option level and others at the contract level. Threshold score and budget were the same for the nine Joint Character Areas, following the national design of the Scheme. The quantity of land entered into the HLS per contract (q_{land}) and total payment received per contract for the land entered into HLS were summed for each contract for all HLS options (aggregation per contract). The average payment rate per contract was obtained by taking the ratio of the total payment received for all HLS options to the total quantity of land entered into HLS for each contract. *Mappy.co.uk* was used to estimate the fastest travelling distances to Hull (most eastern city), Leeds and Manchester (most central and south-western cities respectively) as two of the biggest conurbations in northern England (Defra, 2000) for each contract. An average of these three distances was then calculated for each contract: by construction, the greater the average distance, the farther away from the major east–west-travelling link in the study area. The data used have been summarised in Table 1.

Table 1

Variables description and statistics

Variable	Description	Units	Mean	SD	Min	Max
q_{land}	Quantity of land entered into the HLS per contract	ha	154	219	3	1,092
	Total payment received per contract for the land entered into HLS	£	100,308	118,705	2,991	564,984
ave_{pr}	Average payment rate per contract	£/ha	1,041	625	337	2,893
ave_{dist}	Average of fastest travelling distances to Hull Leeds and Manchester	km	117	23	70	171

Log-linear regressions were performed using STATA 9 (StataCorp, 2005), by regressing the quantity of land entered into HLS (q_{land}) over the payment rate per contract (ave_{pr}) and the average distance to the three main cities (ave_{dist}). The HLS data sample is truncated as HLS successful entrants are mostly selected from a population of farmers enrolling into the (O)ELS part of the Environmental Stewardship Scheme, and only operating HLS contract data were available. Both truncated and OLS regressions on the log-transformed variables for the given sample led to similar results; so, the OLS results (log-linear model) only are reported in Table 2.

Table 2

Log-linear regression results for estimating the quantity of land entered into HLS

	Coefficients
ave_{pr} (SE)	−2.0*** (0.3)
ave_{dist}	−2.5*** (0.8)
Constant	29.5*** (5.1)
N	46
R^2	0.52
Adjusted R^2	0.49
Breusch–Pagan test (heteroskedasticity)	
$\chi^2(1)$	0.21
P	0.65
Durbin–Watson	
$d(3, 46)$	2.26
P	0.65

Note: Values are significant at *10%, **5% and ***1% levels.

Under a given budget constraint and controlling for the weighted environmental benefit per hectare (distance to cities), the quantity of land entered is hypothesised to decrease for higher average payment rates (Hypothesis 1). A negative coefficient for the average payment rate per contract is consequently expected in the regression analysis. With land closer to cities having a higher environmental value per hectare, for constant payment rates, the quantity of land entered is hypothesised to decrease as the distance from the main cities increases. A negative coefficient for the average distance to main cities is thus expected in the regression analysis (Hypothesis 2).

The adjusted R^2 value is relatively high (49%) for cross-sectional data, possibly reflecting the fact that the sample is drawn from the same area with similar characteristics. All coefficients display the expected negative signs, and both the coefficients for average payment rates and for the average distance to main cities were found significant at 1%. No heteroskedasticity was detected (Breusch–Pagan/Cook–Weisberg test: $\chi^2(1) = 0.21$; $P = 0.65$). First-order autoregressive errors [AR(1)] would be the most likely to arise for the spatially ordered data but were not found statistically significant [Durbin–Watson $d(3, 46) = 2.26$].

As expected, the quantity of land entered significantly decreases as the payment rates increase (i.e. increasing foregone agricultural incomes) providing evidence that, for a given environmental non-use benefit per hectare, more land is enrolled into the HLS in lower payment regions (Hypothesis 1). Therefore, for a given budget, and given the same environmental non-use benefit per hectare for all regions, more land overall will be entered into the HLS across all regions from lower payment areas, resulting in a higher total environmental benefit from the Scheme, and an associated increase in the cost effectiveness of the Scheme.

Also as expected, the quantity of land entered is negatively related to the average distance to main cities, i.e. a decreasing quantity of land is entered for decreasing environmental value. Therefore, there is some evidence that, for regions with the same payment rate (i.e. same agricultural land value) but varying environmental benefit weights (represented by distance to the main cities), more land is enrolled into the HLS from areas of higher environmental benefit (i.e. closer to the main cities) under a given budget constraint (Hypothesis 2). Provided that the distance to the main cities (capturing use value) is a good indicator of environmental value as assumed in this case, HLS contract allocation seems to reflect some differentiation of environmental use value by region, and therefore increased cost effectiveness of the Scheme.

4. Conclusion

The Environmental Stewardship Scheme, because of incentive incompatibility and asymmetric information, has the potential for adverse selection for the land entered into the Scheme, leading to reduced cost effectiveness of the Scheme. However, we hypothesise that adverse selection into its HLS component could be reduced by the explicit selection of contracts based on environmental use and non-use benefit criteria embedded into the HLS policy design, combined with the operation of a total payment budget constraint. To evaluate these hypotheses our empirical research focuses on Scheme selection allowing both for the impact of spatially differentiated payment rates (reflecting differentiated costs of foregone agricultural income of entering HLS) in the context of uniform environmental non-use benefits and for differentiated environmental use benefits per hectare (inversely related to distances to main cities) as design mechanisms operating to reduce adverse selection and thereby increase cost effectiveness.

The results show that differences in payment rates between two regions are significantly negatively related to the amount of land admitted into the Scheme for each landscape region. This provides evidence of the capturing of increased environmental non-use benefits by exploiting spatial differentiation of payment rates, thereby reducing adverse selection, and thus increasing Scheme cost effectiveness. In addition, differences in environmental benefit weights between regions (as measured by travelling distance to cities) were found to be significantly negatively related to the amount of land admitted into the Scheme for each landscape region. For landscape regions with the same payment rates (i.e. of the same agricultural value), differential weighting of the public use benefit from environmental goods and services provided by agriculture (as measured here) thus appears to be reflected into the regulator's allocation of contracts, thereby also reducing the adverse selection problem and increasing the Scheme's cost effectiveness.

Further research could control for parish income or population, as these could be expected to influence the willingness to pay for conservation (Brunstad *et al.*, 1999). In addition, the Scheme's operation and allocation mechanisms were revised in 2008, with applications targeted spatially within the same administrative region, with an increased budget. As a result, it would be interesting to analyse contract allocation from 2008, in order to further assess the role of the budget constraint as a mechanism involved in increasing Scheme cost effectiveness.

References

Bateman, I. J., Day, B. H., Georgiou, S. and Lake, I. 'The aggregation of environmental benefit values: Welfare measures, distance decay and total WTP', *Ecological economics*, Vol. 60, (2006) pp. 450–460.

Boatman, N. D., Ramwell, C., Parry, H., Jones, N., Bishop, J., Gaskell, P., Short, C., Mills, J. and Dwyer, J. *A Review of Environmental Benefits Supplied by Agri-Environmental Schemes.* FST20/79/041 (Land Use Policy Group, 2008).

Brunstad, R. J., Gaasland, I. and Vardal, E. 'Agricultural production and the optimal level of landscape preservation', *Land Economics*, Vol. 75, (1999) pp. 538–546.

Connor, J. D., Ward, J. R. and Bryan, B. 'Exploring the cost effectiveness of land conservation auctions and payment policies', *Australian Journal of Agricultural and Resource Economics*, Vol. 52, (2008) pp. 303–319.

Defra. *Yorkshire and the Humber: Geographic Area and Physical Context.* (London: Department for Environment, Food and Rural Affairs, 2000). Edition: 1/10/2000. Last updated: 17/8/2005. Available at: http://www.defra.gov.uk/erdp/docs/yhchapter/yhsection11/default.htm. Last accessed: 22/9/2008.

Defra. *Environmental Stewardship: Look after Your Land and be Rewarded.* PB10487 (London: Department for Environment, Food and Rural Affairs, 2005a). Available at: http://www.defra.gov.uk/erdp/schemes/es/default.htm. Last accessed: 6/7/2007.

Defra. *Higher Level Stewardship handbook: Terms and conditions and how to apply.* PB10382 (London: Department for Environment, Food and Rural Affairs, 2005b). Available at: http://www.defra.gov.uk/erdp/pdfs/es/hls-handbook.pdf. Last accessed: 22/6/2007.

Feng, H. 'Green payments and dual policy goals', *Journal of Environmental Economics and Management*, Vol. 54, (2007) pp. 323–335.

Fleischer, A. and Tsur, Y. 'Measuring the recreational value of agricultural landscape', *European Review of Agricultural Economics*, Vol. 27, (2000) pp. 385–398.

Fraser, R. 'Land heterogeneity, agricultural income forgone and environmental benefit: An assessment of incentive compatibility problems in environmental stewardship schemes', *Journal of Agricultural Economics*, Vol. 60, (2009) pp. 190–201.

Fraser, R. and Fraser, I. *The Implications of Information Asymmetries for Agri-environmental Policies* (2006). Paper presented to the OECD Workshop on Information Deficiencies in Agri-environmental Policies, Paris, June. Available at: http://www.oecd.org/agr/meet/idap.

Hanley, N., Schläpfer, F. and Spurgeon, J. 'Aggregating the benefits of environmental improvements: Distance-decay functions for use and non-use values', *Journal of Environmental Management*, Vol. 68, (2003) pp. 297–304.

Hanley, N., Colombo, S., Mason, P. and Johns, H. 'The reform of support mechanisms for upland farming: Paying for public goods in the severely disadvantaged areas of England', *Journal of Agricultural Economics*, Vol. 58, (2007) pp. 433–453.

Hendrickx, F., Maelfait, J., Van Wingerden, W., Schweiger, O., Speelmans, M., Aviron, S., Augenstein, I., Billeter, R., Bailey, D., Bukacek, R., Burel, F., Diekotter, T. I. M., Dirksen, J., Herzog, F., Liira, J., Roubalova, M., Vandomme, V. and Bugter, R. O. B. 'How landscape structure, land-use intensity and habitat diversity affect components of total arthropod diversity in agricultural landscapes', *Journal of Applied Ecology*, Vol. 44, (2007) pp. 340–351.

Latacz-Lohmann, U. and Schilizzi, S. *Auctions for Conservation Contracts: A Review of the Theoretical and Empirical Literature* (2005). Project No: UKL/001/05. Available at: http://www.scotland.gov.uk/Resource/Doc/93853/0022574.pdf. Last accessed: 14/1/2008.

Moxey, A., White, B. and Ozanne, A. 'Efficient contract design for agri-environment policy', *Journal of Agricultural Economics*, Vol. 50, (1999) pp. 187–202.

OECD. *Agriculture and the Environment: Lessons Learned from a Decade of OECD Work.* (2004). Available at: http://www.oecd.org/dataoecd/15/28/33913449.pdf. Last accessed: 25/6/2007.

Robinson, R. A. and Sutherland, W. J. 'Post-war changes in arable farming and biodiversity in Great Britain', *Journal of Applied Ecology*, Vol. 39, (2002) pp. 157–176.

Schwarz, G., Moxey, A., McCracken, D., Huband, S. and Cummins, R. *An analysis of the Potential Effectiveness of a Payment-by-Results Approach to the Delivery of Environmental Public Goods and Services Supplied by Agri-Environment Schemes.* (2008). Report to the

Land Use Policy Group, UK, 108 pp. Macaulay Institute, Pareto Consulting and Scottish Agricultural College.

StataCorp. *stata Statistical Software: Release 9* (College Station, TX: StataCorp LP, 2005).

Thomson, K. J. and Whitby, M. C. 'The economics of public access in the countryside', *Journal of Agricultural Economics*, Vol. 27, (1976) pp. 307–320.

Wu, J. and Babcock, B. A. 'Contract design for the purchase of environmental goods from agriculture', *American Journal of Agricultural Economics*, Vol. 78, (1996) pp. 935–945.

JAE Journal of Agricultural Economics

Journal of Agricultural Economics, Vol. 62, No. 2, 2011, 330–339
doi: 10.1111/j.1477-9552.2011.00291.x

Chapter 13

Farmer Compensation and its Consequences for Environmental Benefit Provision in the Higher Level Stewardship Scheme

Emmanuelle Quillérou, Rob Fraser and Iain Fraser[1]

(Original submitted April 2010, revision received September 2010, accepted January 2011.)

Abstract

The Environmental Stewardship Scheme (ESS) provides payments to farmers for the provision of environmental services based on forgone agricultural income. Consequently, farmers with a relatively low opportunity cost of agricultural land will be particularly attracted to apply for entry into the ESS within a given payment region. This article tests whether there exists a significant relationship between Higher Level Stewardship (HLS) Scheme entry and agricultural yields. Empirically, HLS participation is found to be negatively related to cereal yields at the farm level. This could be associated with 'auspicious selection' of land into the Scheme, with greater 'value for money' provided by the higher entry of land with lower agricultural forgone income but higher environmental benefit within the region.

Keywords: *Agri-environment*; *contract*; *Environmental Stewardship*; *principal-agent*.

JEL classifications: *D78, D82, H44, Q18, Q58.*

1. Introduction

In Quillérou and Fraser (2010), we focused on the English Higher Level Stewardship (HLS) Environmental Scheme's contract allocation between regions, where we showed that the budget constraint on total payments to farmers encourages the

[1] Emmanuelle Quillérou was a PhD student at the Kent Business School, University of Kent, Canterbury, CT2 7PE, UK. E-mail: emmanuelle_quillerou@yahoo.fr for correspondence. Rob Fraser is Professor of Agricultural Economics at the School of Economics of the University of Kent, and also Adjunct Professor of Agricultural and Resource Economics at the University of Western Australia. Iain Fraser is a Reader in Agri-Environmental Economics at the School of Economics, University of Kent. We are particularly grateful to the Editor-in-Chief, as well as to two anonymous reviewers for their very helpful comments on previous versions.

selection of land in 'low cost' regions. As long as 'low cost' regions provide similar environmental benefits to 'high cost' regions, the budget constraint on spending potentially improves overall cost-effectiveness. In this note, we focus on an empirical assessment of farmers' HLS option selection for entry into the Scheme within a given payment region.

Since 1992, the Common Agricultural Policy has been subject to a series of reforms that have gradually transferred support from agricultural production toward the provision of environmental goods and services. Under the WTO, these payments are constrained to 'the extra costs or loss of income involved in complying with the government programme' (annex 2, articles 1 and 12, WTO, 2009). Since 2005, the main agri-environmental scheme in England has been the Environmental Stewardship Scheme (ESS) (Defra, 2005). ESS is a national scheme composed of two tiers: the lower tier Entry Level Stewardship/Organic Entry Level Stewardship (ELS/OELS) Schemes with general agri-environmental requirements; the higher tier HLS Scheme with more specific environmental requirements and higher levels of environmental commitment.

The ELS Scheme employs a whole-farm approach. Any farmer and landowner can participate and receive a five-year contract (Defra, 2005). The ELS Scheme relies on self-selection by farmers of the environmental options they will undertake from a prespecified 'menu'. For each option selected there is a corresponding number of points reflecting the nationally estimated agricultural income forgone (Defra, 2005). An ELS/OELS Scheme agreement is guaranteed providing a farmer meets a 30-point (60-point) target per hectare. This in turn yields a corresponding payment of £30/ha (£60/ha) (Defra, 2005).

The higher tier HLS Scheme targets more complex types of agri-environmental activities and land use management (Defra, 2005). In common with the ELS Scheme, it is left to an individual farmer to select farm-specific land management options from a prespecified set for each of which there is a predetermined fixed per unit payment. However, entry into the HLS Scheme is at the discretion of Natural England, the operating authority. Natural England selects applications by employing a scoring and threshold mechanism and selecting contracts that provide 'good "value for money"' (Defra, 2005).

The spatial differentiation from 2005 to 2007 has been based on the 159 Joint Character Areas and areas of the English countryside with 'similar' landscape character, each with a specific association of wildlife and natural features (Defra, 2005, 2006). Each of the Joint Character Areas has a corresponding set of environmental targets against which bids submitted to the HLS Scheme are scored, with additional points for enhancing a Site of Special Scientific Interest (SSSI) or a Scheduled Monument (Defra, 2005). All scored applications are then pooled for all Joint Character Areas within the same administrative region (roughly corresponding to Government Office Regions). Finally, a threshold entry decision criterion (i.e. cut-off score) is set for all Joint Character Areas within the same administrative region, reflecting the available budget for the Scheme, and all applications that attain a score greater than the regional threshold are offered a contract. The scheme targeting was revised in 2008 with the adoption of a map-based targeting overlapping the Joint Character Areas.

On the basis of recent evidence, the relationship between the forgone agricultural income (the approximate basis for the HLS Scheme menu prices) and the environmental *physical* benefits provided by conservation schemes seems to be limited at best (Naidoo and Iwamura, 2007; Haines-Young, 2009), or negative (Goulding, 2000; Dallimer *et al.*, 2009; Hanley *et al.*, 2009; Kleijn *et al.*, 2009). This suggests a negative correlation between the forgone agricultural income and *social* environmental value. If so, the HLS Scheme is incentive compatible and is probably to be associated with an 'auspicious selection'[2] of land, with higher 'value for money' (Defra, 2005), contrary to Fraser and Fraser (2006) and Fraser (2009).

To date, the economics literature on adverse selection in agri-environmental scheme design and implementation has been based on theoretical analyses of contract design mechanisms (Wu and Babcock, 1996; Moxey *et al.*, 1999; Feng, 2007). Currently, there exists very little research that has attempted to examine this information problem empirically. The examples that do exist in the literature have considered policy cost-effectiveness issues relating to auction mechanisms (Stoneham *et al.*, 2003; Latacz-Lohmann and Schilizzi, 2005; Connor *et al.*, 2008; Windle and Rolfe, 2008) or to (spatial) benefit targeting (Langpap *et al.*, 2008; Hajkowicz, 2009; Merckx *et al.*, 2009). One exception (Quillérou and Fraser, 2010) focused on HLS Scheme contract allocation between (landscape) regions.

In Section 2, we test whether a significant relationship exists between HLS Scheme entry and agricultural yields. We then discuss the consequences of this finding for environmental benefit provision, and the achievement of 'good "value for money"' (Defra, 2005). The final section of the article provides a summary and conclusions.

2. Data, Analysis and Results

In this section, we test whether a significant relationship exists between HLS Scheme entry and agricultural yields.

The farm-level data used for this analysis come from a survey collected and described in Bailey *et al.* (2009). This survey includes various farm characteristics (size, farm type); agricultural characteristics (crops, yields, prices, self-assessed profitability relative to similar farms in the same area); environmental scheme characteristics (in particular HLS, ELS, Countryside Stewardship Scheme, Environmentally Sensitive Area scheme); socio-economic characteristics (farm status of respondents, in full-time or part-time farming, years in farming); and postcode (area code only). Agricultural yields for the complete dataset have been found to be in line with national averages by Bailey *et al.* (2009), so the data can be considered reasonably representative. Most of the data are on arable or mixed farms. There has been a relatively high uptake of the HLS Scheme by cereal farms: 27% of number of farmers and 40% of the area (Boatman *et al.*, 2007). For the sample data, each farm was spatially matched with government office regions using its postcode area (using ArcGIS, ESRI, 2006). Postcode areas often overlap across several government office regions, hence only entries that could be allocated to a single government office region were retained for the analysis. This yielded a sample of 135 observations.

Fifty-eight percent of the sample farms are in the HLS Scheme or intend to enter in the next three years, which is much higher than the national average (0.5% of holdings in 2006) (Boatman *et al.*, 2007). This over-representation of HLS Scheme

---

[2] We are grateful to an anonymous reviewer for pointing this out and suggesting this term.

farmers could limit the generalisation of the results to the full farmer population for this empirical analysis. Differences in yield averages between crops are mostly due to the number of zero-observations, and not to a difference in the range of yields. Sample observations were mostly in the South East and the South West, which is in keeping with actual HLS Scheme contracts (Boatman *et al.*, 2007). But, our sample has the lowest number of farms in the North West instead of Yorkshire and the Humber.

Although the preferred dependent variable is the quantity of land entered into the HLS Scheme per farm, these data are not available from this dataset. An indicator of whether farms were already entered into the HLS Scheme, or intended to enter within the next three years, was used. Therefore, a binary variable (i.e. HLS Scheme entry/non-entry) was constructed to include both current entries and intended entries. All intended entries were considered as effective entries, as most farms were already enrolled into the Environmentally Sensitive Area Scheme or Countryside Stewardship Scheme (both schemes have now been replaced by the Environmental Stewardship), or into the ELS Scheme (lower tier).

In terms of independent variables, farm size (Total farm area) was included as this has previously been found to potentially influence participation in agri-environmental schemes (Bonnieux *et al.*, 1998; Boatman *et al.*, 2007; Defrancesco *et al.*, 2008; Hynes and Garvey, 2009). More generally, the adoption of the latest English agri-environmental schemes has been found to depend on farm structural characteristics and farm size. For example, these agri-environmental schemes are often less attractive for intensive production systems and smaller holdings. Also, scheme participation tends to be higher for cereal farms (Boatman *et al.*, 2007).

The number of arable crops (Number of crops) was employed as an explanatory variable, as the sum of the types of wheat and barley cropped. The number of farm activities (Number of farm activities) was derived from the types of farm recorded in the dataset (one activity for arable only or livestock only farms, two for mixed farms), as this is expected to influence participation (Boatman *et al.*, 2007; Hynes and Garvey, 2009).

Yield variables for different cereal crops (i.e. wheat for milling or animal feed, barley for animal feed) and other crops (as surveyed) were included as explanatory variables.

A question asking farmers to self-assess their relative level of profitability was included in the questionnaire. This information has been used by employing two dummy variables that take the form less profitable and more profitable, with the classification equally profitable retained as the reference level. Farmer status was included in the analysis as a dummy variable (one for farm manager and zero for farm owner or tenant farmer). To date in the literature there is mixed evidence regarding the impact of farm tenure on Scheme participation (see Wynn *et al.*, 2001; Defrancesco *et al.*, 2008; Hynes and Garvey, 2009). We also included a dummy variable of whether respondents were in full-time agriculture (Full-time) as opposed to part-time farming or agribusiness.

The number of years (Year decider) respondents have been the main decision-makers on the farm is included as an explanatory variable, as farmer age has been found as a significant explanatory variable in previous studies (e.g. Bonnieux *et al.*, 1998; Wynn *et al.*, 2001; Hynes and Garvey, 2009). Education level, measured as a category variable, is also included, which has been found to be negatively related to participation in agri-environmental schemes by previous research studies (Bonnieux *et al.*, 1998; Defrancesco *et al.*, 2008).

Finally, government office region dummies were included so as to control for between-region variations (with the East of England region taken as reference) of agricultural and environmental characteristics and of different HLS Scheme budgets.

In summary, the explanatory variables used to determine entry to the HLS Scheme are: total farm area; number of different crops (for wheat and barley); number of farm activities; yields of three crops (milling wheat, feed wheat and barley); relative level of profitability (dummies); type of farmer (farm manager by reference to farm owner and tenant farmer); number of years as main decision-maker (Year decider); and government office regions (dummies). A statistical summary of the variables employed is reported in the Appendix (Table A1).[3]

Given the form of the dependent variable, we employed limited-dependent variable regression methods. A logit regression model was estimated with the marginal effects reported in Table 1. These are calculated at the point of the sample mean.

The pseudo R^2 value is low (16% – Table 1), as expected for cross-sectional data. The Likelihood Ratio (LR) Chi-squared test statistic is significantly different from zero (*P*-value of 0.0859), suggesting the parameters are jointly significant. Nevertheless, only five of the explanatory variables are significantly related to entry to the HLS Scheme.

The total farm area and number of crops (structural factors) have a significant positive influence on HLS Scheme entry (respectively at a 10% and 5% level of significance), which is consistent with the findings of Boatman *et al.* (2007). The marginal effect for total farm area is, however, very low (0.0% increase in HLS participation for each extra hectare of farm land).

The marginal effects for yields of wheat and barley for feed crops are also found statistically significant (respectively at a 5% and 10% level of significance). Being in full-time agriculture has a positive influence on HLS Scheme entry (at a 5% level of significance), contrary to the findings of Hynes *et al.* (2008) for the Irish REPS. This discrepancy could be due to the HLS Scheme being designed as the highest tier of the ESS, globally more environmentally demanding and with 10-year agreements. It could also be due to differences in farming in England and Ireland, or to differences in Scheme design especially with respect to the types of environmental goods and services being valued or the type of farming implicitly supported.

Most of the explanatory variables suggested in the literature have not been found significant here. This would suggest that there is no simple and reliable theoretical model of participation appropriate for this dataset.

In summary, entry (i.e. participation) in the HLS Scheme significantly decreases with increasing yields of crops for feed wheat and barley within the different government regions (as no regional dummy was found significant). This result implies

---

[3] All estimations were performed using Stata 9 (StataCorp, 2005). All pairs of variables display very low correlation coefficients, with most coefficients < 20% for each pair of variables. The correlation coefficient between the number of farm activities and each of the crop yields is between 40% and 50%. The correlation coefficient between Total farm area and the Farm manager dummy is the highest at around 52%. These coefficients are reported here in relation to the possible existence of collinearity, which appears limited.

Farmer Compensation and its Consequences for Environmental Provision   335

Table 1

Logit regression results of HLS Scheme participation

Variable	Marginal effects	
	dy/dx	SE
Total farm area	0.000*	0.000
Number of crops	0.216**	0.098
Number of farm activities	0.143	0.109
Yield wheat milling	−0.018	0.017
Yield wheat feed	−0.033**	0.015
Yield barley feed	−0.035*	0.018
Yield other crops	0.005	0.008
Less profitable	0.019	0.161
More profitable	−0.086	0.128
Farm manager	−0.157	0.181
Full-time	0.312**	0.153
Year decider	−0.003	0.005
Education	0.041	0.048
East Midlands	−0.090	0.168
North East	0.215	0.197
North West	0.114	0.282
South East	−0.014	0.163
South West	−0.233	0.151
West Midlands	−0.181	0.212
Yorkshire and the Humber	−0.078	0.190
Number of observations	135	
Log-likelihood	−77.39	
LR χ^2 (20)	29.10*	
Pseudo R^2	0.158	

Notes: *, significant at a 10% level; **, significant at a 5% level; ***, significant at a 1% level of significance.

that there is some evidence of farmers entering land of lower agricultural quality (yield) than average into the HLS Scheme. This finding is consistent with the results of studies by Shoemaker (1989), Osterberg (1999, cited by Ferraro, 2008), Osterburg and Nieberg (1999, cited by Latacz-Lohmann and Schilizzi, 2005), and Osterburg (2001), which showed higher participation rates in regions of poorer soils, lower yields and a lower share of intensive crops, and a generally lower intensity of land use (hill areas). In addition, this finding is consistent with the most recent studies of higher participation in the Irish agri-environmental scheme (REPS) for more extensive systems of farming (less environmentally degrading) or for lower soil quality (Hynes and Garvey, 2009).

The study of Rygnestad and Fraser (1996) showed that farmers had an incentive to set aside their lower yielding land to minimise the impact of the set-aside requirement on their production income. This 'adverse selection' of lower yielding land by farmers reduced the cost-effectiveness of the policy's attempts to reduce output. However, Rygnestad and Fraser (1996) also showed that this lower yielding land exhibited greater potential for nitrate leaching from fertiliser application, resulting

336   *Emmanuelle Quillérou, Rob Fraser and Iain Fraser*

in an 'auspicious selection' of land set aside from the perspective of environmental benefits.

In the context of this study, such 'auspicious selection' would also be occurring if the lower yielding land being offered for participation in the HLS Scheme was similarly providing a greater environmental benefit in terms of reduced nitrate leaching or enhanced habitat provision than other land not being offered for participation. Moreover, if such a negative correlation between agricultural income and environmental benefit could be demonstrated to apply for land selected into the HLS Scheme, then this finding would imply improved cost-effectiveness of the Scheme. This would further support the findings of Quillérou and Fraser (2010) regarding the beneficial impact of design features of the HLS Scheme on its cost-effectiveness.

3. Conclusion

This article has examined the selection by farmers of land for entry into the HLS Scheme within a region of common payments for participation. Section 2 of this article focused on determinants of farmers' participation in the HLS Scheme, including cereal yields.

The results show that HLS Scheme participation as measured here is not well explained by the variation in most of the explanatory variables suggested in the literature. In our sample, participation is significantly influenced by the yields of feed wheat and barley, total farm area, the number of crops and whether farmers are in full-time agriculture. Within a given region, farmer participation in the HLS Scheme is significantly negative related to farm yields. These results might, however, not be representative of the whole farmer population in relation to the over-representation of HLS Scheme farmers in the sample. The regional effects might also not be found significant here because of the dataset regional spread and structure.

The same type of analysis could be applied to types of options other than just the arable ones (e.g. for grassland options). It would also be interesting to apply the same approach, controlling for landscape regions (lower geographical level than government office regions), to test whether the relationship holds at a lower level of analysis.

Nevertheless, the Scheme objective – the provision of 'good "value for money"' (Defra, 2005) – would be achieved so long as there is a negative correlation between environmental benefit and the opportunity cost of provision (yield), as suggested by empirical studies. In this case, the Scheme would result in 'auspicious' rather than adverse selection, with lower yielding/higher environmental benefit land being enrolled in the HLS Scheme. In addition, this within-region finding would further support the between-region design benefit features of the HLS Scheme identified by Quillérou and Fraser (2010).

References

Bailey, A. S., Bertaglia, M., Fraser, I. M., Sharma, A. and Douarin, E. 'Integrated pest management portfolios in UK arable farming: Results of a farmer survey', *Pest Management Science*, Vol. 65, (2009) pp. 1030–1039.

Boatman, N., Jones, N., Garthwaite, D. and Bishop, J. *Evaluation of the Introduction and Operation of Environmental Stewardship: Final report*. Defra project No. MA01028. (York:

Central Science Laboratory, 2007). Available at: http://randd.defra.gov.uk/Document. aspx?Document = MA01028_6197_FRP.pdf (last accessed 4 February 2008).

Bonnieux, F., Rainelli, P. and Vermersch, D. 'Estimating the supply of environmental benefits by agriculture: A French case study', *Environmental and Resource Economics*, Vol. 11, (1998) pp. 135–153.

Connor, J. D., Ward, J. R. and Bryan, B. 'Exploring the cost effectiveness of land conservation auctions and payment policies', *Australian Journal of Agricultural and Resource Economics*, Vol. 52, (2008) pp. 303–319.

Dallimer, M., Acs, S., Hanley, N., Wilson, P., Gaston, K. J. and Armsworth, P. 'What explains property-level variation in avian diversity? An inter-disciplinary approach', *Journal of Applied Ecology*, Vol. 46, (2009) pp. 647–656.

Defra. *Higher Level Stewardship Handbook: Terms and Conditions and how to Apply.* PB10382. (Department for Environment, Food and Rural Affairs, 2005). Available at: http://www.defra.gov.uk/erdp/pdfs/es/hls-handbook.pdf (last accessed 22 June 2007).

Defra. *Targeting Statements.* (Department for Environment, Food and Rural Affairs, 2006). Available at: http://www.defra.gov.uk/erdp/schemes/jca-ts/default.htm (last accessed 30 January 2008).

Defrancesco, E., Gatto, P., Runge, F. and Trestini, S. 'Factors affecting farmers' participation in agri-environmental measures: A northern Italian perspective', *Journal of Agricultural Economics*, Vol. 59, (2008) pp. 114–131.

ESRI. ArcGIS Desktop: Release 9.2. (ESRI, 2006).

Feng, H. 'Green payments and dual policy goals', *Journal of Environmental Economics and Management*, Vol. 54, (2007) pp. 323–335.

Ferraro, P. J. 'Asymmetric information and contract design for payments for environmental services', *Ecological Economics*, Vol. 65, (2008) pp. 810–821.

Fraser, R. 'Land heterogeneity, agricultural income forgone and environmental benefit: An assessment of incentive compatibility problems in Environmental Stewardship Schemes', *Journal of Agricultural Economics*, Vol. 60, (2009) pp. 190–201.

Fraser, R. and Fraser, I. The implications of information asymmetries for agri-environmental policies. Paper Presented to the OECD Workshop on Information Deficiencies in Agri-Environmental Policies, June, (Paris, 2006). Available at: http://www.oecd.org/agr/meet/idap.

Goulding, K. 'Nitrate leaching from arable and horticultural land', *Soil Use and Management*, Vol. 16, (2000) pp. 145–151.

Haines-Young, R. 'Land use and biodiversity relationships', *Land Use Policy*, Vol. 26 (Suppl. 1), (2009) pp. S178–S186.

Hajkowicz, S. 'The evolution of Australia's natural resource management programs: Towards improved targeting and evaluation of investments', *Land Use Policy*, Vol. 26, (2009) pp. 471–478.

Hanley, N., Tinch, D., Angelopoulos, K., Davies, A., Barbier, E. B. and Watson, F. 'What drives long-run biodiversity change? New insights from combining economics, palaeoecology and environmental history', *Journal of Environmental Economics and Management*, Vol. 57, (2009) pp. 5–20.

Hynes, S. and Garvey, E. 'Modelling farmers' participation in an agri-environmental scheme using panel data: An application to the rural environment protection scheme in Ireland', *Journal of Agricultural Economics*, Vol. 60, (2009) pp. 546–562.

Hynes, S., Farrelly, N., Murphy, E. and O'Donoghue, C. 'Modelling habitat conservation and participation in agri-environmental schemes: A spatial microsimulation approach', *Ecological Economics*, Vol. 66, (2008) pp. 258–269.

Kleijn, D., Kohler, F., Báldi, A., Batáry, P., Concepción, E. D., Clough, Y., Díaz, M., Gabriel, D., Holzschuh, A., Knop, E., Kovács, A., Marshall, E. J. P., Tscharntke, T. and Verhulst, J. 'On the relationship between farmland biodiversity and land-use intensity in Europe', *Proceedings of the Royal Society B*, Vol. 276, (2009) pp. 903–909.

338   *Emmanuelle Quillérou, Rob Fraser and Iain Fraser*

Langpap, C., Hascic, I. and Wu, J. 'Protecting watershed ecosystems through targeted local land use policies', *American Journal of Agricultural Economics*, Vol. 90, (2008) pp. 684–700.

Latacz-Lohmann, U. and Schilizzi, S. *Auctions for Conservation Contracts: A Review of the Theoretical and Empirical Literature*. Report to the Scottish Executive Environment and Rural Affairs Department Project No: UKL/001/05. (2005), Available at: http://www.scotland.gov.uk/Resource/Doc/93853/0022574.pdf (last accessed 14 January 2008).

Merckx, T., Feber, R. E., Riordan, P., Townsend, M. C., Bourn, N. A. D., Parsons, M. S. and Macdonald, D. W. 'Optimizing the biodiversity gain from agri-environment schemes', *Agriculture, Ecosystems & Environment*, Vol. 130, (2009) pp. 177–182.

Moxey, A., White, B. and Ozanne, A. 'Efficient contract design for agri-environment policy', *Journal of Agricultural Economics*, Vol. 50, (1999) pp. 187–202.

Naidoo, R. and Iwamura, T. 'Global-scale mapping of economic benefits from agricultural lands: Implications for conservation priorities', *Biological Conservation*, Vol. 140, (2007) pp. 40–49.

Osterberg, B. Agri-environment programmes in Germany – implementation, acceptance and aspects of their evaluation. *1st Workshop on the Management and Monitoring of Agri-Environment Schemes*, 23–24 November, (Ispra, Italy, 1999).

Osterburg, B. 'Agri-environmental programs and the use of soil conservation measures in Germany', in D. E. Stott, R. H. Mohtar and G. C. Steinhardt (ed.) *Sustaining the Global Farm – Selected Papers from the 10th International Soil Conservation Organization Meeting, May 24–29, 1999*. (West Lafayette: International Soil Conservation Organization in cooperation with the USDA and Purdue University, 2001, pp. 112–118).

Osterburg, B. and Nieberg, H. Regional acceptance of agri-environmental schemes and their impacts on production, incomes and environment – the case of Germany. *IX European Congress of Agricultural Economists*, 24–28 August, (Warsaw, Poland, 1999).

Quillérou, E. and Fraser, R. 'Adverse selection in the Environmental Stewardship Scheme: Does the Higher Level Stewardship Scheme design reduce adverse selection?' *Journal of Agricultural Economics*, Vol. 61, (2010) pp. 369–380.

Rygnestad, H. L. and Fraser, R. W. 'Land heterogeneity and the effectiveness of CAP set-aside', *Journal of Agricultural Economics*, Vol. 47, (1996) pp. 255–260.

Shoemaker, R. 'Agricultural land values and rents under the conservation reserve program', *Land Economics*, Vol. 65, (1989) pp. 131–137.

StataCorp. Stata Statistical Software: Release 9. (College Station, TX: StataCorp LP, 2005).

Stoneham, G., Chaudhri, V., Ha, A. and Strappazzon, L. 'Auctions for conservation contracts: An empirical examination of Victoria's BushTender trial', *Australian Journal of Agricultural and Resource Economics*, Vol. 47, (2003) pp. 477–500.

Windle, J. and Rolfe, J. 'Exploring the efficiencies of using competitive tenders over fixed price grants to protect biodiversity in Australian rangelands', *Land Use Policy*, Vol. 25, (2008) 388–398.

WTO. *Legal Texts: Marrakesh Agreement*. (WTO, 2009) Available at: http://www.wto.org/english/docs_e/legal_e/14-ag_02_e.htm (last accessed 15 December 2009).

Wu, J. and Babcock, B. A. 'Contract design for the purchase of environmental goods from agriculture', *American Journal of Agricultural Economics*, Vol. 78, (1996) pp. 935–945.

Wynn, G., Crabtree, B. and Potts, J. 'Modelling farmer entry into the environmentally sensitive area schemes in Scotland', *Journal of Agricultural Economics*, Vol. 52, (2001) pp. 65–82.

Farmer Compensation and its Consequences for Environmental Provision   339

Appendix

Table A1

Variable description and statistics of regression sample ($N = 135$)

Variable	Units	Mean	SD	Min	Max
HLS entry	Dummy	0.58	0.50	0	1
Total farm area	ha	385.21	439.72	5.26	2,374.00
Number of crops		1.70	0.91	0	4
Number of farm activities		1.50	0.50	1	2
Yield wheat milling	t/ha	3.62	4.26	0	10.20
Yield wheat feed	t/ha	5.36	4.25	0	11.25
Yield barley feed	t/ha	2.44	3.43	0	10.00
Yield other crops	t/ha	2.97	8.90	0	101.00
Less Profitable	Dummy	0.11	0.32	0	1
More Profitable	Dummy	0.24	0.43	0	1
Farm manager	Dummy	0.14	0.35	0	1
Full-time	Dummy	0.88	0.32	0	1
Year decider	Years	21.80	11.58	0	55
Education	Categories	3.78	1.10	1	5
East Midlands	Dummy	0.13	0.33	0	1
North East	Dummy	0.07	0.25	0	1
North West	Dummy	0.02	0.15	0	1
South East	Dummy	0.14	0.35	0	1
South West	Dummy	0.19	0.40	0	1
West Midlands	Dummy	0.06	0.24	0	1
Yorkshire and the Humber	Dummy	0.10	0.30	0	1

JAE Journal of Agricultural Economics

Journal of Agricultural Economics, Vol. 63, No. 1, 2012, 56–64
doi: 10.1111/j.1477-9552.2011.00327.x

Chapter 14

Moral Hazard, Targeting and Contract Duration in Agri-Environmental Policy

Rob Fraser[1]

(Original submitted April 2011, revision received July 2011, accepted September 2011.)

Abstract

This article extends the multi-period agri-environmental contract model of Fraser (Journal of Agricultural Economics, Vol. 55, (2004) pp. 525–540) to include a more realistic specification of the inter-temporal penalties for non-compliance, and therefore of the inter-temporal moral hazard problem in agri-environmental policy design. It is shown that a farmer has an unambiguous preference for cheating early over cheating late in the contract period based on differences in the expected cost of compliance. It is then shown how the principal can make use of this unambiguous preference to target monitoring resources intertemporally, and in so doing, to encourage full contract duration compliance.

Keywords: *Agri-environmental policy; contract duration; moral hazard; targeting.*

JEL classifications: *D86, Q18, Q58.*

1. Introduction

In the last decade or so researchers have begun investigating the moral hazard problem in relation to agri-environmental policy. In such policies, farmers voluntarily participate in the production of environmental goods and services in return for payment. However, farmers are also required to incur costs in providing these goods and services. As a consequence, farmers have an incentive not to comply with these requirements, depending both on their likelihood of avoiding detection, and on the penalties for non-compliance if caught cheating. It follows that the policy design problem is to manage farmer behaviour to minimise the negative impact of the moral hazard problem on the policy's cost-effectiveness (see Choe and Fraser, 1999; Ozanne *et al.*, 2001; Fraser, 2002). However, virtually all these studies, including the most recent, have framed the policy design problem within an atemporal context, choosing instead to investigate a range of circumstantial complications such as heterogeneity among farmers and the relative effectiveness of alternative policy mechanisms (see Lankoski and Ollikainen, 2003; Kampas and

---

[1] Rob Fraser is with the School of Economics, University of Kent. E-mail: r.w.fraser@kent.ac.uk for correspondence.
I am grateful to two anonymous reviewers and the Editor for their helpful comments on previous versions of this paper.

White, 2004; Hart and Latacz-Lohmann, 2005; Ozanne and White, 2007; Lanko-ski *et al.*, 2010). This static framing of the policy design problem, while justifiable in terms of keeping the theoretical specification of the problem manageable, is nevertheless in clear contrast to the design of actual agri-environmental policies, which are typically based on a multi-year contract duration. For example, Natural England (2010) specifies a 10-year contract period for the Higher Level Steward-ship Scheme.

One exception to these static studies of the moral hazard problem in agri-environ-mental policy design is Fraser (2004), which uses a multi-period framework to investigate the potential benefits of 'targeting' the use of monitoring resources to enforce compliance. In Fraser's multi-period model this 'targeting' involves separat-ing farmers into two groups for monitoring purposes: those who have previously been caught cheating; and those who have not.[2]

However, while Fraser's multi-period model enables farmer behaviour to be managed over time to improve policy cost-effectiveness, his specification of the farmer's dynamic decision problem is very simple. In particular, the penalties for non-compliance are specified as being independent of the time period within which non-compliance is detected. Moreover, this static specification of penalties is in contrast to actual agri-environmental policies where there is typically a clear inter-temporal dimension to the penalties for non-compliance. For example, for Natural England's Higher Level Stewardship Scheme (HLS), it is stated that pen-alties may involve the withholding of 'part or all of any future payments due under your agreement' as well as the recovery of (with 'interest charged') 'part or all of the payments already made to you under the agreement' (Natural England, 2010, p. 11).

It should be recognised that each of the above components of the HLS policy's penalty system is designed to mitigate different aspects of the inter-temporal moral hazard problem. Specifically, by threatening farmers with the withholding of future payments if caught not complying, Natural England is discouraging such farmers from cheating early in the contract period for fear of losing all future benefits of participation; and by threatening farmers with the recovery (with 'interest charged') of past payments if caught not complying, Natural England is discouraging such farmers from cheating late in the contract period for fear of having to repay all past benefits of participation.

The aim of this article was to extend the multi-period model of Fraser (2004) so that it contains a more realistic specification of inter-temporal penalties, and there-fore of the inter-temporal moral hazard problem. In so doing, it will investigate both the relative incentives for farmers to cheat early and/or late in their contract period, and the potential for the principal to use the targeting of monitoring resources to further mitigate the inter-temporal moral hazard problem.[3]

The structure of the article is as follows. Section 2 first sets out the extension of the multi-period model of Fraser (2004) so that it contains an inter-temporal specifi-

---

[2] See Heyes (2000) for a review of other regulation literature which analyses the concept of 'targeting'.

[3] Literature in this context seems very thin. One exception is Rice and Sen (2008), which examines the inter-temporal moral hazard problem in relation to basketball players in the WBA.

Rob Fraser

cation of the penalties for non-compliance. It then examines the implications of this specification for a farmer's incentives to cheat early and/or late in the contract period. In particular, it is shown that a farmer will have an unambiguous preference for cheating early over cheating late, although cheating all the time, or none of the time, may be superior alternatives to occasional cheating. Next, section 3 provides a numerical analysis of the model of section 2. This numerical analysis enables both an evaluation of the role of the main parameter values of the model in determining farmer behaviour, and an evaluation of the potential for the targeting of monitoring resources to further mitigate the inter-temporal moral hazard problem. The paper concludes with a summary of the paper's implications for agri-environmental policy design.

2. The Model

2.1 Extending the model of Fraser (2004)

Fraser (2004) uses a two-period decision context to capture the 'early' and 'late' aspects of contract duration for a risk-averse farmer. In this context the farmer considers the present value of expected utility from four alternatives (with no allowance for altruistic or public good motivations):

1 complying in both periods;
2 complying in the first period, but not the second;
3 complying in the second period, but not the first;
4 not complying in both periods.

The farmer's income (I_i) in each period of complying is given by:

$$I_i = B + x - y \qquad (1)$$

where:

I_i = income in period i (i = 1, 2);
B = income independent of participation;[4]
x = payment for participating;
y = cost of complying; and
x > y.

Note that if the farmer chooses not to comply, and is not caught, then:

---

[4] Note that specifying B to be known with certainty excludes a role for uncertain production income in determining compliance behaviour such as has been analysed by Fraser (2002) and Yano and Blandford (2009). These studies show that risk averse farmers are less likely to comply in the presence of uncertain production income if compliance risk is a substitute for production income risk (i.e. land taken out of production), but more likely to comply if non-compliance increases overall income risk. This general effect has been excluded in what follows in order to simplify the analysis of the interplay between contract duration and compliance behaviour. But in this context it could influence the choice between full and occasional non-compliance depending on its specification. I am grateful to an anonymous reviewer for pointing this out to me.

Moral Hazard, Targeting and Contract Duration in Agri-Environmental Policy 59

$$I_i = B + x. \tag{2}$$

However, if the farmer chooses not to comply, and is caught, then a penalty is incurred.

In Fraser (2004) this penalty was specified simply as a proportion of the payment for participating in that period (i.e. x), and was therefore independent of the contract duration.[5] In what follows this feature of the model of Fraser (2004) is modified to reflect an inter-temporal penalty system. Specifically, a farmer caught cheating in period 1 is penalised not just by the recovery of the payment for participation in that period (i.e. x), but also by the withdrawal of future benefits through exclusion from participation in period 2. As outlined previously, this feature of the penalty system is designed to discourage cheating early in the contract period. In addition, a farmer caught cheating in period 2 is penalised not just by the recovery of the payment for participation in that period (i.e. x), but also by the recovery, with interest, of the payment for participation in period 1 (i.e. $x (1 + r)$; where $r =$ the rate of interest), to discourage cheating late in the contract period.

Inserting this penalty system into the model of Fraser (2004) means that the present value of the expected utility ($E(U)$) from the four alternative farmer behaviours is given by[6]:

$$U(I_{TTT2}) = U(B + x - y) + U(B + x - y)/(1 + r) \tag{3}$$

$$EU(I_{TIC2}) = U(B + x - y) + (pU(B + x) + (1 - p)U(B - x(1 + r)))/(1 + r) \tag{4}$$

$$EU(I_{CIT2}) = p(U(B + x) + U(B + x - y)/(1 + r)) + (1 - p)(U(B) + U(B)/(1 + r)) \tag{5}$$

$$EU(I_{CIC2}) = pU(B + x) + (1 - p)U(B) + (p(pU(B + x) + (1 - p)U(B - x(1 + r))) \\ + (1 - p)U(B))/(1 + r) \tag{6}$$

where:

$p =$ probability of not being monitored in each period;

$U(I_{TTT2}) =$ present value of utility of income from complying in both periods;

$EU(I_{TIC2}) =$ present value of expected utility of income from complying in period 1, but not in period 2;

$EU(I_{CIT2}) =$ present value of expected utility of income from not complying in period 1, but complying in period 2;

$EU(I_{CIC2}) =$ present value of expected utility of income from not complying in both periods.

Note that in equations (3–6) it has been assumed that the probability of not being monitored is known in advance by the farmer, and is the same in both periods. The

---

[5] Note, however that with the introduction of targeting in Fraser (2004) a farmer caught cheating in period 1 would also experience an increase in the probability of being monitored in period 2.

[6] In what follows, the subscript 'T' represents complying behaviour (symbolising 'truthful behaviour'), whereas the subscript 'C' represents cheating behaviour.

Rob Fraser

latter assumption will be relaxed subsequently to consider the potential benefits of inter-temporal targeting of participants. Note also that the rate of discount of future income has been assumed equal to the rate of interest charged on recovered payments for participation within the penalty system.

An examination of equations (3–6) reveals that the key policy parameters in determining the relative size of utility from always complying with expected utility from always not complying are the probability of not being monitored (p) and the relative size of benefits and costs of complying ($x-y$). For example, if p is relatively low and ($x-y$) is relatively high, then it is expected that the farmer would comply in both periods, whereas if p is relatively high and ($x-y$) is relatively low, then it is expected that the farmer would not comply in both periods.

However, further evaluation of the relative size of equations (3–6), and in particular the size of equations (4) and (5) relative to equations (3) and (6) is analytically ambiguous dependent on the numerical values of the key policy parameters p and ($x-y$).

2.2 Cheating early or late?

Despite the analytical ambiguity of the size of equations (4) and (5) relative to equations (3) and (6), it is nevertheless possible to examine the relative incentives to comply early or late in the contract period. For a risk averse farmer this can be done by considering both the expected income and the variance of income from behavioural alternatives (2) and (3) (i.e. either cheating late or cheating early). In particular:

$$E(I_{TIC2}) = B + x - y + p(B+x)/(1+r) + (1-p)(B - x(1+r))/(1+r) \quad (7)$$

while:

$$E(I_{CIT2}) = p(B+x) + (1-p)B + p(B+x-y)/(1+r) + (1-p)B/(1+r) \quad (8)$$

Equations (7) and (8) can be rearranged and simplified to give:

$$E(I_{TIC2}) = B + B/(1+r) + px(1 + 1/(1+r)) - y \quad (9)$$

$$E(I_{CIT2}) = B + B/(1+r) + px(1 + 1/(1+r)) - py/(1+r) \quad (10)$$

It follows from a comparison of equations (9) and (10) that the present value of expected income from cheating early exceeds that of cheating late. Note, however, that this difference arises not from a difference in the expected benefit of cheating (i.e. $px(1 + 1/(1+r))$) but rather from a difference in the expected costs of complying (i.e. $py/(1+r) < y$).

Next consider the variance of the present value of income from cheating late compared with cheating early. In particular[7]:

$$\text{Var}(I_{TIC2}) = p(x + x/(1+r) - px(1+1/(1+r)))^2 + (1-p)(-px(1+1/(1+r)))^2 \quad (11)$$

while:

---

[7] Recall that $\text{Var}(x) = E(x - E(x))^2$

Moral Hazard, Targeting and Contract Duration in Agri-Environmental Policy 61

$$\text{Var}(I_{CIT2}) = p(x + x/(1 + r) - y/(1 + r) - px(1 + 1/(1 + r)) + py/(1 + r))^2$$
$$+ (1 - p)(-px(1 + 1/(1 + r)) + py/(1 + r))^2 \tag{12}$$

Equations (11) and (12) can be rearranged and simplified to give:

$$\text{Var}(I_{TIC2}) = p(1 - p)(x(1 + 1/(1 + r)))^2 \tag{13}$$

$$\text{Var}(I_{CIT2}) = p(1 - p)(x(1 + 1/(1 + r)) - y/(1 + r))^2 \tag{14}$$

It follows from a comparison of equations (13) and (14) that the variance of the present value of income from cheating early is less than that of cheating late.

Therefore, these comparisons show that a (risk neutral and a) risk averse farmer will always prefer the alternative of cheating early to that of cheating late in the contract period because it features both a higher present value of expected income and a lower variance of the present value of income. Moreover, the basis of this preference stems not from a difference in the expected benefits of cheating, but rather from a difference in the expected costs of complying.

Finally in this section, note that because of this unambiguous preference for cheating early compared to cheating late, the potential arises for the principal to consider targeting monitoring resources away from those farmers who are in the late phase of their contract period and towards those farmers who are in the early phase of their contract period. In so doing, the principal may be able to discourage early cheating without incentivising late cheating. This inter-temporal aspect of targeting is explored further in the numerical analysis of the next section.

3. Numerical Analysis

In order to undertake a numerical analysis of the model in section 2 it is necessary to specify both a particular form for the farmer's utility function, and a set of parameter values to act as a base case.

In what follows the utility function is specified to take the constant relative risk aversion form[8]:

$$U(I) = \left(\frac{I^{1-R}}{1 - R} \right) \tag{15}$$

where:

R = coefficient of relative risk aversion $(-U''(I).I/U'(I))$. In addition, the following parameter values are chosen for a base case: $B = 12$; $x = 10$; $y = 7$; $R = 0.2$, 0.6; $r = 0$; $p = 0.75$, 0.5.

On this basis, the top two panels of Table 1 contain details of the base case results in terms of the present value of expected utility for the four behavioural alternatives.

There are two main pairs of parameter value trade-offs illustrated by the results in Panels 1 and 2 of Table 1. The first of these is between the certain level of income independent of participation (B) and the level of risk aversion of the farmer (R). In

---

[8] See Pope and Just (1991) for empirical evidence to support this specification.

62   *Rob Fraser*

Table 1

Results of the numerical analysis[a]

	$U(I_{T1T2})$	$EU(I_{T1C2})$	$EU(I_{C1T2})$	$EU(I_{C1C2})$
Panel 1 ($p = 0.75$)				
$R = 0.2$	21.82	22.57	23.86	23.97
$R = 0.6$	14.77	14.67	15.37	14.28
Panel 2 ($p = 0.5$)				
$R = 0.2$	21.82	19.40	21.99	19.87
$R = 0.6$	14.77	13.34	14.75	12.01
Panel 3 ($R = 0.2$)				
$p = 0.5$	21.82	19.40	21.99	19.87
$p_1 = 0.4$; $p_2 = 0.6$	21.82	20.67	21.24	19.69

Note: a: $B = 12$; $x = 10$; $y = 7$; $r = 0$.

this case increasing B increases the expected level of income relative to the variance of income, which means that cheating becomes less important in determining the value of expected utility. As a consequence, an associated increase in R would be needed to neutralise the diminished role of risk-taking in determining behaviour caused by the increase in B. This also means that an increase in R for given B makes cheating less attractive than complying, as illustrated by comparing the results for $R = 0.2$ and 0.6 in Panel 1 for $U(I_{T1T2})$ relative to $EU(I_{C1C2})$. It follows that for much larger values of B, cheating would occur even for larger values of R, while for $R = 0$ cheating would occur even for $B = 0$ (because $E(I_{C1C2}) > I_{T1T2}$).

The second main pair of parameter value trade-offs, as already identified in section 2, is between the two policy parameters of the probability of not being monitored (p) and the net benefit of complying ($x-y$). In this case, as p is decreased the likelihood of being caught cheating is increased and so, for given ($x-y$), complying becomes relatively more attractive, as illustrated by a comparison of the results in Panels 1 and 2 for $R = 0.2$ and $U(I_{T1T2})$ relative to $EU(I_{C1C2})$. It follows that for even smaller values of p cheating becomes more unlikely even for smaller net benefits of complying. Alternatively, as p is increased towards 1, cheating becomes more likely even for larger net benefits of complying.

In addition, a comparison of the results in Panels 1 and 2 illustrates the potential problem of occasional cheating rather than always complying or always cheating. In particular, in Panel 1 (i.e. with $p = 0.75$) cheating behaviour can be seen to be relatively attractive compared with complying. However the form of cheating depends on the level of risk aversion of the farmer, with the more risk averse farmer ($R = 0.6$) preferring the less risky alternative of cheating occasionally (i.e. $C1T2$) to that of always cheating.[9] Whereas in Panel 2 (i.e. with $p = 0.5$) complying

---

[9] Further in this context, an increase in the rate of interest (r) generally reduces the weight of period 2 in determining the expected utility of the four alternatives. However, unreported numerical analysis shows that if initially always cheating is only just preferred to occasional cheating (i.e. $C1T2$), then an increase in r can lead to a switch in preference towards occasional cheating. In this case, an increase in r acts similarly to an increase in R by discouraging cheating in period 2 (for example this applies in Panel 1 for $R = 0.2$ if r is increased to 0.05). I am grateful to two anonymous reviewers for drawing this special case to my attention.

behaviour increases in attractiveness, but the less risk averse farmer ($R = 0.2$) still prefers cheating occasionally.

Finally, we can consider the potential for the inter-temporal targeting of monitoring resources. In particular, given the unambiguous preference for cheating early over cheating late in the contract period, the potential arises for the principal to target monitoring resources away from farmers who are in the late phase of their contract period and towards those farmers who are in the early phase of their contract periods. This potential is illustrated in Panel 3 of Table 1 which is based on the Panel 2 parameter values for $p = 0.5$ and $R = 0.2$ and considers reallocating monitoring resources away from those farmers in period 2 of their contract and towards those farmers in period 1 of their contract. Specifically, this is done by increasing the probability of not being monitored for those farmers in period 2 from 0.5 to 0.6, and decreasing the probability of not being monitored for those farmers in period 1 from 0.5 to 0.4. The results of this inter-temporal targeting of monitoring resources on the present value of the expected utility of each behavioural alternative are presented in the second row of Panel 3. These results show that the consequence of this inter-temporal targeting is both to increase the expected utility of cheating late, and to decrease the expected utility of cheating early, but such that complying in both periods becomes the most preferred option, even though the farmer knows the relative likelihood of being monitored in each period. In other words, by trading off some of the relative disadvantage of the cheating late option the principal is able to use the extra monitoring resources to discourage the cheating early option to the point where full contract duration compliance is preferred.

4. Conclusion

Most recent contributions to agri-environmental policy design have framed the moral hazard problem within an atemporal context. One exception to this is the study of Fraser (2004), which uses a multi-period contract framework to analyse the moral hazard problem, but specifies the inter-temporal components of the farmer's decision problem in a very simple way. In particular this specification fails to incorporate the inter-temporal dimension to the penalties for non-compliance which is characteristic of actual agri-environmental policies, and which is designed to discourage non-compliance both early and late in the contract period.

Section 2 extends the model in Fraser (2004) and examines the implications for a farmer's incentives to cheat early and/or late, or not at all, in the contract period. In particular, we show not only which parameters play a key role in determining these incentives, but also that a farmer will have an unambiguous preference for cheating early over cheating late in the contract period based on differences in the expected cost of compliance.

Section 3 provides a numerical evaluation of the role of the main parameter values of the model in determining farmer behaviour and then illustrates the potential for the principal to target monitoring resources inter-temporally, by exploiting the unambiguous preference for cheating early over cheating late in the contract period. In particular, it is shown that the principal can reallocate monitoring resources away from farmers late in their contract period and towards farmers early in their contract period, and in so doing discourage the cheating early option sufficiently for full contract compliance to become the preferred option, even though farmers are assumed to know the *ex ante* probabilities of being monitored in both periods.

We conclude that the targeting of monitoring resources away from farmers in the late stage and towards farmers in the early stage of their contract period has the potential to mitigate the inter-temporal moral hazard problem.

References

Choe, C. and Fraser, I. 'Compliance monitoring and agri-environmental policy', *Journal of Agricultural Economics*, Vol. 50, (1999) pp. 468–487.

Fraser, R. W. 'Moral hazard and risk management in agri-environmental policy', *Journal of Agricultural Economics*, Vol. 53, (2002) pp. 475–487.

Fraser, R. W. 'On the use of targeting to reduce moral hazard in agri-environmental schemes', *Journal of Agricultural Economics*, Vol. 55, (2004) pp. 525–540.

Hart, R. and Latacz-Lohmann, U. 'Combating moral hazard in agri-environmental schemes: a multiple-agent approach', *European Review of Agricultural Economics*, Vol. 32, (2005) pp. 75–91.

Heyes, A. G. 'Implementing environmental regulation: Enforcement and compliance', *Journal of Regulatory Economics*, Vol. 17, (2000) pp. 107–129.

Kampas, A. and White, B. 'Administrative costs and instrument choice for stochastic non-point source pollution', *Environmental and Resource Economics*, Vol. 27, (2004) pp. 109–133.

Lankoski, J. and Ollikainen, M. 'Agri-environmental externalities: a framework for designing targeted policies', *European Review of Agricultural Economics*, Vol. 30, (2003) pp. 50–75.

Lankoski, J., Lichtenberg, E. and Ollikainen, M. 'Agri-environmental program compliance in a heterogeneous landscape', *Environmental and Resource Economics*, Vol. 47, (2010) pp. 1–22.

Natural England (2010) *NE227 – Higher Level Stewardship: Environmental Stewardship Handbook*, Third Edition. Available at: http://naturalengland.etraderstores.com/Natural EnglandShop/NE227. Last accessed: 5/12/2011.

Ozanne, A. and White, B. 'Equivalence of input quotas and import charges under asymmetric information in agri-environmental schemes', *Journal of Agricultural Economics*, Vol. 58, (2007) pp. 260–268.

Ozanne, A., Hogan, T. and Colman, D. 'Moral hazard, risk aversion and compliance monitoring and agri-environmental policy', *European Review of Agricultural Economics*, Vol. 38, (2001) pp. 329–347.

Pope, R. D. and Just, R. E. 'On testing the structure of risk preferences in agricultural supply analysis', *American Journal of Agricultural Economics*, Vol. 73, (1991) pp. 743–748.

Rice, J. B. and Sen, A. 'Moral hazard and long-term guaranteed contracts: Theory and evidence from the NBA (2008)'. Available at: http://www.econdse.org/seminar/seminar52.pdf. Last accessed: 5/12/2011.

Yano, Y. and Blandford, D. 'Use of compliance rewards in agri-environmental schemes', *Journal of Agricultural Economics*, Vol. 60, (2009) pp. 530–545.

Chapter 15

Price Insurance, Moral Hazard and Agri-environmental Policy[*]

Rob Fraser

School of Economics

University of Kent

Abstract

Motivated by recent EC proposals to "strengthen risk management tools" in the CAP in relation to farmers' increased exposure to market price risk, this paper draws attention to a potential negative consequence of such a change in the CAP — an associated increase in cheating behaviour by farmers in the context of environmental stewardship. A theoretical framework for this policy problem is developed and used not just to illustrate the problem, but also to propose a solution — specifically to combine the introduction of CAP-supported policy changes which reduce farmers' exposure to market-based risk with changes in environmental stewardship policies which increase the riskiness of cheating and thereby discourage such behaviour.

Introduction

During the last two decades the key reforms to the European Union's Common Agricultural Policy (CAP) have been initially to reduce price support for agricultural production in favour of direct payments as "uncoupled" farm income support and, more recently, to shift farmer income support from agriculture-based payments ("Pillar 1") to environment-based payments ("Pillar 2"). Important consequences of these two changes are: (i) that for agricultural production farmers are now exposed to far greater market price risk than previously, (ii) that by contrast the "production" of environmental goods and services receives known payments and is therefore risk-free income, and (iii) that given (i) and (ii), farmers have been strongly attracted to environmental stewardship options such as field margins ("buffer strips") which replace the uncertain income from crop production with

---

[*]Paper presented to the Agricultural Economics Society Annual Conference, Warwick University, April 2012.

guaranteed payments for providing enhanced habitants, and where these payments are based on the average foregone agricultural income — in effect the substitution of agricultural production by the production of environmental goods and services, coupled with the replacement of uncertain income by its average level (see for example Natural England, 2011).

Most recently, the European Commission's discussion document "The CAP towards 2020" has canvassed a set of further reform options for this policy (European Commission, 2010). One of the core components of these reform options, possibly further motivated by the strong variations in food prices in recent years, has been to "strengthen risk management tools" — specifically to advocate CAP support for farmers to deal with their far greater exposure to market price risk — typically in the form of market-based risk management options such as forward pricing, futures markets and price insurance schemes. Moreover, such proposals seem to have widespread support — perhaps based on their common use in US agriculture and their World Trade Organisation (WTO)-acceptability. For example, "Defra's position is that price volatility is best managed by encouraging the development of market based solutions such as futures markets or insurance" (Environment, Food and Rural Affairs Committee April 2011, paragraph 218), while the European Centre for International Political Economy advocates that the EU "assist farmers in employing financial risk management tools, promote the creation of risk-sharing markets, and subsidise private insurance schemes" (ECIPE, 2008, p. 4).

Give this policy reform background, the aim of this paper is to draw attention to one of the potential negative consequences for farmer behaviour of a CAP-supported reduction in market price risk for agricultural production: an associated increase in the risk of cheating by farmers in relation to environmental stewardship. In particular, a reduction in market price risk, by reducing the overall riskiness of farmer income, may encourage cheating behaviour by farmers in the context of their payments for producing environmental goods and services.[1]

However, having identified this problem as a consequence of CAP support for reducing market price risk, the paper also identifies a solution to this policy problem — an associated policy-based increase in the riskiness of cheating behaviour in the context of environmental stewardship.

The structure of this paper is as follows: Section 1 first develops a theoretical framework which identifies the policy problem and then provides a numerical illustration of its impact on farmer behaviour. Subsequently, Section 2 outlines the theoretical framework for the policy-based solution to this problem, and also

---

[1] Note that this paper builds on previous contributions by Fraser (2002) and Yano and Blandford (2009, 2011) which have highlighted the interplay between production income risk and non-compliance risk in determining a farmer's overall income risk — with consequent implications for farmer behaviour.

numerically illustrates its operation. The paper concludes with a brief summary and discussion of its policy implications.

Section 1: The Policy Problem

1.1 *Theoretical framework*

The central feature of this framework is the introduction of area-based payments for removing land from agricultural production and instead producing environmental goods and services — with the payment for this environmental provision being based on the average foregone agricultural production income from the designated area. Note that the most common farm of such area-based payments are field margins, or "buffer strips", which protect field boundaries as habitats and are of a specified width — for example six metres (see Natural England, 2011).

Given this specification, the area-based payment will in effect represent the substitution of uncertain income from agricultural production with guaranteed income set at the average level of agricultural production income:

$$x = \bar{p}q \qquad\qquad (1)$$

where:

x = environmental stewardship payment for the specified area

$\bar{p}$ = expected market price of agricultural output

q = agricultural output from the specified area.

Note that with this specification it is assumed that there is no yield variability in agricultural production.

Moreover, given that agricultural production income from the specified area will have a variance given by:

$$q^2 Var(p)$$

where: $Var(p)$ is the variance of the market price of agricultural output, then it follows that a risk averse farmer will always prefer the guaranteed environmental stewardship payment to the uncertain agricultural production income, and therefore this farmer will always choose to participate in this form of environmental steward-ship rather than choosing not to participate and instead to produce agricultural output on the specified area.

However, this farmer also has the behavioural option of cheating by accepting the environmental stewardship payment, but still producing agricultural output on the specified area in order to receive both the guaranteed environmental stewardship payment without providing the environmental stewardship, and the uncertain agricultural production income. Note that both of these actions are risky activities and the farmer's choice between this form of cheating and instead behaving truthfully and accepting x in return for removing the specified land from production will depend on the following factors:

(i) the level of risk aversion of the farmer,
(ii) the probability of being caught cheating $(= b)$,
(iii) the penalty if caught cheating $(= tx, \; where \; t \geq 1)$, and
(iv) the riskiness of agricultural production income from the specified area $(= q^2 Var(p))$.

More specifically, for a particular farmer the decision is based on whether:

$$U(x) \lessgtr E(U(Ic)) \tag{2}$$

where:

$$U(x) = \text{certain utility from behaving truthfully}$$
$$E(U(Ic)) = \text{expected utility from cheating.}$$

Given this specification, income from cheating (Ic) will be:

$$Ic = x + pq \text{ if not caught}$$
$$= x + pq - xt \text{ if caught,} \tag{3}$$

and taking account of the probability of being caught (b):

$$E(Ic) = \bar{p}q + x(1 - bt) \tag{4}$$

$$Var(Ic) = q^2 Var(p) + x^2 t^2 (1 - b)b \tag{5}$$

where:

$$E(Ic) = \text{expected income from cheating}$$
$$Var(Ic) = \text{variance of income from cheating}^2$$

Bearing in mind that:

$$x = \bar{p}q \tag{6}$$

an examination of equation (4) shows that if:

$$bt \leq 1 \tag{7}$$

then

$$E(Ic) > x \tag{8}$$

and in this case whether:

$$U(x) \lessgtr E(U(Ic)) \tag{9}$$

will depend both on the level of risk aversion of the farmer, and on the size of $Var(Ic)$ — which as shown by equation (5) is dependent both on the riskiness of agricultural production income and on the riskiness of cheating behaviour.

---

[2]This expression for $Var(Ic)$ is derived in the Appendix.

Moreover, the policy problem outlined in the Introduction can now be identified within this theoretical framework. Specifically, consider initially the situation where in the absence of CAP-support for reduced market price risk:

$$E(Ic) > x \qquad (10)$$

but:

$$U(x) > E(U(Ic)) \qquad (11)$$

because of the overall riskiness of cheating behaviour, and as a consequence the farmer chooses to behave truthfully.

Then suppose that CAP-support for reduced market price risk is introduced in the form of actuarially-fair price insurance.[3] As a consequence, $Var(p)$ is decreased, so that $Var(Ic)$ is also decreased. Therefore, the possibility arises that a farmer who chooses to behave truthfully in the absence of such price insurance, now finds that the decrease in $Var(Ic)$ associated with the introduction of price insurance results in:

$$U(x) < E(U(Ic)) \qquad (12)$$

so that this farmer now prefers to cheat by both accepting the environmental stewardship payment and producing agricultural output on the specified land — with the associated removal of the provision of environmental goods and services on this land.

This policy problem, and the role of various parameter values in determining its occurrence is illustrated numerically in the next sub-section.

1.2 *Illustration of the policy problem*

In order to undertake a numerical analysis which illustrates the policy problem identified in the previous sub-section, first assume the following parameter values as a Base Case:

$$x = 100; \quad \bar{p} = 10; \quad CV_p = 0.35; \quad q = 10; \quad t = 2; \quad b = 0.4.$$

Note at this point that with $t = 2$ and $b = 0.4$:

$$bt < 1$$

and as a consequence:

$$E(Ic) = 120 > x = 100$$

which, as shown in sub-section 1.1, is a requirement for cheating behaviour to potentially be preferred. In addition, assume the attitude to risk of the farmer

---

[3] Actuarially-fair price insurance means that although the farmer is provided with a guaranteed minimum price which therefore both increases the expected price and decreases the variance of price, the cost of this insurance provision is set equal to the increment in the expected price, so that overall only $Var(p)$ is affected.

can be represented by the mean-variance framework and the constant relative risk aversion functional form.[4]

$$E(U(I)) = U(E(I)) + \frac{1}{2}U''(E(I)) \cdot Var(I) \tag{13}$$

where:

$$U(I) = I^{(1-R)}/(1 - R)$$

and $R =$ constant coefficient of relative risk aversion $= -U''(I) \cdot I/U'(I)$ where: $U''(I)$ is the second derivative of the utility function ($U''(I) < 0$).

Finally consider the alternative specifications of the impact of the price insurance scheme on the existing variability of market price: (i) where CV_p is reduced from 0.35 to 0.25 and (ii) where CV_p is reduced from 0.35 to 0.15.

On this basis Table 1 contains details of the numerical results regarding the levels of expected utility from cheating and truth-telling behaviour for a range of attitudes to risk and the alternative impact of the price insurance scheme on CV_p.[5]

Table 1 shows that in the absence of a price insurance scheme only the least risk averse farmer ($R = 0.25$) finds cheating to be preferred to truth-telling behaviour (i.e. 44.93 > 42.16). In addition, Table 1 shows that following the introduction of a price insurance scheme which reduces CV_p from 0.35 to 0.25 it remains the case that only the least risk averse farmer prefers to cheat. However, if with the introduction of the price insurance scheme CV_p is reduced from 0.35 to 0.15, then in this case the farmer with the middle level of risk aversion ($R = 0.5$) now finds cheating behaviour is preferred to truth-telling (i.e. 20.04 > 20.00). It follows that this scenario illustrates the policy problem identified in sub-section 1.1 — specifically that a price insurance scheme, by reducing the overall riskiness of income, will generally increase the attractiveness of cheating behaviour (note all values for $E(U(Ic))$ in Table 1 are increased for lower values of CV_p) and, as a consequence, the potential arises for this increase to result in a farmer switching from behaving

Table 1   The policy problem.

	R		
	0.25	0.5	0.75
$U(x)$	42.16	20.00	12.65
$E(U(Ic))$ for $CVp = 0.35$	44.93	19.85	12.30
$E(U(Ic))$ for $CVp = 0.25$	45.12	19.96	12.36
$E(U(Ic))$ for $CVp = 0.15$	45.25	20.04	12.39

[4]See Hanson and Ladd (1991) and Pope and Just (1991) for arguments supporting these assumptions.

[5]Note from Hazell, Jaramillo and Williamson (1990) that a CV_p of 0.35 is consistent with historical evidence for the world wheat market. Also note that Newbery and Stiglitz (1981) suggest levels of R between 0.5 and 1.2 are consistent with most empirical estimates.

truthfully to cheating. In addition, it can be concluded from the results in Table 1 that the more successful the price insurance scheme is in reducing market price risk, the more likely this switch in behaviour is to occur. Finally, Table 1 shows that this switching behaviour is more likely among farmers with moderate levels of risk aversion, where both the incentive to cheat and the aversion to income variability have a role in determining behaviour.

Section 2: The Policy Solution

2.1 *Theoretical framework*

Drawing on the mainstream economics contributions of Polinsky and Shavell (1979) and Kaplow and Shavell (1994) it is clear that the most straightforward, if politically unacceptable, way to discourage cheating is to increase the penalty that follows being caught. This can be demonstrated using the theoretical framework of sub-section 1.1 where it can be seen that both the expected penalty $(E(z))$ from being caught cheating:

$$E(z) = xtb \tag{14}$$

and the variance of income $(Var(z))$ associated with being caught cheating:

$$Var(z) = x^2 t^2 (1 - b)b \tag{15}$$

are increased by an increase in t:

$$\frac{\partial E(z)}{\partial t} = xb > 0 \tag{16}$$

$$\frac{\partial Var(z)}{\partial t} = 2x^2 t(1 - b)b > 0. \tag{17}$$

However, as shown in Fraser (2002), for risk averse farmers it is also possible to discourage cheating simply by increasing the riskiness of cheating, and without increasing the expected penalty from cheating. In particular because the expected penalty associated with cheating is linear in the two compliance parameters, b and t, but the variance of income associated with cheating is non-linear in b and t, it is possible to utilise the concept of an expected penalty preserving increase in the riskiness of cheating in order to discourage a risk averse farmer from cheating. More specifically, Fraser (2002) shows that an increase in t which is offset in terms of its impact on $E(z)$ by a decrease in b, so that the expected penalty is unchanged, will nevertheless increase the riskiness of cheating and thereby act to discourage farmers from such behaviour. Moreover, Fraser (2002) argues that such changes in the non-compliance parameters not only have the desirable feature of discouraging cheating while leaving the expected penalty if caught unchanged, but also reduce the costs of policy enforcement through the reduction in monitoring effort that occurs with a decrease in the probability of being monitored (b). Therefore, on both these counts an expected penalty preserving change in the values of the compliance parameters is likely to be more politically acceptable than just an increase in the penalty if caught cheating.

In the following sub-section the numerical example of sub-section 1.2 is further developed to illustrate how this approach to exploiting the risk aversion of farmers to discourage cheating can solve the problem identified previously.

2.2   *Numerical illustration of the policy solution*

The policy problem as previously identified is that the decrease in the riskiness of cheating behaviour that follows the introduction of a CAP-supported market price insurance scheme has the potential to cause farmers to switch from behaving truthfully to cheating by accepting payment for but not providing environmental goods and services and instead producing agricultural output on specified land.

The policy solution proposed in the previous sub-section is to combine the introduction of the CAP-supported price insurance scheme with an adjustment in the compliance parameters of the environmental stewardship policy which leaves the expected penalty from being caught cheating unchanged, but which increases the riskiness of cheating as outlined in Fraser (2002).

To illustrate this policy solution consider two alternative adjustments in the compliance parameters from their Base Case values of $t = 2$ and $b = 0.4$. Specifically:

$$(a) \quad t = 2.4; \quad b = 0.333$$

$$(b) \quad t = 4; \quad b = 0.2$$

Note that in both cases the expected penalty if caught cheating $(E(z))$ is unchanged but the variance of income associated with being caught cheating $(Var(z))$ is increased (and the cost of monitoring resources is reduced). Table 2 contains details of the impact of combining this environmental stewardship policy change with the introduction of a CAP-supported price insurance scheme. In particular, the results in Table 2 shown that for change (a) in the compliance parameters (i.e. $t = 2.4$;

Table 2   The policy solution.

	R		
	0.25	0.5	0.75
$U(x)$	42.16	20.00	12.65
$E(U(Ic))$ for $CVp = 0.15$; $t = 2$; $b = 0.4$	45.25	20.04	12.39
$E(U(Ic))$ for $CVp = 0.15$; $t = 2.4$; $b = 0.333$	44.25	19.43	12.12
$E(U(Ic))$ for $CVp = 0.15$; $t = 4$; $b = 0.2$	40.21	17.00	11.01

$I_i =$ income in period $i (i = 1, 2)$

$b = 0.333$) the example of the policy problem illustrated in Table 1 for a farmer with an attitude to risk represented by $R = 0.5$ no longer applies — that is the farmer now finds that continuing to behave truthfully remains the preferred choice because the reduced riskiness of cheating brought about by the price insurance scheme is more than offset by the increased riskiness of cheating brought about by the change in the policy compliance parameters.

Finally in this sub-section, the potential for an expected penalty preserving change in the compliance parameters of the environmental stewardship policy to ameliorate the problem of cheating behaviour is illustrated by the impact of change (b) in these parameters. In particular, the bottom row of results in Table 2 show that for this policy change even the least risk averse farmer now prefers behaving truthfully to cheating.

Conclusion

This paper has been motivated by recent EC proposals to provide CAP support to "strengthen risk management tools" such as futures markets and market price insurance (EC, 2010). The aim of such support is to enable farmers to reduce their exposure to market price risk, typically by removing to some extent this risk from them by using market-based mechanisms. The aim of the paper has been not just to draw attention to a potential negative consequence of such a change in the CAP — specifically an associated increase in cheating behaviour by farmers in relation to environmental stewardship — but also to provide a solution to this policy problem.

Section 1 outlined a theoretical framework for identifying this policy problem and demonstrated how CAP-supported price insurance would reduce the overall riskiness of cheating behaviour — thereby potentially enabling an expected increase in income associated with cheating behaviour to dominate a farmer's decision process. This outline was further developed with a numerical illustration of the policy problem — specifically showing how, with the introduction of CAP-supported price insurance, a farmer could switch from behaving truthfully by accepting payment for taking land out of agricultural production and as required using it to provide environmental goods and services, to cheating by accepting such a payment but continuing to produce agricultural output on the specified land. It was also shown that the extent of this policy problem depended both on the extent to which the price insurance scheme removed market price risk, and the level of risk aversion of the farmer.

Section 2 then proposed a solution to this policy problem based on the demonstration in Fraser (2002) that cheating behaviour can be discouraged simply by exploiting the risk aversion of the farmer and increasing the riskiness of cheating behaviour. Specifically this can be done using the concept of an expected penalty preserving change in the two compliance parameters, the penalty itself and the probability of being monitored, which not only increases the riskiness of cheating behaviour but also reduces the costs of monitoring. Therefore, by combining the introduction of CAP-supported price insurance with such a change in the environmental stewardship policy it was shown using a numerical example how the potential for incentivising cheating behaviour by reducing market risk can be removed — even for farmers with relatively low levels of risk aversion.

The policy implications of this paper are two-fold. First, policy charges should not focus on market-based risk to the exclusion of other types of risk in determining farmer behaviour because such behaviour is based on the broader notion of income risk, which itself is a composite of multiple sources of risk. Second, exploiting the risk aversion of farmers can be a powerful method of ensuring appropriate delivering by farmers of desired policy outcomes — both in the context of agricultural production and in the context of the provision of environmental goods and services.

References

Environment, Food and Rural Affairs Committee (2011) *The Common Agricultural Policy after 2013*. [Online] Available at: http://www.publications.parliament.uk/pa/cm201011/cmselect/cmenvfru/671/67113.htm (Accessed 15th April 2011).

European Centre for International Political Economy (2008) *Reforming the EU's Common Agricultural Policy: Health Check, Budget Review, Doha Round*. Policy Brief No. 06/2008 (Valentin Zahnt) ISSN 1653–8994.

European Commission (2010) *The Common Agricultural Policy (CAP) towards 2020 — Meeting the food, national resources and territorial challenges of the future*. [Online] Available at: http://ec.europa.eu/agriculture/cap-post2013/communication/index_en.htm (Accessed 18th November 2011).

Fraser R. W. (2002) Moral hazard and risk management in agri-environmental policy, *Journal of Agricultural Economics* 53(3): 475–487.

Hanson, S. D. and Ladd, G. W. (1991) Robustness of the mean-variance model with truncated probability distributions, *American Journal of Agricultural Economics* 73(2): 436–445.

Hazell, P. B. R., Jaramillo, M. and Williamson, A. (1990) The relationship between world price instability and the prices farmers receive in developing countries, *Journal of Agricultural Economics* 41(2): 227–241.

Kaplow, L. and Shavell, S. (1994) Accuracy in the determination of liability, *Journal of Law and Economics* 37(1): 1–15.

Natural England (2011) *Environmental Stewardship*. [Online] Available at: http://www.naturalengland.gov.uk/ourwork/farming/funding/es/default.aspx (Accessed 16th May 2011).

Newbery, D. M. G. and Stiglitz, J. E. (1981) *The Theory of Commodity Price Stabilisation*. Oxford: Clarendon Press.

Polinsky, M. and Shavell, S. (1979) The optimal trade-off between the probability and magnitude of fines, *American Economic Review* 69(5): 880–891.

Pope, R. D. and Just, R. E. (1991) On testing the structure of risk preferences in agricultural supply analysis, *American Journal of Agricultural Economics* 73(3): 743–748.

Yano, Y. and Blandford, D. (2009) Use of compliance rewards in agri-environmental schemes, *Journal of Agricultural Economics* 60(3): 530–545.

Yano, Y. and Blandford, D. (2011) Agri-environmental policy and moral hazard under multiple sources of uncertainty, *European Review of Agricultural Economics* 38(1): 141–155.

Appendix

$$Var(Ic) = \int^{p} (1-b)[pq + x - E(Ic)]^2 f p dp$$

$$+ \int^{p} b[pq + (1-t)x - E(Ic)]^2 f p dp \tag{A1}$$

With:

$$E(Ic) = \bar{p}q + x(1 - bt)$$

the first term on the right-hand-side of (A1) may be rearranged and simplified to give:

$$(1-b)q^2 Var(p) + (1-b)x^2 t^2 b^2 \tag{A2}$$

While the second term on the right-hand-side of (A1) may be rearranged and simplified to give:

$$bq^2 Var(p) + bx^2 t^2 (1-b)^2 \tag{A3}$$

Combining (A2) and (A3) and simplifying gives:

$$Var(Ic) = q^2 Var(p) + x^2 t^2 (1-b)b \tag{A4}$$

JAE Journal of Agricultural Economics

Journal of Agricultural Economics, Vol. 64, No. 3, 2013, 527–536
doi: 10.1111/1477-9552.12035

Chapter 16

Presidential Address

To Cheat or Not To Cheat: Moral Hazard and Agri-environmental Policy

Rob Fraser[1]

Abstract

This Address examines the moral hazard problem in agri-environmental policy. It begins with a theoretical analysis of moral hazard in this context, including the identification of eight potential causes of cheating behaviour among farmers. But is cheating behaviour among farmers actually a problem for agri-environmental policy? And if it is, which are the statistically significant causes of concern? The answer seems to be: "we don't know" as there are currently no empirical analyses of the moral hazard problem and its causes in agri-environmental policy. On this basis I analyse a set of policy solutions – to a problem for which we have no evidence of its causes or extent!

Keywords: *Moral hazard; agri-environmental policy.*

JEL classifications: *C93, D03, H23, Q52, Q58.*

1. Introduction

In mainstream economics principal-agent theory is focussed on designing a policy so that it successfully leads to actions on the part of agents which deliver outcomes desired by the principal. In effect, an ideal policy results in agents doing what is in their best interests, but this, due to careful policy design, also achieves the principal's policy objective(s). Economists have identified two main problems with policy design in this context: the adverse selection problem and the moral hazard problem. These two problems are typically referred to jointly under the heading of "asymmetric information" – and each has the same effect on the policy outcome: reduced cost-effectiveness.

In the last decade or so I have done research on both these problems in relation to the design of agri-environmental policy.[2] However, this Presidential Address is focussed on moral hazard.

---

[1]Rob Fraser is Professor of Agricultural Economics, School of Economics, University of Kent, UK. E-mail: R.W.Fraser@kent.ac.uk for correspondence.
[2]See Fraser (2001, 2009), Quillerou and Fraser (2010), and Quillerou *et al.* (2011) in the context of adverse selection. And see Fraser (2002, 2004 and 2012) in the context of moral hazard.

The structure of the Address is as follows: Section 2 examines the causes of the moral hazard problem in agri-environmental policy, both from a theoretical and an empirical perspective. On this basis Section 3 identifies a set of agri-environmental policy solutions to the moral hazard problem. The Address ends with a brief Conclusion.

2. The Agri-environmental Policy Problem

As stated in the Introduction, the moral hazard problem leads to reduced cost-effectiveness of the policy outcome. In general terms, cheating behaviour by agents reduces the effectiveness of outcomes, and leads to cost increases for the principal as it attempts to prevent such behaviour. The following theoretical analysis establishes the potential causes of the moral hazard problem in agri-environmental policy, with the aim of developing a set of hypotheses relating to the causes of this problem, which could be tested by empirical research.

Consider a farmer who has two sources of income: agricultural production income and agri-environmental policy payments. In what follows, agricultural income (B) is net of production costs and is uncertain, with a mean $E(B)$ and variance $\text{Var}(B)$. Participation in the agri-environmental scheme has two components: a payment for participation (x) and a cost of compliance (y). In what follows both of these values are assumed to be known.[3]

Because the farmer is assumed to be already committed to participating in the agri-environmental scheme, the payment x is guaranteed. However, incurring the cost of compliance y is the farmer's choice. If the farmer chooses to comply with the requirements of participation and so incur the cost of compliance (i.e. to behave truthfully), then expected income ($E(I_t)$) is given by:

$$E(I_t) = E(B) + (x - y). \tag{1}$$

If instead the farmer chooses not to incur the cost of compliance (i.e. to cheat), then income (I_c) will depend on whether the farmer is caught not complying:

$$I_c = B + x \text{ if not caught}$$

and:

$$I_c = B + x - xt \text{ if caught,}$$

where t is the parameter reflecting the penalty associated with being caught cheating. In this case, setting the probability of being caught as p, expected income from cheating ($E(I_c)$) is given by:

$$\begin{aligned} E(I_c) &= E(B) + (1 - p)x + p(x - xt) \\ &= E(B) + x - pxt. \end{aligned} \tag{2}$$

Note also that the variance of income from behaving truthfully ($\text{Var}(I_t)$) is given by:

---

[3]The cost of compliance could be a combination of foregone production income and a cost of implementing the agri-environmental measure. This implies y could be uncertain, but this possibility is ignored for simplicity in what follows.

To Cheat or Not To Cheat 529

$$\text{Var}(I_t) = \text{Var}(B) \tag{3}$$

while the variance of income from cheating ($\text{Var}(I_c)$) is given by:[4]

$$\text{Var}(I_c) = \text{Var}(B) + (1 - p)px^2t^2. \tag{4}$$

A comparison of equations (3) and (4) shows that the variance of income from cheating is unambiguously larger than the variance of income from behaving truthfully:

$$\text{Var}(I_c) > \text{Var}(I_t). \tag{5}$$

It follows from equation (5) that, for a risk-averse farmer, if the expected income from cheating is less than or equal to the expected income from behaving truthfully, then behaving truthfully is unambiguously preferred to cheating.

Therefore, if cheating is in some situation to be preferred by a risk-averse farmer, there is the following "Incentive Compatibility Condition" (ICC):

$$E(I_c) < E(I_t). \tag{6}$$

Recalling equations (1) and (2), satisfying this condition thus requires:

$$E(B) + x - pxt < E(B) + x - y$$

which simplifies to:

$$y < pxt. \tag{7}$$

In words, equation (7) says that if a risk-averse farmer prefers – in some situation – to cheat, that is, for the moral hazard problem to be a policy concern, then the cost of compliance must exceed the expected penalty from being caught cheating. As a consequence, equation (7) provides four hypotheses suitable for testing with empirical research:

H1: Cheating is more likely the higher are the costs of compliance (y).

H2: Cheating is more likely the lower is the probability of being caught (p).

H3: Cheating is more likely the lower is the payment for participation (x).

H4: Cheating is more likely the lower is the penalty parameter if caught (t).

(all other things being equal).

Given that the "Incentive Compatibility Condition" is not satisfied, the risk-averse farmer's choice of behaviour then depends on the "Risk-Return Balance" (RRB). Using the expected utility framework this implies that the choice of behaving truthfully or cheating depends on:

$$E(U(I_t)) > \text{ or } < E(U(I_c)) \tag{8}$$

where:

$E(U(I_t))$ = expected utility from behaving truthfully, and
$E(U(I_c))$ = expected utility from cheating.

---

[4]Equation (4) is derived from the statistical definition: $\text{Var}(x) = E(x - E(x))^2$; and the assumed independence of uncertain production income and the risk of being caught cheating. See Fraser (2012b) for details.

530   *Rob Fraser*

Moreover, using the mean-variance framework of expected utility analysis shows that the farmer's expected utility of income can be decomposed into two main components:

$$E(U(I)) = U(E(I)) + 1/2\ddot{U}''(E(I))\text{Var}(I) \tag{9}$$

where:

$U(E(I))$ = utility from expected income (>0), and

$U''(E(I))$ = second derivative of the farmer's utility function (<0).

Note from equation (9) that the first term on the right-hand-side is positive, while the second term is negative. In addition, the "Incentive Compatibility Condition" not being satisfied implies that:

$$U(E(I_c)) > U(E(I_t)), \tag{10}$$

while equation (5) implies:[5]

$$\text{Absolute Magnitude } (U''(E(I_c)) \cdot \text{Var}(I_c)) > \text{Absolute Magnitude } (U''(E(I_t)) \cdot \text{Var}(I_t)). \tag{11}$$

Therefore, the "Risk-Return Balance" in equation (8) will depend on the relative strengths of the inequalities in equations (10) and (11). In words, for a risk-averse farmer, does the greater expected income from cheating justify the greater income risk?

As a consequence, equations (8), (10) and (11) together provide three more hypotheses suitable for testing with empirical research:

H5: Cheating is more likely the higher is expected income from agricultural production (E(B)).

Specifically, the higher is $E(B)$ the smaller (in magnitude) is $U''(E(I))$, so the inequality in income risk between cheating and behaving truthfully diminishes in importance relative to the inequality in utility from expected income in determining the farmer's behaviour. In other words, the main (income-generating) game for the farmer is agricultural production, and so participation in the agri-environmental scheme is just a side-line activity, suitable for an occasional "flutter" by cheating.

H6: Cheating is more likely the smaller is the variance of income from agricultural production (Var(B)).

Similar to H5, for smaller Var(B) the inequality of income risk diminishes in relative importance in determining the farmer's behaviour. And in other words, the farmer's income from agricultural production seems "safe" and so taking a "risk" by cheating on the agri-environmental scheme seems on balance worthwhile.[6]

H7: Cheating is more likely the less risk averse is the farmer (the smaller in magnitude is U''(E(I))).

---

[5]Note that for $E(I_c) > E(I_t)$, it follows that the absolute magnitude of $U''(E(I_c))$ will be smaller than that of $U''(E(I_t))$. However, for levels of risk aversion consistent with empirical estimates, this difference is trivial in percentage terms compared with typical differences between the magnitudes of Var(I_c) and Var(I_t).

[6]Note in this context that a policy of reducing farmers' exposure to market risk by supporting prices or providing price insurance may, as a consequence, encourage cheating behaviour in relation to an agri-environmental scheme. See Fraser (2012b) for details.

Again similar to H5 and H6, for a smaller magnitude of $U''(E(I))$ the inequality of income risk diminishes in relative importance in determining the farmer's behaviour. And again in other words, for lower risk aversion the farmer is increasingly attracted to the expected income benefits despite its greater riskiness.

Finally in this section, I'd like to recall the theoretical contribution of my paper in the *JAE* in 2012 (Fraser, 2012a). This paper used a two-period framework for analysing the moral hazard problem to investigate whether cheating was more likely "early" or "late" in the farmer's contract to participate in the agri-environmental scheme. This analysis showed that:

$$E(I_{CIT2}) > E(I_{TIC2}) \tag{12}$$

and that:

$$\mathrm{Var}(I_{CIT2}) < \mathrm{Var}(I_{TIC2}). \tag{13}$$

In words, not only does the expected income from cheating "early" exceed that from cheating "late", but also the variance of income from cheating "early" is less than that from cheating "late". As a consequence, this paper showed that a risk-averse farmer would unambiguously prefer cheating "early" to cheating "late" in their contract period:

> H8: *Cheating is more likely early than late in a farmer's agri-environmental contract period.*

In summary, the theoretical analysis in this section has identified eight hypotheses relating to causes of the moral hazard problem in the context of agri-environmental policy which are suitable for testing with empirical research.

The next section was to have considered the empirical research to date investigating the causes and extent of the moral hazard problem in this context. However, I can find no empirical evaluations of the causes of the moral hazard problem in agri-environmental policy.[7]

3. The Agri-environmental Policy Solutions

The prospects for evidence-based policy solutions in relation to the moral hazard problem in agri-environmental policy are currently rather bleak. However, my aim in this section is to use the theoretical analysis in Section 2, and the associated eight hypotheses, for empirical research in order to suggest a set of policy solutions. In what follows I consider three alternative approaches: i) increasing the expected cost of being caught cheating; ii) increasing the riskiness of cheating, and iii) targeting farmers who are more likely to cheat.

3.1. *Increasing the expected cost of being caught cheating*

The focus in this section is on the "Incentive Compatibility Condition", which contains three policy parameters (p, x and t) that can be manipulated to increase the expected cost of being caught cheating:

$$y < pxt. \tag{7'}$$

---

[7]One attractive, though cavalier option in this case is outlined in an online Appendix.

As explained in Section 2.1, the right-hand-side of equation (7′) is the expected cost of being caught cheating, so increasing the size of this expected cost increases the likelihood of the ICC being met, in which case cheating is unattractive, even to a risk neutral farmer. Alternatively, if the ICC is not satisfied, then increasing the expected cost of being caught cheating will reduce the magnitude of inequality (10) in the "Risk-Return Balance":

$$U(E(I_c)) > U(E(I_t)) \tag{10'}$$

thereby increasing the likelihood of the "Risk-Return Balance" favouring truthful behaviour for a risk-averse farmer.[8]

More specifically: H2 suggests that cheating is less likely the higher is the probability of being caught (p); H3 suggests that cheating is less likely the higher is the payment for participation (x); and H4 suggests that cheating is less likely the higher is the penalty parameter (t).[9]

However, while in principle the policy-maker has the choice of increasing any one or more of these policy parameters in order to increase the expected cost of being caught cheating, the cost to the policy-maker of changing each of these parameters is likely to be very different. In particular, increasing x requires increasing agri-environmental payments to all farmers, regardless of their behaviour. On this basis, I would expect this policy option to be the most expensive way to increase the expected cost of being caught cheating. Alternatively, increasing the probability of being caught cheating requires increased monitoring activities, with their associated higher costs. Finally, increasing the penalty parameter seems to me to be the cheapest option, requiring possibly only an increased operational use of the legally available range of penalty levels.[10]

3.2. Increasing the riskiness of cheating

Equation (4) shows that the variance of income attributable specifically to the penalty for being caught cheating ($\text{Var}(C)$) is given by:

$$\text{Var}(C) = (1-p)px^2t^2 \tag{14}$$

which in turn shows that the riskiness of cheating is non-linear in the three policy parameters p, x and t. This is in contrast to the expected penalty from being caught cheating ($E(C)$), which from equation (7) is given by:

$$E(C) = pxt \tag{15}$$

and which is clearly linear in p, x and t.

---

[8] It should be noted from equation (4) that increasing each of p, x and t (as long as $p < \frac{1}{2}$) will also increase the variance of income from cheating, thereby also helping to shift the RRB towards behaving truthfully.

[9] See the mainstream economics contributions of Polinsky and Shavell (1979) and Kaplan and Shavell (1994) for the origin of these observations.

[10] In this context, personal communications with HMRC have informed me that the applied penalty levels in the case of taxation non-compliance are typically well below legal maximums. Note also that in James Mirrlees' long-lost paper titled "The theory of moral hazard and unobservable behaviour: Part 1" the "unpleasant" main result is that "penalties of unlimited severity are optimal" (1999, p.12). And there is no "Part 2"!

To Cheat or Not To Cheat 533

As demonstrated in Fraser (2002), this difference creates the opportunity to ameliorate the moral hazard problem by just exploiting the risk aversion of farmers. In particular, the policy-maker has the option to manipulate the two policy parameters p and t in such a way as to leave the expected penalty from being caught unchanged, but at the same time increasing the variance of income attributable to the penalty from being caught. To see this consider Table 1, which is adapted from Fraser (2002).

Table 1
Impact of mean-penalty preserving changes in p and t on Var(C)

p	t	$E(C)$	Var(C)
0.90	0.56	350	13,611
0.76	0.67	350	40,833
0.50	1	350	122,500
0.25	2	350	367,500
0.10	5	350	1,102,500

Note: x = 700.
Source: Adapted from Fraser (2002).

Specifically, Table 1 shows that by simultaneously increasing the penalty parameter (t) and decreasing the probability of being monitored for compliance (p), but doing so in a linear combination, the policy-maker is able to leave the expected cost of being caught cheating unchanged, but increase the riskiness of cheating. In so doing, the ICC is left unaffected by the policy changes, but the RRB is shifted towards truthful behaviour for a risk-averse farmer. Moreover, in so doing the policy-maker is able to reduce the cost of monitoring compliance without providing any encouragement to cheating behaviour.

In other words, while I suggested in Section 3.1 that the cheapest policy option for reducing the moral hazard problem by increasing the expected cost of being caught cheating was to do so by increasing the penalty parameter (t), I am suggesting instead here that by not just increasing t but also reducing p, the policy-maker can both reduce the moral hazard problem and reduce the policy's operating costs. This opportunity can only be described as a "win–win" for the policy-maker.

3.3. Targeting farmers who are more likely to cheat

Both the policy solutions in Sections 3.1 and 3.2 involve across-the-board changes to policy parameters in the sense that they affect all farmers involved in the agri-environmental scheme. However, an alternative approach is to target the potential source of the moral hazard problem: those farmers who are thought to be more likely to cheat. Such an approach may not necessarily involve any increase in costs, rather it aims to increase the policy's cost-effectiveness by re-allocating monitoring resources away from farmers who are less likely to cheat and towards those more likely to do so.[11] In effect, although there are no explicit changes in overall policy parameters, this re-allocation involves increasing the probability of being caught cheating particularly

---

[11]See Fraser (2004) and Fraser and Fraser (2005) for previous examples of targeting in this context.

534   *Rob Fraser*

for those farmers who are likely to change their behaviour for the benefit of the scheme's cost-effectiveness.

Furthermore, looking again at H1, H5, H6, H7 and H8 provides a range of additional suggestions for such targeting of monitoring resources towards those farmers who are more likely to be contributing to the moral hazard problem. More specifically:

1   H1 suggests targeting those farmers who have relatively high compliance costs. Such farmers may be those whose farms have particular landscape or spatial characteristics which increase the costs of compliance, or they may be farmers with relatively high debt levels, and which are likely to be exacerbated by the need to finance compliance costs.

2   H5 suggests targeting those farmers for whom participation in the agri-environmental scheme is a relatively minor component of their total expected income, and so they are more likely to treat participation as an opportunity for an occasional "flutter" by cheating.

3   H6 suggests targeting those farmers for whom agricultural production is a relatively safe source of income, so that increasing their income risk by cheating is a minor consequence. Such farmers may be those for whom production is subject to relatively low yield uncertainty, and/or those who face relatively small market price risk.

4   H7 suggests targeting those farmers with relatively low risk aversion. In this context, although there is no empirical evidence for the UK of diverging attitudes to risk among farmers, a study by Bardsley and Harris (1987) of Australian farmers' attitudes to risk found large variations among farmers between the main agricultural regions of the pastoral zone, the wheat–sheep zone and the high rainfall zone. In particular, farmers in the diversified and therefore relatively low income risk region of the wheat–sheep zone were found to have relatively high estimated levels of risk aversion compared to those farmers involved in the relatively high income risk activities of the pastoral and high rainfall zones.

5   However, note that if such a divergence were to apply in the UK, then it implies that the targeting of low income risk farmers suggested by H6 is also likely to be geographically divergent from the targeting of low risk aversion farmers suggested by H7.

6   H8 suggests targeting those farmers who are relatively early in their contract period of participation in the agri-environmental scheme as such farmers are more attracted to the opportunity to avoid compliance costs than those late in their contract period.

I think the overall conclusion from this analysis of targeting is that it is not a simple matter, with the above discussion identifying five (possibly) different types of farmer to target. Moreover, the consequent likelihood of increased costs associated with managing its complexity may undermine its attraction – and perhaps instead endorse the attraction of a simple across-the-board policy approach such as suggested in Sections 3.1 and 3.2.

4. Conclusion

This Presidential Address has examined the moral hazard problem in agri-environmental policy. It began with a theoretical analysis of moral hazard in this context, including the identification of eight potential causes of cheating behaviour among farmers (Section 2).

But is cheating behaviour among farmers actually a problem for agri-environmental policy? And if it is, which are the statistically significant causes of concern? The answer seems to be: "we don't know" – there are currently no empirical analyses of the moral hazard problem and its causes in agri-environmental policy.

Which brings us to Section 3 – my analysis of a set of policy solutions – to a problem for which we have no evidence of its causes or extent!

Yet the fact of the matter is that we know cheating behaviour by UK farmers does occur, as personal communications with Defra confirm.[12] We just do not have any evidence of its potential causes – which (further) undermines the (complex) concept of targeting (see Section 3.3) as a policy solution – that is, we don't know who or what to target with the available monitoring resources.

As a consequence, I think we are left with just the across-the-board policy solutions as discussed in Sections 3.1 and 3.2 – primarily in my view those involving the two policy parameters of the probability of being caught cheating, and the consequent penalty. Moreover, we know that increasing the probability of being caught requires an increase in monitoring resources, and is therefore likely to be the most costly of these approaches. Whereas increasing the penalty if caught is likely to be relatively cheap to implement. And finally, as I've shown in Section 3.2, if you want to get fancy and focus on exploiting the risk aversion of farmers, then you can both increase the penalty and decrease the probability of being caught in a way which just increases the riskiness of cheating and thereby discourages risk-averse farmers from such behaviour – while at the same time providing a reduction in monitoring costs.

Either way, in view of the absence of empirical evidence relating to the moral hazard problem in the context of agri-environmental policy, I would currently advocate a relatively low cost approach to solving a problem we know so little about in reality.

Supporting Information

Additional Supporting Information may be found in the online version of this article:
  Appendix S1. Make Up The Data

References

Bardsley, P. and Harris, M. 'An approach to the econometric estimation of attitudes to risk in agriculture', *Australian Journal of Agricultural Economics*, Vol. 31, (1987) pp. 112–126.

Fraser, R. W. 'Using principal-agent theory to deal with output slippage in the European Union set-aside policy', *Journal of Agricultural Economics*, Vol. 52, (2001) pp. 29–41.

Fraser, R. W. 'Moral hazard and risk management in agri-environmental policy', *Journal of Agricultural Economics*, Vol. 53, (2002) pp. 475–487.

Fraser, R. W. 'On the use of targeting to reduce moral hazard in agri-environmental schemes', *Journal of Agricultural Economics*, Vol. 55, (2004) pp. 525–540.

---

[12]I actually have a spreadsheet of monitoring outcomes provided to me by Johannes Sauer (now at the University of Kiel) which he obtained from Defra. This spreadsheet catalogues a set of observed incidents of non-compliance by farmers in relation to the Higher Level Stewardship Scheme.

536   *Rob Fraser*

Fraser, R. W. 'Land heterogeneity, agricultural income foregone and environmental benefit: an assessment of incentive compatibility problems in environmental stewardship schemes', *Journal of Agricultural Economics*, Vol. 60, (2009) pp. 190–201.

Fraser, R. W. 'Moral hazard, targeting and contract duration in agri-environmental policy', *Journal of Agricultural Economics*, Vol. 63, (2012a) pp. 56–64.

Fraser, R. W. *Price Insurance, Moral Hazard and Agri-environmental Policy*. Paper presented to the Agricultural Economics Society Annual Conference, University of Warwick, April, 2012b.

Fraser, R. W. and Fraser, I. M. 'Targeting monitoring resources to enhance the effectiveness of the CAP', *EuroChoices*, Vol. 4, (2005) pp. 22–27.

Kaplow, L. and Shavell, S. 'Accuracy in the determination of liability', *Journal of Law and Economics*, Vol. 37, (1994) pp. 1–15.

Mirrlees, J. A. 'The theory of moral hazard and unobservable behaviour: Part 1', *Review of Economic Studies*, Vol. 66, (1999) pp. 3–21.

Polinsky, M. and Shavell, S. 'The optimal trade-off between the probability and magnitude of fines', *American Economic Review*, Vol. 69, (1979) pp. 880–891.

Quillerou, E. and Fraser, R. W. 'Adverse selection in the Environmental Stewardship Scheme: Does the Higher Level Stewardship Scheme design reduce adverse selection?' *Journal of Agricultural Economics*, Vol. 61, (2010) pp. 369–380.

Quillerou, E., Fraser, I. M. and Fraser, R. W. 'Farmer compensation and its consequences for environmental benefit provision in the Higher Level Stewardship Scheme', *Journal of Agricultural Economics*, Vol. 62, (2011) pp. 330–339.

Chapter 17

Reflections, Looking Around and Looking Ahead

17.1 Reflections

One of the reviewers of the proposal for this book suggested removing Part A (and expanding Part B) because "no one is talking about set-aside anymore". So is this book relevant? I think it is, and I think so primarily because its whole is greater than the sum of its parts.[1]

More specifically, my view is that this is a book:

(i) for policy researchers in general — based on my experiences as a policy researcher over twenty-five years,

(ii) for researchers using principal-agent theory — again based on my experience of applying this methodology in the context of the EU's agricultural land use policy, and

(iii) for researchers interested in the development of the CAP over the last twenty-five years from its "productivity" phase through its "competitiveness" phase and onto its current "sustainability" phase — and where I think the most prominent feature of change has been the introduction and subsequent modification of an agricultural land use policy component to the CAP.

So in the following subsections I will reflect on my research experiences from each of these perspectives with the aim of drawing out some "lessons learned" in the process.

17.1.1 *Reflections on doing policy research*

I started doing policy research in the 1980s because I thought policy was "relevant" and that is what I wanted to be as an economist. What I didn't realise initially is

---

[1]Moreover, having been abolished in 2008, set-aside has been brought back in the "CAP Reform 2014–2020" — but it is now to be called an "ecological focus area". See section 17.3 for a discussion of the rationale behind this recent "reincarnation" of set-aside.

that doing policy research can often be a race against time — in particular both to undertake the research and to get it published before the policy changes!

Moreover, this problem seemed to be particularly acute as an agricultural policy researcher in Australia in the 1980s as the Australian government embarked on a process of "deregulation" involving the dismantling of such agricultural policy "greats" as the wool industry's "Buffer Stock Scheme" and the wheat industry's "Guaranteed Minimum Price Scheme" (see for example Fraser, 1984 and Fraser, 1988) — which might explain why in the late 1980s I shifted my attention (as a policy economist) from Australian agricultural policy to the CAP (see for example Fraser, 1991). But I think it was the introduction of voluntary set-aside into the CAP in 1988 which particularly caught my policy researcher's eye, primarily because the idea of being paid *not* to work seemed so extraordinary! (See Chapter 2.) However, little did I realise then how this mere seedling of an agricultural land use policy would grow into the prominent role it now has in the CAP, and no doubt with more growth to come in the future (see section 17.3).

So what have I learned about being a policy researcher during this 25 year period?

First, as alluded to already, doing policy research is definitely a race against time, even within the mighty CAP — just think about the May 1992 CAP Reform (heralding the self-titled "competitiveness" phase of the CAP), followed by only a short "transition period" before the Agenda 2000 reforms were being debated (and themselves heralding the "sustainability" phase of the CAP). And since then there have been numerous changes in the form of "adjustments" and "health checks", all featuring substantial prior periods of "negotiation" and subsequent periods of "implementation".

If you already are a policy researcher, you will know what I mean, and if you are aspiring to become one, then here is my main piece of advice: get in early! More specifically, it is a mistake to wait until the new policy has even been agreed before you start researching it — instead read the tea leaves of the negotiations and get going as soon as you can. And if in the final brush-off a 15% change becomes a 12% change, then you can always adjust your analysis to take this into account (in fact a comparison of what was planned and what was agreed can often be a good basis for a policy research paper — see Chapter 7 as an example of this — published in 1999 but based on the yet-to-be implemented Agenda 2000 CAP Reform).

Second, could you avoid this "race against time" by simply being a policy researcher who focuses on the ex post evaluation of policies? Well you could, but this approach has in my view two important weaknesses:

(i) the so-called "absence of the counterfactual" — we only experience one reality, so the opportunities to have a clear comparison of the "policy-on" situation with the "policy-off" situation are thin indeed — especially when you are talking about a policy that is applied at the national level (let alone the international level like the CAP), and

(ii) given the dynamic nature of policy, being an ex post policy evaluator more or less puts you in the category of being an economic historian rather than a policy advisor (which I think is where the action is!).

So there is no doubt in my mind that the ex ante evaluation of policy is the place to be from the point of view of relevance (and based primarily on model simulations — see below). Moreover, being involved before the implementation of the policy potentially gives you the additional opportunity to explore the options for improving the policy's design as well as evaluating its performance — which opens the door to you having impact on the design of the actual policy (highly prized in the UK in these days of the REF!). Note that I will discuss in more detail the lessons I've learned about improving policy design in the next subsection.

Finally, I think building models and simulating the impact of alternative policies is the best way to undertake ex ante policy evaluation (and also to investigate improving policy design). But should you work with a "small" model or a "big" model? In my case I started out as a policy researcher trying to follow both these paths. More specifically, in the 1980s I trained to become a user of the (then-called) ORANI model of the Australian economy developed under the leadership of Peter Dixon (see Dixon *et al.*, 1982). ORANI was a very large general equilibrium model of the Australian economy (with something like 112 industries in its specification), and was capable of being used to evaluate a wide range of policy and other impacts on the Australian economy (see for example Fraser, 1986a and Fraser and Salerian, 1987). But at the same time I also was exploring the advantages of the "small" model approach, which is intrinsically "partial equilibrium" but which I think allows the researcher increased flexibility in the specification and analysis of policy impacts (see for example Fraser, 1985 and Fraser, 1986b).

In this case I don't think any one approach is superior, and perhaps ideally you would be in a position to implement both approaches. But there is no escaping the considerable financial resources required to develop and maintain large models, so in times of increasingly scarce research funding, that is something to bear in mind. And remember, you can always take the route of comparing your "small" model results with those of the "big" models (I think Chapter 7 is also a good example of taking this approach).

17.1.2 *Reflections on using principal-agent theory*

Although my early research published in this book adopted a framework of evaluating the impact of a (principal's) policy on the behaviour and circumstances of an individual producer (agent), it was not until the late 1990s that I started to make explicit use of principal-agent theory in my research.[2]

---

[2]For this I am grateful to my friend, Uwe Latacz-Lohmann (currently Professor of Agricultural Economics at the University of Kiel).

More specifically, Chapters 2 to 7 report research which undertakes an evaluation of the impact of various changes in the CAP on the production decisions and financial circumstances of individual EU farmers. Whereas Chapter 8 explicitly adopts the principal-agent methodology and therefore is able not just to evaluate the impact of the CAP's set-aside policy, but also to identify improvements in the design of this policy which, if adopted, would reduce the problem of output slippage which reduces the cost-effectiveness of this policy, both because of adverse selection and moral hazard behaviour by farmers.

To me as a policy economist this is the real strength of using principal-agent theory — it enables you to expand the scope of your research from one of just using models to simulate the impact of a given policy change on producers (and their behaviour) to one of being able both to modify the design of this policy and to re-evaluate its impact in order to identify a better policy outcome for society.

In my view identifying improvements in policy design in this way is an important opportunity for a policy researcher to have a direct impact on the actual policy implemented — an opportunity not to be missed! As a consequence, my explicit use of principal-agent theory as a method for both designing and evaluating a policy ex ante is pervasive in the research reported in Part B of this book.

However, I should emphasise that my personal preference for using principal-agent theory to undertake ex ante policy simulations is not to undermine the importance of other approaches to ex ante policy simulations — and particularly those provided by "big" models. As stated in the previous subsection, my own early research experience with using a "big" model was fruitful, I just didn't have the personal circumstances for maintaining this activity.

So rather than take a position that one modelling approach is superior to another, I think the way to go is to acknowledge the "comparative advantage" of different approaches and in so doing hopefully deliver better policy decision-making. In particular, I have already argued that "small" models are more "flexible", despite being only "partial" in their evaluation of policy. This in itself suggests that it would be better to use "small" models (based on the principal-agent framework) to undertake a "partial" assessment of potential policy design improvements, and then use a "big" model to evaluate the "general" impact of such policy design improvements. And I wouldn't mind betting that different policy researchers themselves have a "comparative advantage" in undertaking one or the other of these types of ex ante policy simulation, which only adds to the value of this suggested complementary modelling approach.

Focussing now more directly on principal-agent theory, we know that it has helped us to identify the general problem of asymmetric information in policy design — and more specifically the twin problems of adverse selection and moral hazard behaviour among agents (both of which reduce the cost-effectiveness of the policy). And it is clear from the range of literature cited in the Introduction to Part B of this book that EU policy researchers have embraced this methodology to evaluate policy design issues within the CAP, particularly since the Agenda 2000 reforms and the implementation of the "sustainability" phase of the CAP.

But a review of these papers, as well as those published as Chapters 9 to 16 of this book, reveals that the vast majority of these papers report theoretical rather than empirical research findings. In fact the research findings reported in Chapters 12 and 13 are the only two empirical studies of the adverse selection problem in agri-environmental policy that I am currently aware of — and, as reported in Chapter 16, empirical assessments of the extent of the moral hazard problem in agri-environmental policy are non-existent.[3]

Which of course creates a problem for the (current) government preference for "evidence-based policy" — i.e. how can we design improved agri-environmental policies without evidence on which to base these improvements?

I will return to this issue of evidence-based policy making in the next sub-section and also in section 17.3 where I look ahead to the future of agricultural land use policy in the EU, but for now I just wanted to emphasise that many of the policy design improvements suggested by the research findings in Chapters 9 to 16 to tackle both the adverse selection and moral hazard problems, and thereby improve the cost-effectiveness of agri-environmental policy, are simply adjustments in the settings of policy instruments, and therefore are likely to be relatively low in cost to implement. Moreover, this feature of my research findings, combined with the current dearth of empirical evidence about the extent of these problems, led me to conclude my Presidential address to the Agricultural Economics Society in 2013 by saying: "I would currently advocate a relatively low cost approach to solving a problem we know so little about in reality".

17.1.3 *Reflections on the development of agricultural land use policy within the CAP*

In Chapter 1 I traced "A brief history of agricultural land use policy within the Common Agricultural Policy". And in that account I relied heavily on the European

---

[3] An empirical analysis by Lippert, Zorn and Dabbert (2014) of the moral hazard problem in the related context of organic livestock farming (in Switzerland) has been published since Chapter 16 was first published. Lippert *et al.* (2014) develop a theoretical model of the "expected farm-individual benefit" from non-compliance (with organic certification standards) from which they derive nine hypotheses regarding the determinants of non-compliance, many of which relate to the hypotheses developed in Chapter 16. However, data limitations mean that most of these hypotheses cannot be tested. Moreover, they are unable to provide an intuitive basis for the only two farm characteristics which they find to be statistically significant in increasing non-compliance: the presence on the farm of processing activities, and livestock diversity on the farm.

Commission's own account of the history of the CAP in which it characterises the evolution of the CAP as having three main phases:

  (i) from 1957 — "productivity",
  (ii) from the May 1992 CAP Reform — "competitiveness", and
  (iii) from the Agenda 2000 CAP Reform — "sustainability".

Moreover, the recently agreed "CAP Reform 2014–2020" looks set to extend the "sustainability" phase at least until 2020 (I will discuss this CAP reform in more detail in section 17.3).

So one thing that stands out for me in this context is the (relative) brevity of the "competitiveness" phase of the CAP — given that we had over 30 years of a CAP focussed on "productivity", and we are now looking at a CAP focussed on "sustainability" for at least 20 years.

And I think the simple explanation for this "competitiveness" phase only lasting 8 years is that while the CAP's "crisis years" of the 1970s and 1980s make it clear that the CAP needed major reform, there was for a decade or so only a clear awareness of what was "bad" about the CAP, not what would make it "good".

More specifically, it was clear into the 1980s that the CAP's price support mechanisms were causing over-production of key agricultural commodities, and in association with this, also some social awareness of the negative environmental consequences of the intensification and extensification of agricultural land use. But the initial focus of reform was on reducing this over-production by: (i) reducing price support and (ii) introducing "compliance set-aside". Moreover, reducing price support (so that EU farmers would become more "competitive" on world markets) was clearly the main game, coupled of course with appropriate direct payments to compensate farmers for the associated income losses.

In other words, even though agricultural land use policy (to protect and enhance environmental goods and services) has now become the centrepiece of the "sustainability" phase of the CAP, at that time its fledging form of "compliance set-aside" (to help reduce over-production) was without doubt the poor cousin of the "competitiveness" phase.

So what brought about the speedy shift from the "competitiveness" phase of the CAP to its on-going "sustainability" phase?

It should be recalled at this point that there had already been calls in the academic literature in the late 1980s for "conservation set-aside" to deliver environmental benefits from agricultural land (see for example Gasson and Potter, 1988). But despite the existence of a social concern about environmental degradation caused by the intensification and extensification of agricultural land use prior to the introduction of a set-aside policy within the CAP, as stated above, there is no doubt that the "compliance set-aside" of the May 1992 CAP Reform was targeted at over-production of agricultural commodities, much like the US's Conservation Reserve Program introduced with the 1985 Farm Bill.

However, what became clear during the 1990s was that farmers, in being forced to set aside agricultural land, were at the same time delivering enhanced environmental benefits from that land — both in terms of reduced negative consequences such as nitrate pollution and soil erosion from cropping, and in terms of increased positive consequences such as improved habitats (see Chapter 7 for research findings in support of these consequences). That is, the *reality* of the "compliance set-aside" policy was that farmers in taking the land out of production that was least detrimental to their production income, were also de-extensifying their land use in ways which were delivering a "win-win" for the levels of environmental goods and services provided by agricultural land.

So my view is that this *evidence* that an agricultural land use policy could deliver environmental benefits, combined with a growing awareness in society of the *value* of environmental goods and services to its well-being, was effective in changing the focus of the CAP in the late 1990s from "competitiveness" to "sustainability". More specifically, this *evidence* set the European Commission on the path of developing an agricultural land use policy within the Agenda 2000 CAP which, although based on the concept of set-aside as a production-control policy, transformed itself into a policy which saw farmers as "environmental stewards" charged with the task of managing their agricultural land to provide environmental goods and services for society, and moreover being appropriately remunerated for this provision within the CAP's budget. And it is worth noting in this context that the direct payments that farmers used to receive as "compensation" for the reduction/removal of commodity price support, and which since the 1990s were increasingly being seen as a "welfare regime for farmers" (see Chapter 1), are now with the continued development of the CAP's "sustainability" phase being transformed into "justified" payments to farmers for their "greening measures" (this issue will be discussed further in section 17.3).

Therefore, while we have little evidence on which to base improvements in the cost-effectiveness of our agri-environmental policies, there is no shortage of evidence that having an agricultural land use policy as a core component of the CAP going forward is an important way to engage farmers in the provision of environmental goods and services for the benefit of society. This must surely be the main lesson to be taken forward from our study of the development of the CAP's agricultural land use policy over the last twenty-five years.

17.2 Looking Around

In this section I make some comments on the challenges of operating an agricultural land use policy in circumstances where there is considerable heterogeneity in terms both of the biophysical components of the agricultural landscape and of the social perception of the value of these components.

These comments are organised in three spatial categories: (i) within the UK, (ii) within the EU, and (iii) outside the EU.

17.2.1 *Within the UK*

"Compliance set-aside" was a relatively simple agricultural land use policy in that it was targeted at arable land. This minimised the degree of heterogeneity in the agricultural landscape affected by the policy, although it didn't stop farmers choosing their least productive land to set aside (see Chapter 6).

However, the UK's environmental stewardship schemes apply to the entire agricultural landscape, while the associated payments for farmers remain based uniformly on the principle of foregone agricultural income.

This means that the cost to society of a farmer's participation in, say, the Higher Level Stewardship Scheme (HLS) depends on the farmer's foregone income from this participation. Moreover, on a per hectare basis these payments will typically be considerably higher for arable land than for grazing land, regardless of the location of these respective hectares.

In my view this creates two problems for the cost-effectiveness of the HLS. The first is that while the payment to a farmer for removing land from production is based on this farmer's foregone agricultural income from this land, the associated environmental benefits provided to society will depend both on each person's perception of the use and non-use environmental value of this land, and on the number of people receiving an environmental benefit from this land.

More specifically, recent empirical research has revealed that people place higher values on some components of the overall agricultural landscape than others (particularly upland areas compared with lowland areas), and that the extent to which people benefit from agricultural landscape depends on its location — with areas of landscape closer to large population centres having higher overall social value (see Hanley *et al.* (2007), Garrod *et al.* (2014), Sen *et al.* (2014)).

And the second problem for the cost-effectiveness of the HLS is that the budget available to fund the HLS is limited by the extent of modulation from Pillar 1 to Pillar 2. This means that, simply in terms of participating hectares, this fixed budget will be able to fund less hectares of participation from cropping regions than from grazing regions.

But I also think that the solution to these problems is clear: Natural England should select land for participation in the HLS in order to maximise the environmental benefits delivered from spending its HLS budget — and this selection process should be based on the following three considerations:

 (i) the type of agricultural landscape surrounding the participating land,
 (ii) the location of the participating land in relation to population centres, and
(iii) the level of payment for the participating land.

By selecting on the basis of (i) and (ii) and consistent with the existing *evidence* on spatial differences in environmental values, Natural England will be maximising the environmental benefit per hectare of participating land, and by conditioning this selection on the basis of (iii) Natural England will be maximising the cost-effectiveness of its budget.

In this context it should also be recognised that the empirical evidence reported in Hanley *et al.* (2007) and in Chapter 13 suggests there is likely in some cases to be a happy overlap between the types of land that have a relatively high landscape value to society and those which have a relatively low level of foregone agricultural income associated with them being taken out of production. And if the extent of this overlap can be realised through Natural England's selection process for participating land, then the outcome is undoubtedly a "win-win" for the delivery of environmental benefits from the HLS.

Finally, these comments will have implications for the role of spatial considerations in the UK's New Environmental Land Management Scheme (NELMS) announced at the end of 2013, implications which will be considered further in section 17.3.

17.2.2   *Within the EU*

I think that one of the most underestimated costs of the UK's Foot and Mouth disease outbreak in 2001 was the social cost of the closure of the countryside. And a similar social "storm" broke out in 2012 with the identification of the Ash Dieback disease threatening to destroy the UK's third most abundant tree species. In other words, I think there is no doubt that the agricultural landscape is of enormous value to UK society and that, as a consequence, the UK government knew it had society's backing when it pushed for 15% modulation from Pillar 1 to Pillar 2 during the 2013 consultation on "CAP Reform 2014–2020".

But does this strong social "demand" for the provision of environmental goods and services by farmers exist elsewhere within the EU? My view is that almost certainly the shadow of heterogeneity is cast once again in this context, and that there is considerable variation within the EU counties in relation to the social perception of the value of the agricultural landscape. This is not to say that there are not other countries in the EU which value very highly components or even the large proportion of their agricultural landscape, but I doubt this is true for all countries in the EU.

Moreover, this heterogeneity can be used to explain the "diversity" of support among EU countries for the degree of modulation to be applied between Pillar 1 and Pillar 2, and hence the amount of funding available to farmers for the provision of environmental goods and services.

But at the same time, the European Commission needs to continue to deal with the growing social perception that direct payments (i.e. Pillar 1) are these days little more than "a welfare regime for farmers" (see Chapter 1). More specifically, it is relatively straightforward for members of society to understand that Pillar 2 funding is for "rural development" and that in this context farmers receive payments in return for "supplying" environmental goods and services. But what is the justification for the direct payments farmers receive from Pillar 1?

In other words, while there might be considerable diversity among EU countries in the extent to which their societies "demand" the "supply" of environmental goods and services from the agricultural landscape, this diversity can be "managed" internally by varying the amount of modulation from Pillar 1 to Pillar 2 (note in this context that the UK government agreed in late 2013 not to increase the extent of modulation in England from 9% to 15%, settling instead for 12% as a compromise between the "demand" and the "supply" sides of the "market" for environmental goods and services). However, justifying the direct payments to farmers from Pillar 1 in societies which are still suffering the economic hardships of the financial crisis of 2008 is more difficult!

As a consequence, I don't think it is particularly surprising that the "CAP Reform 2014–2020" now features a powerful incursion of "greening measures" into the domain of direct payments as a way of (partially) justifying these payments to farmers which have long since (i.e. May 1992) lost their original justification (as "compensation" for reduced price support). This issue of "greening measures" in the "CAP Reform to 2020", which themselves represent a new (future) expansion in the scope of the EU's agricultural land use policy, is discussed more in section 17.3.

17.2.3   *Outside the EU*

The United States and Australia

It is clear from Ervin (1988) that the US's Conservation Reserve Program (CRP), introduced with the 1985 Farm Bill, was the antecedent for the CAP's voluntary set-aside scheme (introduced in 1988). But whereas the May 1992 CAP Reform subsequently converted voluntary set-aside into "compliance set-aside", in effect making it compulsory for EU farmers to participate, the CRP has remained throughout its existence a voluntary participation programme, despite a series of changes since 1985 in its structure and scope.

Moreover, although it is acknowledged that land participating in the CRP may also provide environmental benefits, both in terms of enhanced habitat and species abundance, the initial motivation and on-going basis of the CRP has been as an agricultural land use policy (with voluntary participation) aimed at the amelioration of the negative consequences of farming, particularly in relation to the soil erosion and water quality problems caused by cropping.

This focus on reducing the negative environmental impacts of farming (and again primarily from cropping) has also been the motivating force behind similar agricultural land use management schemes in Australia — but again with the distinguishing feature of voluntary participation (with the exception of regulations against the clearing of remnant vegetation).

So whereas the EU was quick to move its agricultural land use policy into the realms of compulsory participation by farmers (and is set to move further with the "greening measures" of the "CAP Reform to 2020"), why have other developed countries such as the US and Australia not taken this step?

I don't think this difference is to do with the history of government support for farm incomes — the US is not unlike the EU in having a long tradition of supporting farmers' incomes with taxation receipts, whereas Australia has typically maintained a system of (industry-based) levies on revenues from production to provide financial assistance where and when needed (with the exception of taxpayer-funded drought relief).

Instead I think this difference is more likely to be due to different perceptions between these countries in the level of "demand" by society for the provision of environmental goods and services from agricultural land. And I think these "demand" differences probably have their origins in the proportion of the population living in or close to the agricultural landscape, and therefore more exposed to the environmental problems created by the farming of this landscape.

Norway and New Zealand

By contrast, Norway and New Zealand are both similar to many EU countries in having a relatively high proportion of their populations living in or close to the agricultural landscape. But their traditions of government support for farm incomes are very different. More specifically, Norway's agricultural policy is much like the EU's CAP in providing substantial long-standing support for farm incomes (largely through tariff barriers, and higher even than those of the EU), while New Zealand is arguably the developed world's best example of "free markets" for agricultural production and trade.

However, in both countries the agricultural landscape is dominated by livestock production (and particularly dairy products), and both countries are now facing a growing social "demand" for this type of farming to improve its environmental impact. In the case of Norway, a country which prides itself on its environmental friendliness (e.g. 100% renewable energy), the particular problem is the greenhouse gas emissions from livestock production. In New Zealand, it is the damage being done to the country's waterways by nitrate leaching as a consequence of intensive livestock feeding practices, which is upsetting a society which historically has benefited considerably from its clean waterways (and in particular for recreational fishing).

Now in the case of Norway the solution to this problem seems relatively straightforward — i.e. the country has a tradition of government support for farm incomes, so it should not be a big step to adopt the EU's May 1992 CAP Reform approach of making some of this support conditional on (in Norway's case, environmental) "compliance" as a part of its agricultural land use policy. But in the case of New Zealand, there is no such traditional of government support for farm incomes, and so the question arises: is the social "demand" for improved environmental consequences from livestock production sufficient to justify the introduction of taxpayer-based financial incentives for farmers to deliver such improvements? And although this raises the perennial issue of "polluter pays" versus "beneficiary pays", to which we know there is no right or wrong economic answer, in the end it will be up to the New Zealand people to make the political decision of whether or not they want to take the novel step of using taxpayer funds to "buy" the desired environmental improvements from farmers, just as the EU has been doing as a central part of its agricultural land use policy since the Agenda 2000 CAP Reform.

17.3   Looking Ahead

In this section I build on this book's analysis of the development to date of an agricultural land use policy as a component of the EU's CAP to make some suggestions about the likely future direction of this policy. I "look ahead" in two contexts: (i) within the EU and (ii) within the UK; and in two stages: (a) the CAP to 2020 and (b) the CAP beyond 2020.

17.3.1   *Within the EU*

(a) *The CAP to 2020*

We have seen that the first phase of an agricultural land use policy as a component of the CAP began in 1988 with the introduction of voluntary set-aside as a production control policy. This, largely ineffective attempt at production control, was followed by the introduction of "compliance set-aside" as a key part of the May 1992 CAP Reform. This change in effect converted set-aside into a compulsory land use policy, still aimed at production control, but with farmers required to participate in order to receive "compensatory payments" for the reductions in price support included in the May 1992 CAP Reform. The third phase of the CAP's agricultural land use policy began with the Agenda 2000 Reform, and as we have seen, coincided with the beginning of the CAP's "sustainability" phase. This phase has seen both the (eventual) removal of set-aside as a production control device (in 2008), and the establishment of the CAP's "Pillar 2", within which farmers are seen as "environmental stewards" and are offered financial incentives to participate (voluntarily) in schemes designed to provide improvements in environmental goods and services from agricultural land. Moreover, within the context of the various minor reforms since 2000 (i.e. 2003, 2008) the funding for Pillar 2 has continued to grow at the expense of the funding for Pillar 1 — i.e. the budget for the CAP's "direct payments" to farmers (historically the "compensatory payments").

Given this background, I think we can now see the announcement in late 2013 of the European Commission's "CAP Reform 2014–2020" as the beginning of a fourth phase of the CAP's agricultural land use policy (see European Commission, 2013 and Allen *et al.*, 2013). More specifically, included in this latest reform is a return to the type of compulsory agricultural land use policy previously manifested as "compliance set-aside" in the 1990s (and subsequently abandoned). But whereas "compliance set-aside" was used as a production control policy, and required farmers to set aside a proportion of their land in order to receive "compensatory payments", the "CAP Reform 2014–2020" features the introduction of "greening measures", and in particular the requirement for farmers to establish an "ecological focus area" comprising (at least) 5% of their land, and where compliance with these measures is a requirement for Farmers to receive 30% of their "direct payments". So in effect the "CAP Reform 2014–2020" has re-introduced "compliance set-aside", where this compliance is once again required in order to receive "payments" under Pillar 1, but where this set-aside land is now called an "ecological focus area".[4]

I think this is a fascinating "recycling" of an earlier phase of the CAP's agricultural land use policy, and based on the discussion in subsection 17.2.3 sets the EU apart from other countries in henceforth *requiring* farmers to participate in providing improved environmental goods and services from agricultural land, rather than just incentivising them to do so (under Pillar 2). Moreover, it coincides with a cessation of the forced shift of CAP funding from Pillar 1 to Pillar 2, thus clearly emphasising a shift from voluntary to compulsory participation by farmers in the CAP's agricultural land use policy going forward. And in addition, the "CAP Reform 2014–2020" contains a proposal to increase the proportion of a farmer's land dedicated to their "ecological focus area" from 5% to 7% in 2017!

Given the financial encouragement provided to the development of Pillar 2 since 2000, and with it both the obvious support for and perceived success of environmental stewardship as a voluntary agricultural land use policy, the question clearly arises as to why this change to compulsory participation in environmental stewardship?

In my view, the answer to this question lies in the "political problem" of "direct payments". More specifically, if we go back to the May 1992 CAP Reform, we can see the origins of such "payments" to farmers as "compensation" for a reduction of previously existing price support, and designed to maintain farm incomes despite this policy change. However, this rationale is now more than 20 years old, and the "payments" have also since been "de-coupled" from production, so that they now just look like a "welfare regime for farmers" (see Chapter 1). It follows that the "direct payments" to farmers under Pillar 1 need a new political rationale, and the

---

[4]Although see the discussion in the next sub-section regarding the option for farmers to grow "nitrogen-fixing crops" to satisfy their "Ecological Focus Area" requirement.

perceived success of farmers as environmental stewards under Pillar 2 would seem to have provided this rationale!

Moreover, as stated previously, the initial policy setting of 5% of a farmer's land set-aside as an "ecological focus area" as a requirement to receive 30% of their direct payments has already been flagged for modification to 7% of their land in 2017. This clearly also raises the prospect of an elevation of the 30% policy setting at some point in the future, not just to encourage compliance with the larger set-aside land requirement, but also to add strength to the political rationale for the continuation of direct payments.

(b) *The CAP beyond 2020*

On-going expansion of the EU, and in particular to include countries with relatively large agricultural sectors, can be expected to put further pressure on the CAP's budget. It follows that the size and rationale for the Pillar 1 budget will come under increasing scrutiny. So what will happen?

It seems to me that there is very strong social support for the role of farmers as environmental stewards, so I don't see any prospect of farmers not continuing to be funded to provide improvements in environmental goods and services from their land. Rather, the question in my mind is whether the direct payments system can withstand the ever-increasing social pressure to make the provision of such environmental improvements both more spatially targeted and, partly as a consequence, more cost-effective. In other words, will environmental stewardship continue as the broadly focussed feature of the "CAP Reform 2014–2020" ostensibly to support farm incomes, or will it change eventually to a demand-driven agricultural land use policy for (more) cost-effectively providing improved environmental goods and services from agricultural land? Given the unending prospect of government budget deficits, and the associated continuing pressure for improved value for money from government spending, I expect the ambition of the "CAP Reform 2014–2020" of prolonging the life of the direct payments system to ultimately fail.

17.3.2   *Within the UK*

(a) *The CAP to 2020*

The complicated governance structure of the UK (comprising England along with the "devolved administrations" of Scotland, Wales and Northern Ireland) means that although the UK government receives the UK's share of the CAP budget, and can itself determine the implementation of the CAP Reform 2014–2020 within England, much of the detail of this implementation outside of England will be determined by the "devolved administrations" (see Allen *et al.*, 2013). As a consequence, in what follows I will refer primarily to the UK government's plans for implementation of this CAP reform within England.

However, this approach is actually not as "unrepresentative" of implications of CAP reform for the entire UK's agriculture as it may seem, because although English agriculture is based on just over 50% of the UK's agricultural land, it also generates almost two-thirds of the UK's share of the CAP budget. In essence this is because England contributes about 80% of the UK's total arable land, and crop-based payments have always dominated the CAP's Pillar 1 (i.e. direct payments) budget. Moreover, England has over 40% of the UK's sheep, over 50% of its cattle, over 70% of its chickens and over 80% of its pigs (see Allen *et al.*, 2013).

And from this budgetary perspective, there are three main aspects to the UK government's implementation of CAP Reform 2014–2020 in relation to agricultural land use (within England):

(i) the extent of modulation (i.e. the balance of the CAP budget between Pillar 1 and Pillar 2),

(ii) the "greening measures" required in relation to Pillar 1 payments, particularly those for the "Ecological Focus Area", and

(iii) the environmental stewardship opportunities in relation to the Pillar 2 budget.

Regarding (i), in 2013 the UK government "modulated" 9% of its CAP budget from Pillar 1 to Pillar 2, primarily to fund its environmental stewardship schemes (mainly the Entry Level Stewardship (ELS) and Higher Level Stewardship (HLS) schemes). And its proposal for 2014 onwards was to increase this proportion to 15% — the maximum amount permitted by the new CAP reform — based on internal research estimating very large benefit-cost ratios for making this adjustment. However, political pressure from farmers saw this adjustment reduced to 12%. Nevertheless, given the UK government's stated preference for using its CAP budget to improve the provision of environmental goods and services from agricultural land, I think that the shift upwards to 15% towards 2020 is inevitable (see further below in relation to the agricultural land use implications of the Pillar 2 budget and the "NELMS").

In relation to the new CAP's "greening measures" this is one context where England's dominance of UK crop production, combined with its powerful uptake of environmental stewardship (and particularly its enthusiastic taking of land out of production with buffer strips and field margins), creates an implementation problem — that of "double funding". Specifically, farmers cannot be paid from both Pillar 1 and Pillar 2 for taking the same hectare of land out of production, so a farmer's 5% "Ecological Focus Area" (required to receive 30% of "direct payments" from Pillar 1) cannot also be receiving environmental stewardship payments for forgone cropping income (i.e. from buffer strips and field margins) from Pillar 2. However, in this case the UK government has decided to exploit an option provided within the new CAP for land planted to "nitrogen-fixing crops" to satisfy the "ecological focus area" requirement.[5] In so doing, the UK government has achieved

---

[5] Admittedly with a "coefficient" of 0.7, which means that farmers will have to plant just over 7% of their land to "nitrogen-fixing crops" to satisfy the 5% requirement.

a sort of land use policy "win-win-win" in that arable farmers can use their land to generate production income while simultaneously satisfying the "ecological focus area" requirement to receive their 30% of "direct payments" from Pillar 1 — and also maintaining their historical contribution of agricultural land to environmental stewardship (along with associated payments) under Pillar 2. However, it should also be acknowledged that environmental groups are somewhat sceptical of the claims made for the nitrate leaching and insect pollinator (i.e. environmental) benefits from growing nitrogen-fixing crops. Therefore, the future of this "solution" to the problem of implementing the "ecological focus area" requirement as the size of this requirement increases towards 2020 is unclear. Nevertheless, in the meantime I think we'll see a lot more peas and beans being grown in England!

Finally, the UK government has announced that from 2015 it will introduce a "New Environmental Land Management Scheme" ("NELMS") to replace its previously existing environmental stewardship schemes (i.e. the ELS and HLS schemes) in distributing its Pillar 2 budget. And although at the time of writing full details of this "NELMS" are yet to be revealed, the UK government has already indicated that this new environmental stewardship scheme will feature a stronger focus on the spatial characteristics of environmental goods and services from the agricultural landscape. Moreover, as previously mentioned in section 17.2, research (i.e. "evidence") provided by Hanley *et al.* (2007), Garrod *et al.* (2014) and Sen *et al.* (2014) would suggest that the social value of recreation in the agricultural landscape is higher both in upland areas and near large population centres. Consequently, I think we can expect in future that applications by farmers to contribute some of their agricultural land to the improved production of environmental goods and services will be "scored" higher (and therefore more likely to be approved) if their agricultural land exhibits such spatial characteristics. It follows that the cost-effectiveness of the UK's environmental stewardship schemes in delivering benefits to society will be improved by this ("evidence-based") closer alliance of participation (i.e. supply) with demand.[6]

(b) *The CAP beyond 2020*

(i) Climate change and agricultural land use policy

One of the main challenges in assessing the implications of climate change for agricultural land use has been the difficulty of mapping the spatial characteristics of climate change onto the agricultural landscape. However, recent research by Fezzi

---

[6]Note that at the end of 2014 further details were announced of "NELMS" — including changing its name to "Countryside Stewardship". And although they remain incomplete, these further details confirmed that Countryside Stewardship "will be more targeted and focused than previous schemes . . . This will encourage applicants to deliver the right environmental management in the correct combinations and in the right places. It will also make sure Countryside Stewardship is good value for taxpayers' money". (p. 1) See: Defra, "Introducing Countryside Stewardship", November 2014 (www.gov.uk/cap-reform).

et al. (2014) has provided valuable insights into the implications of climate change for agricultural land use across the UK and from 2020 to 2060.

Using spatially-disaggregated climate change projections form the UK's Climate Impact Programme (UKCIP, 2009) combined with a spatially-heterogeneous econometric model of agricultural land use decision-making developed by Fezzi and Bateman (2011), Fezzi *et al.* (2014) are able to provide detailed projections of changes in UK agricultural land use patterns induced by the impact of projected climate changes, particularly in relation to temperature and precipitation, on farm gross margins across a range of agricultural production activities.

The Fezzi *et al.* (2014) results are based primarily on a climate change projection across the UK of warmer, drier summers (i.e. the growing season). On this basis, and given the limitations of their econometric model, while they express some doubt about the impact of climate change on the UK's cropping regions (which may need to adapt towards non-traditional crops which respond well to warmer, drier growing seasons such as field tomatoes, nuts and stone fruit), their main finding is for climate change to "boost the potential for shifts out of low intensity pastoral activities towards higher return options" (p. 199). In particular, "the number of dairy cows is, *ceteris paribus*, expected to increase significantly" (p. 210), in conjunction with a substantial shift (i.e. in each case about 20% of the total) of agricultural land use from rough grazing to permanent grassland, particularly in the West and North of the UK.

So what are the implications of these adaptations to climate change for agricultural land use policy in the UK, and particularly in relation to the provision of environmental goods and services in the agricultural landscape?

On the supply side, the shift of agricultural land use in the (largely upland) West and North from rough grazing to permanent grassland to support high(er) value dairy production will also increase the payments to farmers (as foregone income) in those areas for participation in environmental stewardship. Therefore, given the (relative) complementarity of livestock production with participation in environmental stewardship, I would expect these climate change-induced adaptations also to increase the provision of environmental goods and services from these areas.

While on the demand side, and given not just the (current) vagaries of UK summers, but also the revealed preference of UK residents for recreation activities in upland areas (see Hanley *et al.*, 2007; Sen *et al.*, 2014), I would expect the climate change-induced warmer, drier summers to lead to increased demand for recreation in the West and North of the UK, and especially for those areas nearer larger population centres (see Garrod *et al.*, 2014).

Therefore, in the context of climate change, it would seem the future bodes well for environmental stewardship in the UK, particularly in high recreation value areas.

(ii) Food security vs energy security vs environmental conservation

A recent report by the University of Cambridge's Institute for Sustainability Leadership (ISL, 2014) highlights the conflicting demands on the UK's agricultural land use arising from the objectives of: "Improved UK food security", "Increased UK energy security", and "Better protection of nature" (as well as "Enhanced recreational space", p. 5). And on this basis, combined with an expected future UK population growth, the ISL forecasts a shortage of UK agricultural land of 2 m hectares by 2030 (a "supply-demand gap" equal to 10% of the existing total, p. 5), even allowing for a range of mitigating factors (such as reduced food wastage).

But given the creation of 2 m new hectares of agricultural land in the UK is not an option, how should this agricultural land use policy problem be solved in society's best interests? My view is that it is important to recognise in this context that both food and energy are what economists define as "traded goods" — and in fact the UK already has substantial levels of imported food and energy. Whereas environmental goods and services provided on agricultural land are what economists define as "non-traded goods (and services)" — in other words they are provided by farmers *in situ* in the agricultural landscape and cannot be imported (although these services can be "exported" in the sense of overseas visitors coming to recreate in the UK's agricultural landscape).

Therefore, it seems to me that, on the basis of what can and can't be traded, the objective of "better protection of nature" (as well as that of "enhanced recreational space") should have a natural priority over food and energy security objectives in the UK's agricultural land use policy beyond 2020.

References

Allen, M., Downing, E., Edwards, T., Seaton, N., and Semple, M. (2013) *CAP Reform 2014–20: EU Agreement and Implementation in the UK and in Ireland*, Research Paper 136/13, House of Commons Library, November.

Dixon, P. B., Parmenter, B. R., Sutton, J. and Vincent, D. P. (1982) *ORANI: A Multisectoral Model of the Australian Economy*, Amsterdam: North-Holland.

Ervin, D. E. (1988) Cropland diversion (set-aside) in the US and the UK, *Journal of Agricultural Economics* 39(2): 183–196.

European Commission (2013) *CAP Reform — An Explanation of the Main Elements*, Memo/13/937, October.

Fezzi, C. and Bateman, I. J. (2011) Structural agricultural land use modelling for spatial agro-environmental policy analysis, *American Journal of Agricultural Economics* 93: 1168–1188.

Fezzi, C, *et al.* (2014) Valuing provision of ecosystem services: The impact of climate change on food production in the United Kingdom, *Environmental and Resource Economics* 57: 197–214.

Fraser, R. W. (1984) On the desirability of an income stabilisation scheme, *Economics Letters* 15: 65–72.

Fraser, R. W. (1985) Severance taxes, uncertainty and natural resources: the effect on investment of the choice of tax base, *Public Finance* 40: 172–181.

Fraser, R. W. (1986a) Three views of the contribution of the extractive industries to the WA economy, *Resources Policy* 12(1): 47–61.

Fraser, R. W. (1986b) Uncertainty and production quotas, *Economic Record* 62(178): 338–342.

Fraser, R. W. and Salerian, S. (1987) Agricultural exports and the West Australian economy, *Australian Journal of Agricultural Economics* 31(1): 74–82.

Fraser, R. W. (1988) A method for evaluating supply response to price underwriting, *Australian Journal of Agricultural Economics* 32: 22–36.

Fraser, R. W. (1991) Price-support effects on EC producers. *Journal of Agricultural Economics* 42(1): 1–10.

Garrod, G., *et al.* (2014) Investigating preferences for the local delivery of agri-environmental benefits, *Journal of Agricultural Economics* 65(1): 177–190.

Gasson, R. and Potter, C. (1988) Conservation through land diversion: a survey of farmers' attitudes, *Journal of Agricultural Economics* 39(2): 340–351.

Hanley, N., *et al.* (2007) The reform of support mechanisms for upland farming: Paying for public goods in the severely disadvantaged areas of England, *Journal of Agricultural Economics* 58(3): 433–453.

Institute for Sustainability Leadership (2014) *The Cambridge natural capital leaders platform: The best use of UK agricultural land*, University of Cambridge.

Lippert, C., Zorn, A. and Dabbert, S. (2014) Econometric analysis of noncompliance with organic farming standards in Switzerland, *Agricultural Economics* 45: 313–325.

Sen, A., *et al.* (2014) Economic Assessment of the recreational value of ecosystems: Methodological development and national and local application, *Environmental and Resource Economics* 57: 233–249.

UK Climate Change Programme (2009) *UK climate projection: briefing report*, Met Office, Hadley, Exeter.

Printed in the United States
By Bookmasters